Syria and Lebanon: Regional Powder Keg

GEW Reports & Analyses Team

Global East-West. London

Contents

1
Introduction
Intertwined Destinies – Syria and Lebanon

Geographical Proximities and Cultural Ties

The historical and cultural linkages that bind Syria and Lebanon have long dictated the tone and substance of their bilateral ties, weaving a dense and multi-layered fabric of common narratives, rituals, and reciprocal influences. The two states, separated by an undulating border yet united by contiguous terrains, have sedimented overlapping chronicles and social transfers in every valley and mountain. The region's ancient polities, from the Phoenician coastal city-states through Assyrian heartlands and Roman provinces to Ottoman district borders, layered a common linguistic and artisanal vernacular that persists in the present-day accents, festivals, and public aesthetics of both societies. This shared past has settled into practices, cosmogonies, and moral axioms that jointly anchor the two peoples. Successive epochs of imperial stewardship, culminating in colonial mandates and the struggles for national autonomy, further braided the two polities, generating a kinetic feedback of migration, commerce, and political cross-fertilisation that renders their separation, in cultural terms, constantly porous.

The intimate geographical proximity of Syria and Lebanon, compounded by centuries of shared migration and trade, has laid the groundwork for a vibrant circulation of food, music, literature, and religious rites. From bustling souks to village gatherings, the blending of these expressions has produced a cultural mosaic that defies the boundaries of modern statehood. While these entangled inheritances have bred a pervasive sense of mutual recognition and communal solidarity, they have simultaneously revealed fault lines, as allegiance to competing identities and external patrons has wrought episodes of friction and discord. Thus, the present-day diplomacy between the two lands cannot be disentangled from the interlaced heritage of movement and adoption that both moulded their peoples and shaped their territories. A careful reading of these cultural geographies is, therefore, the indispensable prelude to any inquiry into the evolving politics that determine how their futures remain, for better or for worse, singular expressions of a shared, albeit contested, inheritance.

The Modern States: Formation and Boundaries

Syria and Lebanon have emerged as modern polities along a trajectory marked by entangled local and imperial logics. Their elemental consolidation occurred against the backdrop of the Ottoman Empire's waning authority and the reordering of territorial and political prerogatives that followed the Great War. With the Ottoman disjunction, the French Mandate descended, recasting a swathe of the Levant, reconstituting provincial boundaries, and substituting colonial guardianship for imperial oversight, an operation that undermined established administrative continuities while inscribing the idea of post-imperial sovereignty on the cartographic and institutional landscape.In 1920, the League of Nations transferred the mandate for the Levant to France, marking a critical watershed in the modern history of the region. The subsequent delimitation of the modern jurisdictions of Syria and Lebanon consolidated these territories for administrative purposes, yet the act was inseparable from indexical disputes and local contestations. The imposed frontiers invited penetrating inquiries into communal identity, ethnonational categorisation, and sectarian allegiance, engendering socio-political entanglements whose contemporary resonance remains manifest. The result was the crystallisation of Syria and Lebanon as separate political bodies, each charting a distinctive trajectory amid successive regional convulsions and the tactical intrigues of global powers. The earlier colonial calculation instituted a topography whose geopolitical relevance outlived the mandate; the enforced frontiers and divisional bureaucracies corroded inherited communal balances and consolidated communal cleavages within a brittle geopolitical grid. The borders and territorial integrity of contemporary Syria and Lebanon thus reveal a compound synthesis involving inherited imperial legacies, foreign directives, and indigenous contestation, rendering the cartography of their sovereignty perpetually contingent. The spatial and demographic realities of these states disclose a dense layering of ethnos, sect, and cultured solidarities, whose mutual entwinement remains a defining characteristic of their political arenas.The rich cultural mosaic of Syria and Lebanon presents profound opportunities for societal flourishing and perpetual difficulty in governance and collective national coherence. Boundary drawing within and between these polities attests to the persistent interplay of cognitive maps and cultural memory that extends throughout the wider Middle East.

Shared Challenges: War, Peace, and Diplomacy

Syria and Lebanon remain inextricably bound by a common inheritance of war, negotiated peace, and diplomatic stratagems. The colonial legacy, compounded by civil divisions and the persistent threat of wider regional conflagration, has left the two states with an accumulative memory of interruptions to sovereignty and stability. Episodes of violence and the rare, fragile interregnums of calm have not only scarred the physical territory but have also reconfigured social hierarchies and institutional competencies on both sides of the international boundary. Simultaneously, the overlapping circuits of regional diplomacy—emphasising temporary alliances, conditional support, and external peace initiatives—have repeatedly recalibrated the distribution of power and consent within Syria and Lebanon. Hence, a rigorous examination of these interlaced ordeals remains essential for understanding the composite forces that continue to shape the political and existential trajectory of both polities.Syria and Lebanon share a history of violence, each conflict a stage on which regional and global powers have repeatedly played their hand. The collapse of the Ottoman Empire, the punitive reshaping of the Levant under the French mandate, and the population movements they unleashed gave rise to fragile political identities still haunted by the search for the dignity of statehood. The flames of Lebanon's Civil War and the more recent catastrophes of the Syrian Civil War both erupted from localised fractures yet spread contagiously outward, inviting outside interventions that were seldom disinterested. In the midst of these recurring catastrophes, intermittent peacemaking endeavours have sought to channel communal energies away from destruction and toward a future of coexistence. Diplomatic channels—whether the quiet behind-the-scenes encouragement of global powers or the more fragile, fortress-like, parallel tracks of Syrian-Lebanese dialogue—have sought to untangle the twin legacies of colonial fragility and Cold War competition. International actors, when they were present, occasionally imparted leverage that turned toward the constructive; yet shifts in the capitals of both countries, driven by priorities that rarely aligned, meant that cautions and incentives could just as easily unravel.Amid these evolving geopolitical pressures, Syria and Lebanon have persistently engaged in the difficult artistry of international diplomacy, striving to preserve their national autonomies in the face of competing imperial and regional interests. The fragile movement among conflict, settlement, and negotiation thus emerges as the key prism through which to discern the historical, political, and humanitarian layers of the two countries' converging trajectories.

Political Landscapes: Influence of Regional Powers

Syria and Lebanon's political environments remain closely enmeshed with regional powers, whose interventions have created enduring patterns in governance, security, and diplomacy. Both the historical record and present crisis reflect how interventions by Arab, Iranian, and external actors have structured the political topographies of the two states. Foremost among the regional influencers is Iran, which, through its extensive network of military, intelligence, and financial resources, has cultivated close ties with multiple Lebanese and Syrian groups. Iran's undisputed backing of Hezbollah, alongside its expansive military logistics to the Assad government, has helped Tehran institutionalise its presence across the Levant, while simultaneously institutionalising the Assad regime. These strategic calculations weave Iran into and through the intersection of state and non-state spheres, generating a cohesive axis that both empowers its proxies and complicates the independence of Lebanese and Syrian governance. Counterbalancing Iranian advances, Saudi Arabia seeks to curtail Tehran's footprint through diplomatic investment, funding of rival militias, and diplomatic negotiations aimed at reshaping regional hegemony. The resulting competition, pronounced in military aid to competing factions and exclusive political outreach, has sharpened sectarian identifications and aggravated chasms within the two states.

Saudi Arabia's backing of selected political and paramilitary factions within the affected state has further entangled the regional order, intensifying pre-existing discord and undermining the integrity of state apparatuses. At the same time, Turkey's engagement in the political evolution of Syria and Lebanon warrants close scrutiny. Ankara's pursuit of objectives tied to frontier security and consolidated regional sway has prompted a sustained military footprint in northern Syria, coupled with the intake of large-scale forced migration. This posture has recalibrated the Syrian conflict's internal equilibriums and, through the entwined sociopolitical fabric, has reverberated across Lebanon's precarious stability. Concurrently, Moscow's presence in the governance spaces of Syria and, more marginally, Lebanon, has grown more visible. The Kremlin's aerial and ground force deployments in defence of the Assad authority have redrawn the Syrian military calculus and have established Russia as a decisive actor in the broader geopolitical contest, guiding negotiating tracks and influencing the longer-term evolution of the Levant.

In summation, regional power engagement continues to exert decisive influence over the political trajectories of Syria and Lebanon, creating interwoven challenges and openings that shape prospects for stability and development on both sides of the border. Grasping the subtle permutations of these interventions is essential for situating Syria and Lebanon within the larger geopolitical environment that informs their choices and constraints. Such an understanding is equally necessary for the formulation of reliable, context-sensitive approaches to conflict de-escalation and durable peace consolidation.

Socioeconomic Interconnections: Trade and Migration

Trade and migration have remained fundamental drivers of the intricate interdependence that characterises Syria and Lebanon, continuously reshaping their socioeconomic contours and binding their peoples through overlapping livelihoods. Long-standing commercial circuits and migratory streams have been instrumental in fostering both economic growth and cultural dialogue, embedding each society within a larger, fluid regional context. Historically, the two states have operated as critical nodes in the exchange corridors linking the Mediterranean to the broader Levant, facilitating the circulation of goods, knowledge, and human capital. Beirut and Latakia, as principal port cities, have attracted traders from the Nile, the Gulf, and the Western Mediterranean, weaving their markets into a shared maritime continuum. In parallel, the porous shared border has permitted the circulation of labour and families, engendering a rich cross-fertilisation of dialects, traditions, and practices that continues to animate everyday life in both countries.

Periodic political discord and armed conflict have not eroded the underlying ties of commerce and cross-border movement; rather, they reveal the remarkable persistence of connected economies and populations. Recently, the Syrian civil war and its ripple effects in Lebanon have reconfigured mobility and trading patterns, generating both difficulties and openings for the two countries. Syrian asylum seekers arriving in Lebanon have tested the nation's services and fiscal resources, igniting discussion of labour market pressures and social assimilation. Concurrently, the rupture of established transit corridors and the tightening of economic sanctions have redefined the commercial terrain, disrupting key sectors and jeopardising household livelihoods along the frontier. Yet, within this turbulence, trading and migrating remain channels through which societies absorb shocks and reconstitute themselves. International and regional commerce is being reconfigured, while initiatives to regulate seasonal employment and expand humanitarian support signal paths for reweaving the dual economic and social fabric of Lebanon and Syria. Throughout the section that follows, we dissect the complex weave of corridors and migrations that unite the two states, illuminating the dynamisms reshaping them and the persistent co-dependencies that chart their collective horizons.

Security Concerns: Border Dynamics and Military Entanglements

The border between Syria and Lebanon is arguably the most telling front in the wider confrontation presently engulfing the Eastern Mediterranean. During the last four decades, the roughly 350-kilometre frontier has evolved into an ever-more porous seam between opposing state and military regimes, proprietary militias, and transnational actors. While Lebanon has hosted rising waves of Syrian refugees, Damascus has deployed border units calibrated likewise for counter-insurgency and counter-smuggling, blurring the distinction between security, support, and coercion. The continued entrenchment of Hezbollah as a quasi-state in southern Lebanon, tasked in part with confronting the Syrian opposition in Qalamoun, has fused state-to-state and substate military calculations, producing, in the process, a dramatic widening of the operational theatre. Syria's fragile political and security architecture is, in turn, peppered by spillover effects from cross-border skirmishes and by constant recalibrations of foreign military assets from rival patrons. Such spatial and vertical ambiguity inhibits coherent security solutions and challenges both Lebanese and Syrian authorities, whose bilaterally agreed protocols on border control remain largely dormant. A concerted response must therefore integrate political reconstruction, the regulation of armed groups, and humane border management into a single, interdisciplinary framework. Only then might the border cease to be a vector of fragmentation and instead gradually evolve into a zone of accountability and rational governance.

Consequently, effective management of evolving border dynamics and military entanglements necessitates a refined strategy that integrates military preparedness with clearly governed diplomatic tracks, humanitarian outreach, and long-term economic revitalisation programmes. Precise boundary clarification, methodical disarmament, and sustained confidence-building exercises remain central to cultivating mutual trust and reducing proximate dangers, thereby laying a credible groundwork for enduring security arrangements. External multilateral engagement is consequently indispensable, providing channels for impartial mediation, well-scoped peace operations, and targeted institutional strengthening. Equally, addressing structural sources of instability—ranging from economic inequities and competition over critical resources to entrenched ideological rifts—remains a non-negotiable requirement for securing a lasting peace and for protecting the welfare of communities situated along the frontier. Ultimately, the compound security dilemmas linked to border dynamics and military entanglement necessitate a comprehensive and cooperative framework that intentionally surpasses conventional military paradigms, aligning with the broader strategic goal of cultivating regional stability, coexistence, and mutual prosperity across the interdependent futures of Syria and Lebanon.

Multilateral Relations: Role in International Affairs

The multilateral diplomatic and institutional framework retains crucial importance in the broader international engagement with Syria and Lebanon, owing to their geographic significance, their interlinked internal fractures, and the overlapping regional and global strategic priorities that converge upon their borders.

Syria and Lebanon remain critical theatres for a dense network of international diplomacy and engagement involving the United Nations, the European Union, the Arab League, and a constellation of states, notably Russia, the United States, Iran, and Saudi Arabia. Each of these multilateral and unilateral actors has, directly and indirectly, shaped the security and stability calculus of the Levant. The two countries' deeply interwoven political and socioeconomic fabric has rendered them a site of rivalry and collaboration for the major global powers, compelling Damascus and Beirut to perform a sustained balancing act between divergent and often competing external agendas. The impact of this multilateral politics extends beyond the bilateral Lebanese–Syrian relationship; it sends ripples through regional configurations, influencing the trajectory of the Syrian civil war, the Israel-Palestine conflict, and the broader Arab political landscape. In parallel, the United Nations has prioritised the humanitarian dimensions of the Syrian crisis by orchestrating aid delivery and championing negotiations, while the European Union has augmented this effort through targeted financial and humanitarian support, aimed at ameliorating the humanitarian fallout of these overlapping crises.

Multilateral initiatives demonstrate the overlapping fates that characterise contemporary Middle Eastern geopolitics. Alongside these efforts, the Arab League remains pivotal, mediating disputes and promoting dialogue—sometimes between the uneasy pair of Syria and Lebanon. Its sustained engagement echoes the collective memory and mutual responsibilities that the Arab states share and reinforces the idea that regional stability requires concerted, rather than unilateral, action. At the same time, external actors, notably Russia, the United States, Iran, and Saudi Arabia, condition the same territory through diverse military, economic, and diplomatic levers. The result is a diplomatic lattice whose permeable fibres both preserve and reconfigure local balances of power. Rivalry and collaboration among these actors extend active conflicts and create moments when compromise, however fragile, becomes plausible. A nuanced appreciation of these overlapping diplomatic circuits is therefore indispensable for anticipating the ramifications of Syria and Lebanon's crises as they ripple across a more interconnected international system.

Humanitarian Considerations: Crisis and Aid Efforts

In the closely intertwined narratives of Syria and Lebanon, humanitarian issues take precedence, dictated by deepening crises and by the scale of aid that struggles to match unfolding need. Conflict, displacement, and the erosion of basic public services continue to mark the humanitarian profile of the region. Syria's compounding violence has fed relentless population flight into Lebanon, testing its already-fragile health systems and social safety nets. National and local relief actors, along with the international community, have deployed life-saving measures, yet the gap between emergency response and the durable solutions so urgently required remains wide. A decade of war in Syria, compounded by the border region's volatility, has placed humanitarian considerations at the core of any credible strategy for regional stability. External actors regularly calibrate aid delivery against a landscape altered by geopolitical rivalries, and the need for secure, unfettered access to affected populations stays unresolved. Effective response hinges upon purposeful coordination among state institutions, international NGOs, and UN bodies, whereby political sensitivities and security vulnerabilities are openly acknowledged and managed. Only through such concerted effort can the immediate suffering of populations at risk be eased, while fostering the longer-term resilience that the region demands.

The ongoing crisis has not only tested the coping capacities of host communities but has also underscored the entanglement of humanitarian operations with global geopolitical currents. Lasting solutions must go beyond immediate relief to account for the enduring sociopolitical dimensions of the displacement, centring on the empowerment of local authorities and the fortification of communal capacities. Equally, the ecological ramifications must not be sidelined: accelerated resource depletion and habitat loss compound the vulnerabilities of displaced and host populations alike. Planning for the future, the coordinated delivery of assistance must blend the immediate imperatives of humanitarian response with the objectives of inclusive, long-term development.

Environmental Factors: Shared Natural Assets

The Syrian and Lebanese geographies, though modest in extent, are braided by a lattice of shared ecological systems and natural resources that carry weight for both countries. From the coastal lowlands to the encircling ranges, a mosaic of ecosystems supports the livelihoods and economies of a dispersed and interlinked populace.

Water resources in the eastern Mediterranean have become a preeminent environmental challenge confronting both Syria and Lebanon. The Litani River, which rises in Lebanon's Bekaa Valley, provides a vital freshwater artery for domestic consumption and agricultural irrigation. After coursing through southern Lebanon, it discharges into the Mediterranean Sea. Yet, accelerated urban expansion, industrial effluents, and outdated irrigation techniques have collectively degraded the river's quality and diminished its dependable flow. The resultant conflict between human dependency and the need to conserve fragile riverine ecosystems demands harmonised policy and management from Beirut and Damascus. At the same time, Syria's Euphrates River undergirds agriculture and rural vitality across its lowland basin. The construction of upstream storage dams and expansion of irrigation schemes have sharpened disputes over equitable water allocations, further intensifying the pressure on this critical supply. The recurring theme of transboundary river management thus acquires added urgency, emphasising the imperative for legally underpinned, cooperative institutional arrangements to resolve joint hydrological problems. On a broader scale, both nations also benefit from a shared Mediterranean coastline, which not only furnishes fisheries and mineral resources but also links regional trade and maritime infrastructure.

The marine environment offers viable avenues for sustainable fisheries and ecotourism, bolstering the economic resilience of coastal towns. Nonetheless, the accelerated decline of marine habitats—driven by overharvesting, pollution, and climate shifts—constitutes an urgent hazard for these shared marine commons, necessitating integrated marine conservation frameworks. Under these escalating pressures, Syria and Lebanon confront a decisive moment in which equitable stewardship of marine resources hinges on coordinated action. Tackling the ecological dimensions of the crisis demands transnational partnerships that place ecosystem viability before transient political interests. Consequently, prioritising joint scientific investigations, harmonising cross-border protective regimes, and crafting transparent mechanisms for managing disagreements become non-negotiable in the effort to sustain these shared marine endowments.

Vision for the Future: Pathways to Cooperation and Stability

The fates of Syria and Lebanon have for generations been woven together by a lattice of history, politics, society, and economy. Looking ahead, the necessity of imagining a trajectory that cultivates collaboration and durable peace between the two societies is clear, since such a trajectory is inextricable from the broader goals of regional security and shared prosperity.

Environmental strains arising from shared natural resources offer states the imperative to reimagine cooperation as the foundation of sustainable stability. Central to this re-imagination is the design of joint, transboundary programmes dedicated to the conservation and prudent stewardship of common assets. Coordinated approaches to water governance, the deployment of renewable energy infrastructures, and habitat protection initiatives can pre-empt the centrifugal pressures of scarcity while nurturing a resilient web of trust and mutual dependency between Syria and Lebanon. By embedding sustainable methodologies and cross-border reciprocity into policy frameworks, both countries can gradually supplant entrenched geopolitical rivalries with a common horizon of shared prosperity. The remit of this cooperative vision, however, cannot be confined to the ecological sphere; it must be woven into the socio-political and economic fabric of the region. Elevating diplomatic exchanges, facilitating intercultural discourse, and designing bilateral economic agreements will be decisive for the emergence of a durable peace. This will require confronting legacies of mistrust, constructing inclusive and accountable governance, and opening corridors for trade and investment that transcend state borders. Finally, harnessing technology and innovative practices can amplify collective efforts, transforming shared challenges into opportunities for joint advancement.

By harnessing pervasive digital connectivity, expanding educational exchange initiatives, and collaboratively confronting health system vulnerabilities, Syria and Lebanon can collaboratively enter an era of sustainable interdependence. Technological innovation, when effectively mobilised, enables knowledge economies to flourish, overcoming the legacies of divided histories. The future envisioned here rests on an inclusive framework that recognises the inseparability of Syrian and Lebanese trajectories. It is distinguished by strategic leadership prepared to sustain dialogue, an institutional resolve to translate empathy into policy, and continuous engagement to cultivate shared cultural and civic respect. The path is undeniably complex, marked by historic and immediate setbacks, yet the enduring promise of joint prosperity and regional stability inspires persistent efforts. In this shared undertaking, the peoples of both countries, supported by their wider environment, can jointly write a narrative of reconciliation and resilient growth.

2
Historical Context
A Shared Past, Divergent Trajectories

Ancient Ties: The Roots of Syrian-Lebanese Relations

Situated at the nexus of the oldest trade routes and cultural corridors, Syria and Lebanon have conserved a common past that continues to inform their present. Throughout antiquity, the Levant's gentle topography and abundant resources sustained the simultaneous rise of settlements and powerful states. From the third millennium BCE, the vines of the Bekaa and the cedar-studded ranges nurtured the city-states of Ugarit, Mari, and Byblos, which exchanged not only pottery and grain but also philosophical texts and hymnody. The ensuing compression of peoples under successive Assyrian, Babylonian, and Persian rule had the dual effect of integrating the districts and accentuating their distinctiveness.

Among these, the Phoenicians of the Levantine littoral pioneered a unified maritime culture that linked Lebanon's cedar wood and Syria's metals to far-flung markets, sowing the early seeds of a relational matrix that would endure through Hellenistic diffusion, Roman provincial governance, and later Islamic empires. The linguistic and ritual inheritances that evolved within these shared arenas of trade, conquest, and ecology laid an enduring matrix of cooperation and reciprocity that centuries of later political contingencies have only periodically interrupted.

The Phoenicians forged a legacy, their mariners charting waters from Syracuse to Cadiz, their bales of Alexandrian purple dye, worth their weight in gold, looping the Mediterranean in prestige and coin. Their networks of signed treaties brought Levantine ports and desert oases into one hesitant political conversation. Fifty leagues east, Damascus commanded the caravans that threaded silk to Phoenician hulls, cotton to Roman belts, ivory to the Emperor's court; the same streets welcomed traders in medicine, geometry, and dialectic. Alexander's armies passed, and the granite squares of Antioch were measured with columns that borrowed from Egyptian, Ionian, and Mesopotamian hands. Later, Rome threaded its roads and aqueducts through the cedar and the Galilee, Antioch and Baalbek lifting marble facades and Senate, their baths scented with Syrian pine. In the centuries shy of the Common Era, the new confession of the crucified swept in with traders and soldiers; desert fathers settled in Hermon's leeward caves, the council at Tyre debated the Nicene creed, and bishops of Damascus and of Tyre signed the same letters to the imperial court. It is through this unbroken ribbon of migrations, settlements, heresies, and entrepôts that the modern Syrian and Lebanese lands, still nearly touching the same Mediterranean, still sharing the same cedar wood, look at each other.

Their joint inheritance constitutes a mosaic of cultures and civilizations, intricately woven by the dual forces of time and geography, and it has quietly furnished the underlying conditions that continue to influence their contemporary ties.

The Ottoman Era: A Patchwork of Provinces

The Ottoman epoch, now frequently invoked as a critical interval in the histories of what we now call Syria and Lebanon, registered a host of deep and interlocking changes. Ottoman sovereignty rendered the lands that comprise modern Syria and Lebanon into separate administrative provinces, each calibrated by its own set of institutional markers and regional character. Istanbul's increasing political centralisation enabled the rise of a layered administrative structure in which central officials, provincial notables, and local chieftains acted in a highly negotiated polity of semi-autonomous jurisdictions. This decentralised matrix, in turn, underscored the divergent yet interdependent paths that would later be taken by Syrian and Lebanese societies. The Ottoman conquest of the Levant in the early 16th century forged a fluctuating political mosaic marked by provisional alliances, sporadic insurrections, and the recalibration of genres of influence. The dual apparatus of provincial governance—vilayet and mutasarrifate—imposed an uneven edifice of legal codes, tax regimes, and ecclesiastical jurisdictions, thereby conferring a calibrated level of institutional and confessional latitude to local elites.

The regime thus inaugurated gave rise to a plurality of competing loyalties and identities that cut across the heterogeneous populations of the territories, embedding the layered divisions that still colour the region's geopolitical currents.

Concurrently, the demographic profile of the Levant underwent decisive transformation under Ottoman rule: the arrival of new populations, resettlements, and migrations, the coercive resettlement of entire ethnic blocks, and the relentless push–pull of migration expanded the ethnic and cultural layering still evident in present-day Syria and Lebanon. Confronted by shifting military and fiscal pressures, the imperial government pursued a calibrated policy of demographic reconfiguration, conferral of land grants to loyal officials, and planned urban expansion; the legacy of these interventions remains etched in the region's social, legal, and spatial codes. Such initiatives not only reconfigured the topography of towns and villages but also recalibrated the compass of social rank, fiscal obligation, and communal allegiance. By 1918, the Ottoman Levant had become a deliberately engineered social mosaic whose internal mechanics had already begun to outlive the polity that had first devised them. Deciphering these layered processes allows scholars to trace the historical trajectory that led to the present alignments of authority and allegiance across the Eastern Mediterranean.

Mandate Period: European Powers Redefining Borders

The failure of the empire and the settlement that ensued reconstructed the Levant's sovereign distinctions through the mandate trench.

Consequently, the territories of Syria and Lebanon passed into the stewardship of European powers, France governing both, while Britain assumed control over Palestine and Transjordan. This era catalysed a complex interplay of European colonial designs and the evolving aspirations of Arab nationalists alongside diverse local communities. For Syria and Lebanon, the mandate period crystallised a decisive moment in the reconfiguration of territorial limits and the formulation of national consciousness. European authorities exercised decisive control in fixing borders and structuring administrations, regularly disregarding the intricate realities of sectarian and ethnic compositions. The enforcement of synthetic boundaries and bureaucratic partitions thereby generated enduring effects, the echoes of which remain audible in the contemporary Middle East. In Lebanon, the French mandate institutionalised a confessional system in which state offices, from the presidency to the parliament, were allocated proportionately to the recognised sectarian groups. This elaborate allocation, while momentarily stabilising, entrenchment laid the groundwork for a frail sectarian equilibrium whose strains periodically erupt. In contrast, Syria's experience was marked by sustained and violent opposition, as local insurrections and burgeoning nationalist leagues repeatedly challenged the imposition of foreign governance and underscored the irreconcilability of colonial authority with indigenous aspirations for sovereign statehood. The colonial interlude of mandate rule forged diverging national courses in Syria and Lebanon, directed by contrasting European designs and domestic pulses. In both territories, however, this same interval witnessed cultural awakening and political vocabulary. Poets, journalists, and intellectuals in Damascus, Beirut, and the hinterlands interrogated the very meanings of political belonging, and through presses, salons, and lectures, insisted upon sovereignty and self-determination as living principles rather than distant promises. External manipulations, whether through the strategic fracturing of ethnic bases or the partial co-opting of local elites, complicated these deliberations, creating a layering of fragmented loyalties that would later metastasise into civil strife. By examining the intricate stratagems of the mandate administrators alongside the reflexive, often contradictory, responses of indigenous society, one discerns in the inter-war decades the sedimented anticipations upon which the fraught state of Syria and Lebanon now rests.

Independence and Early Alliances: Divergence Begins

The end of European colonial rule ushered Syria and Lebanon into independence but also laid the first bricks of their contrasting futures. The years immediately following the formal handover crystallised the political choices each country would make. Lebanon, fragile yet determined, formalised a sectarian power-sharing pact intended to translate its confessional mosaic into political stability; each religious community gained its share of representation and administration. Syria, by contrast, surveyed a population of overlapping religious and ethnic constituencies and sought to forge a singular national identity while managing centrifugal pressures. These formative years produced political architectures that would resonate across the shared border. Lebanon's practice of reciprocal sectarian bargaining began to crystallise into formal parties and informal clientelist networks, while Syria gradually centred power in its own party and security apparatus, projecting authority over a fragmented society. The interactions thus patterned between the two neighbours would oscillate between competition and conditional cooperation. As both nations navigated their first years of sovereignty, they also cultivated early linkages to foreign patrons, which would compound their divergent paths and embed each into a wider geopolitical field.

Lebanon, balancing itself on a diplomatic tightrope, skilfully cultivated its partnerships with France and the United States while preserving its traditional orientation towards Arab capitals, especially Cairo and Riyadh. Meanwhile, Syria oriented its foreign policy towards the Soviet bloc and the wider socialist world, presenting a clearly opposing geopolitical trajectory. The resulting agreements, forged between the late 1940s and the early 1950s, not only mirrored the divergent ideological cosmologies of the two states but also planted the seeds for later contested regional entanglement. Each state's prize assets—Lebanon's fortified-segment of economic liberalism counterposed with Syria's obsession with territorial recovery—were further complicated by competing projects of political legitimacy. Both nations confronted the dual task of graphically delineating their nationhood while absorbing internal and external pressures that sought to dictate their role within the emergent Arab order. The connections established during this early post-colonial phase still inform the present-day balance of power, highlighting how the foundational break between Lebanese pluralism and Syrian centralism forged the geopolitical fissures that now endure.

Post-Colonial Politics: Parallel but Distinct Paths

After the rupture with colonial rule, Syria and Lebanon pursued separate post-colonial paths, shaped by separate political, social, and economic realities. Each country retained the legacy of French mandate rule, and both professed a common impulse for self-rule, yet they practised their new sovereignty in different registers.In Syria, the decades after European colonial withdrawal were marked by ongoing military coups and widespread political turbulence as rival groups contested control. The turbulence eventually enabled the Baath Party to consolidate power, culminating in Hafez al-Assad's seizure of the presidency in 1970. Assad's government established a firmly centralised authority that profoundly shaped Syria's domestic order and directed its strategic posture with Lebanon. Lebanon, after obtaining independence, surfaced its own intractable difficulties. The power-sharing arrangements imposed by the French mandate produced a fragile equilibrium among its diverse religious and sectarian groups, which in turn obstructed the formation of durable state institutions. The persistence of rival political blocs, reinforced by foreign intervention, further strained Lebanon's efforts to secure internal cohesion. The 1943 National Pact, which ostensibly allocated official positions in accordance with sectarian identity, institutionalised a confessional framework that both recognised and perpetuated the country's demographic pluralism. While Lebanon endeavoured to project itself as an open and cosmopolitan centre, Syria, under the influence of President Gamal Abdel Nasser, pursued the ambitious project of Arab nationalist unity.This ideological pivot—positioned to galvanise the Arab world against imperialism and colonialism—complicated the already intricate bilateral ties between Syria and Lebanon. The divergent trajectories charted by the two states in the post-colonial epoch generated a dense weave of competing interests and overlapping aspirations. Common motifs—nation-building, difficult transferences of sovereignty from colonial regimes, and the search for enduring political order—appeared in both polities, yet the specific courses these ambitions followed illuminated the distinctive obstacles confronting each. Within the frame of post-colonial political reconfiguration, Syria and Lebanon sequentially articulated separate national narratives and institutional legacies, thus laying the groundwork for the multifaceted relations and reciprocal influences that persist in the contemporary period.

The Lebanese Civil War: Implications for Bilateral Relations

The Lebanese Civil War 1975–1990 introduced seismic shifts into the bilaterally negotiated terrain between Syria and Lebanon. The multilayered and internally stratified character of that conflict redefined the contours of both societies and generated legacies whose resonance would extend into the governance and diplomacy of the following decades.The civil conflict was propelled by entrenched sectarian rivalries, stark socio-economic inequities, and contests for political hegemony, factors that coursed across borders and rearranged the regional geopolitical landscape. In the war's opening phase, Damascus deepened its military presence in Lebanon to consolidate its regional sway and to harness the disorder in pursuit of its own strategic imperatives. While Syrian forces were ostensibly deployed to re-establish order and safeguard Syrian national interests, their presence ignited vehement opposition from Lebanese groups that viewed outside intervention as an erosion of sovereignty. Such incursions produced a re-forged interface between the two states, now marked by an imbalance of power that bred a chronic mutual distrust. Against this backdrop, the civil war's convoluted matrix of allegiances and enmities further strained Syrian-Lebanese ties. Lebanon was transmuted into a battleground for external powers, each underwriting a differing militia according to its own strategic calculus. The resulting fragmentation, compounded by persistent outside meddling, widened the chasm of mistrust and enshrined an instability resistant to the cultivation of sincere bilateral collaboration. The legacy of the civil war thus came to exist as an enduring shadow, its aftereffects still informing the complex entanglement of Syrian and Lebanese national interests.The entrenchment of Syrian influence in Lebanon was marked by military presence and the unambiguous installation of a Syrian protectorate that recalibrated the regional order. Lebanon's political and security frameworks were rendered instrumental to Syrian objectives, generating institutional dependency that provoked widespread disquiet among Lebanese constituencies. The enduring civil war legacy, and Syria's decisive role in structuring post-conflict Lebanon, highlighted the intricate and often conflictual underpinnings of the bilateral engagement. Competing historical narratives and the fresh wounds of war sustained a low-grade friction that complicated advances toward a partnership marked by mutual respect and equilibrium. The civil war, therefore, remains the original rupture, continually refracting contemporary Syrian-Lebanese interactions through a prism of wartime memory and unresolved distrust.

Hafez al-Assad's Influence: A Decade of Control

In the unsettled decade that followed the formal conclusion of Lebanon's civil strife, Hafez al-Assad emerged as the decisive actor whose policies and posturing charted the regional order. Syrian President from 1971 to 2000, Assad deployed a calculus of military, political, and economic instruments to entrench Lebanese dependency, consolidating Syrian hegemony over the post-war apparatus while simultaneously courting rival Lebanese elites to fracture potential opposition.This chapter examines the intricate dimensions of Assad's rule and the implications for the political, social, and economic contours of both Syria and Lebanon. The Syrian leader's Lebanon policy rested on overlapping alliances, calibrated interventions, and shifting power configurations. By nurturing specific Lebanese groups and stationing Syrian troops, Assad sought to reinforce Syrian hegemony while adjusting to a fluid regional environment. The presence of the Syrian armed forces inaugurated sweeping modifications to Lebanon's domestic equilibrium and inhibited the already tenuous post-war recovery, etching a durable mark upon the country's political architecture. Assad's conduct and doctrines, in turn, redefined the bilateral nexus, influenced the regional balance, and reverberated across the wider geopolitical arena. By astutely negotiating Lebanon's fragmented sectarian landscape and managing external stakeholders, Assad consolidated Syria's status as a pivotal actor, though this consolidation aggravated sectarian divisions and precipitated future instability. The approach garnered mixed responses: it won allegiance in particular segments while generating opposition and persistent animus, both in Lebanon and in the international arena. The complexity of this period was further deepened by decisive geopolitical transitions—the fading of the Cold War, the evolving Arab-Israeli confrontations, and the rise of new regional configurations.These developments created a complex landscape of challenge and opportunity for the Assad regime, compelling Damascus to reorient its relations with Beirut and to manoeuvre skilfully within a shifting web of external pressures. Hafez al-Assad's imprint on regional security infrastructures has proved indelible, having structured alliances and solidified fault lines that remain salient in present-day geopolitics. A focused analysis of Hafez's fifteen-year dominance of Lebanon thereby illuminates the nuanced choreography of power, the mechanisms of cross-border intervention, and the mutual entanglement of state actors within a continuously unstable regional theatre.

Rebuilding Lebanon: Syria's Role in the Post-War Era

Syria's engagement during Lebanon's post-war reconstruction was multifaceted, rooted in both strategic ambition and regional posturing. By reinforcing its military deployment and orchestrating political manoeuvres, Damascus sought to tether Lebanon firmly to its orbit, perceiving Beirut's geopolitical configuration as indispensable to Syrian national security. The consequent militarisation of Lebanese politics crystallised governance arrangements that favoured Damascus and inoculated its brokers against reformist pressures. At the same time, this manoeuvre obscured emergent civil actors and obscured calls for a more equitable distribution of power. Sociologically, the Syrian imprint rendered sectarian elites more reliant on external backing, whilst simultaneously entrenching distinct localised grievances that persisted well beyond the reconstruction phase. Internationally, Syria's persistent dominance attracted condemnation, galvanising Western isolation tactics and galvanising Lebanese nationalists who rallied against perceived Syrian tutelage. Ultimately, though Syria's footprint restored a modicum of order, its stewardship of post-war Lebanon reproduced the very cleavages civil war reconstruction had ostensibly sought to transcend, inhibiting the consolidation of a coherent, nationally driven recovery agenda. At the same time, Lebanon remained fractured along the fault line between factions that accepted Syrian involvement and those that rejected it, aggravating internal discord and hindering the twin tasks of reconstruction and reconciliation. The strategies adopted for reviving Lebanon's shattered economy and eroded social fabric were therefore inseparable from the terms under which Syria engaged the country once the guns were silent. The Syrian state, supported by its allies, identified numerous entry points for deepening cross-border economic coordination, aiming both to secure immediate reparative gains and to consolidate its political weight. Although several of these cross-national programmes did, in principle, respond to humanitarian urgency in both nations, in practice they repeatedly tilted in ways that advanced Syrian priorities. The cumulative effect forced Lebanon to confront recurring difficulties in consolidating its autonomy and crafting a distinct trajectory of recovery. Furthermore, Syrian involvement did not stop at the border; its repercussions reverberated across the Levant and beyond, reconfiguring coalitions, breeding proxy clashes, and unsettling diplomatic circuits. The modalities of Syrian governance in Lebanon were thus enmeshed in a web of regional equations—its fraught dealings with key Arab states, shifting great power orientations, and the fluctuating balance of intra-Arab rivalry. Such layered interaction complicated, rather than clarified, the parameters of Lebanon's post-war reintegration, subjecting both promise and peril to the ongoing calibration of Syrian regional strategies. In sum, Syria's imprint on Lebanon's recovery was neither unilateral nor linear; it manifested the converging logics of national imperatives, regional calculus, and external power interaction. As Lebanon undertook the difficult processes of reconstruction and societal healing, Syrian involvement offered both assistance and hindrance, imprinting its own character on Beirut's path into the new century.

21st Century Developments: From Cooperation to Discord

The first years of the twenty-first century brought to Syrian-Lebanese relations a sequence of alternating cooperation and discord. When the devastating Lebanese civil war finally ceded to reconstruction, the newly rebuilding state, aware of its vulnerable institutions, briefly anticipated a revival of reciprocal engagement, and Damascus presented itself as an essential partner in the twin projects of political stabilisation and economic revival. Syrian officials championed joint enterprises and border regulation, projecting an image of regional solidarity. Yet, as reconstruction stagnated and the regional order refocused on the consequences of the Iraq war, deeper rifts re-emerged. Competing visions for political sovereignty, economic autonomy, and, crucially, security control re-asserted themselves. Simultaneously, the role of external actors intensified. Washington, the Gulf, Tehran, and, to a lesser extent, Moscow began recalibrating their positions toward Syria and Lebanon, tempting each side with conditional aid and diplomatic support to isolate competitors. The very instruments intended to stabilise the region—aid benchmarks, ceasefire brokerage, and security partnerships—were thus reinterpreted as tactical leverage. The cumulative effect re-energised dormant distrust and reinvigorated the historical disputes that had never fully receded beneath the surface.

The early twenty-first century also revealed sharply contrasting political trajectories for Syria and Lebanon, which in turn deepened their mutual estrangement. Throughout this period, Lebanon was preoccupied with chronic elite rivalries entrenched along sectarian lines, while Syria was consumed by the eruption of civil war and the reconfiguration of its own regime. These overlapping yet separate crises reframed bilateral relations, illustrating how internal disorder can decisively redirect external diplomacy. The emergence of Hezbollah as a pivotal actor further complicated the picture, given its militia footprint in Lebanon and its perennial rehearsals of insubordination toward the Syrian state. Regime anxieties about the group's Iranian nexus, accentuated by Saudi and Israeli impulses to destabilise the axis, catalysed a cautious and at times combative Syrian response. Such cross-cutting pressures gradually dissipated the minimal political alignment that still lingered after the Syrian withdrawal from Lebanon in 2005. By the second decade, it was clear that the accumulation of domestic fractures, geopolitics, and the spectre of sectarian war had decisively reoriented Damascus and Beirut away from the collaborative histories of the past, making estrangement the more durable equilibrium.

The future paths of Syria and Lebanon, once closely linked, now appear increasingly contested, complicating numerous initiatives aimed at rebuilding mutual comprehension and fruitful cooperation. The fallout from this state of affairs extends beyond the immediate borders of either country, highlighting once again the continuing relevance of the shifting ties that bind Syria to Lebanon.

Reflecting on History: Lessons for Contemporary Challenges

In confronting the contemporary difficulties that confront Syria and Lebanon, it is essential to situate current negotiations within the longer, comparative history that has moulded their conjoined fates. A critically informed survey of their common and diverging narratives reveals durable political logics, helping to clarify the layered character of today's geostrategic picture. The historical record documents recurrent interweaving of mutual assistance and mutual stress, permitting recognition of the structural pressures that have ordered the bi-national interaction over centuries. Repeated sequences of diplomatic synchrony and subsequent withdrawal, achieved within broader regional and global theatres, echo within present diplomatic deadlocks. A careful rereading of key historical junctures thus discloses layered precedents that inform the countries' reactions to disputes today, yielding conceptual scaffolds for delineating responses to the multilayered conflicts that will shape the early 21st century in the Levant.

The complex weave of past events illustrates how intertwined political, cultural, and socio-economic forces have consistently reconfigured the destinies of Syria and Lebanon. Beginning with the ancient currents that linked these territories and continuing through the colonial impositions and the struggles for independence, each period has left distinctive imprints on collective identity and future ambitions. Insight drawn from this chronicle illuminates the contemporary dilemmas now facing both countries. By returning to history's reservoir, one discerns the multiple levels of interconnectedness and the stubborn residues that still inform the present. Such an anchored comprehension allows for a measured assessment of how to advance, guided by the tempered judgement that only long-term reciprocal experience, both convergent and divergent, can provide.

3
The Syrian Civil War
Catalyst for Regional Instability

The Dawn of Conflict: Origins and Early Developments

The Syrian civil war erupted from a confluence of political repression, economic instability, and social fracture that had accumulated over decades. Enduring popular discontent with Bashar al-Assad's authoritarian governance was amplified by a lack of political pluralism, discriminatory economic practices, and pervasive graft. The spread of revolts during the Arab Spring emboldened Syrians to stage the first demonstrations in March 2011, demanding reforms. The regime's violent retaliations, beginning with mass arrests of youth activists and escalating to the shelling of urban centres, radicalised the protests and spread the uprising across the country. Peaceful marches gave way to disparate paramilitary movements, each forging its own doctrine, from secular nationalism to political Islam. Outside powers, motivated by geopolitical rivalries and sectarian alignments, began supplying armaments and funding, aggravating the fracturing of the rebel ranks and the proliferation of jihadist groups. Consequently, the original grievances mutated, as the war's destructive momentum reconfigured identities and the logic of survival, embedding the country in a protracted, multinational civil war.For a substantial segment of the Syrian populace, the early demands for political reform quickly evolved into calls for the regime's ouster, a shift catalysed by the authorities' brutal reprisals and by their persistent refusal to engage seriously with genuine complaints. In parallel, the regime, recognising the fracturing of the social contract, resorted to escalating military reprisals while simultaneously framing the uprising in explicitly sectarian and counter-terrorist terms, branding dissenters as traitors and extremists. This rhetorical strategy served both to justify extreme violence and to drive wedges among communities, thereby entrenching a brutal, self-reinforcing cycle. The conflict's internationalisation—marked by rival state intervention according to strategic, doctrinal, and sectarian calculations—added complexity and durable violence, as proxy battles fed into the civil war's increasingly fragmented and brutal character. The cumulative effect of these forces transformed the early protests into a civil war of indefinitely escalating scope and misery, with reverberations across the neighbouring states and the geopolitical order of the entire Levant.

From Protest to War: Escalation Dynamics and Motivations

The passage from demonstrative dissent to organised violence represented a decisive fracture in Syria's historical flow, inaugurating a spiral of ruin and regional peril. The forces propelling this metamorphosis were numerous, and their interwoven logic drew on political repression, shifting social alliances, and the deliberate interventions of foreign states, each vector exacerbating the others and overriding the window for negotiated resolution.

Initially, widespread demands for democratic governance and the eradication of systemic corruption travelled through every stratum of Syrian society, animated by the Arab Spring that invigorated the region. Yet, when these demands collided with the regime's firmly rooted authority, the national scene erupted into open rupture. The trajectory that followed was animated by a lattice of motives—decades of repression, bleak socioeconomic prospects, and deep-seated sectarian cleavages. The rapid endorsement of armed resistance by formerly peaceful activists, compounded by the regime's indiscriminate retaliation, rapidly escalated the struggle into a drawn-out, ruinous war. The fracturing of the opposition into rival militias, each pursuing divergent programmes and foreign patronage, established a turbulent battleground where ever-shifting allegiances and competing imperatives multiplied the violence. Concurrently, regional and global powers, pursuing their own strategic interests, stoked the fire and fortified mutually contradictory discourses, deepening the war's stubborn obstinacy. The intersection of these centrifugal forces set in motion a vicious cycle that engulfed the state in flames, forging a milieu in which negotiated resolution receded, and the humanitarian toll multiplied without respite.

Consequently, deciphering how peaceful protests escalated into protracted civil war requires a thorough analysis of multilayered domestic, regional, and global factors, illuminating the intricate motivations that thrust Syria into a lasting and harrowing conflict.

Key Players: Domestic Factions and Leaderships

The Syria conflict has unfolded within a densely interwoven environment of domestic actors, each motivated by divergent political, social, and territorial imperatives. A nuanced analysis of these factions, together with the hierarchies that sustain them, is indispensable for any assessment of the war's complexity and its regional aftershocks. Central to the struggle are the armed forces and security apparatus that remain steadfastly loyal to President Bashar al-Assad; their Alawite-led command is confronted by a lattice of rebel brigades and militia groups that span a broad ideological spectrum. Despite a shared animus toward the regime, the opposition has been characterized by fragmentation: secular nationalists, Salafist militias, ethnonational militias, and later, jihadist contingents, fractiously compete for dominance, territorial gains, and, ultimately, legitimacy. The ascendancy of the Islamic State of Iraq and al-Sham, and its later incarnation as ISIS, injected a radical core into the anti-regime constellation, restructuring territorial control and compounding the emerging humanitarian catastrophe.

Additionally, Kurdish forces, most notably the People's Protection Units (YPG), have asserted control over large swathes of northeast Syria, establishing a degree of local governance that has altered the territorial and political calculus of the civil war. Their consolidation of authority has forced both the regime and other non-state actors to recalibrate their objectives. Yet, the YPG's rise cannot be disentangled from external actors whose military, logistical, and political contributions have sustained and, at times, redirected different camps. Iran and Russia have delivered arms, fighters, and political legitimacy to Damascus, while the U.S. and a coalition of European and Gulf states have intermittently channelled assistance to a fragmented spectrum of opposition brigades, fearful of the consolidated sway that either the regime or its foreign patrons might otherwise accrue. The broader region's actors, none of whom subscribe to a common Syria agenda, have layered their own imperatives atop the war's pre-existing fissures: Ankara has deployed cross-border forces to inhibit Kurdish autonomy and entrench a belt of loyal Sunni enclaves, while Gulf capitals have recalibrated their commitments in line with both sectarian calculations and the calculus of U.S.-Iran competition. The interplay of these divergent agendas has refracted hostilities, deepened fragmentation, and occasioned a humanitarian toll that outstrips the capacity of international agencies to alleviate. The persistence and revival of violence in Syria thus underscore the inextricability of its civil war from a broader geopolitical chessboard, wherein local agency is always overdetermined by regional and global patrons, and the prospect of a negotiated settlement recedes further.

International Entanglements: The Role of Global Powers

The Syrian Civil War has been shaped as much by its internal factions and neighbourhood rivalries as by the competing interests of global powers. The crucible of the conflict has drawn direct foreign intervention in both visible and subterranean forms, altering its internal dynamics and radiating effects throughout the wider region. Russia stands as one of the primary global architects of the war's evolution, having reinforced the Assad regime through concentrated military intervention, capability transfers, and strategic diplomacy. These actions have not only buttressed Moscow's client state but have also secured its military foothold and influence throughout the Eastern Mediterranean. The United States has countered with its own calibrated presence, channelling arms and resources to selected opposition entities while also executing precision strikes designed to degrade both the Islamic State and other extremist networks. This American posture has, paradoxically, complicated the conflict's already dysfunctional alliance patterns by introducing a competing—though sometimes overlapping—set of objectives. At the same time, regional heavyweights Iran and Turkey have woven their respective interests into the conflict's fabric: Tehran has dispatched manpower and money to cement a peripheral corridor to the Mediterranean, while Ankara has aimed to contain Kurdish autonomy and fortify its own security perimeter. The result is a conflict that, far from being resolvable by its domestic actors, is irreversibly threaded through a web of foreign stakeholders whose ambitions continue to intersect—often at cross-purposes.Iran's commitment to the Assad regime and its sponsorship of militia networks have ensnared Tehran more deeply in the Syrian morass, accentuating the sectarian contours of the war.

Concurrently, Ankara's cross-border operations, designed to inhibit Kurdish autonomy and carve out security corridors, complicate the already dense lattice of allegiances and enmities. The entry of these regional and global powers has not merely extended the fighting; it has reverberated through the entire Middle Eastern security architecture. The collision of their objectives has fractured the regional order, with rival interventions intensifying hostilities and redrawing geopolitical lines. The resulting mosaic of shifting alliances, enmities, and contests for influence now extends well beyond the territory of Syria. As the international community weighs the repercussions of its involvement, the overlapping designs of these outside actors persist in directing the trajectory of the war and perplexing efforts to secure a durable peace and regional stability.

Humanitarian Crisis: Impact on Civilians and Response Mechanisms

The humanitarian catastrophe arising from the Syrian civil war has exerted an unprecedented toll on civilian populations, both inside Syria and in the bordering states that have sheltered its refugee waves.The sheer scale of suffering and displacement is beyond comprehension, with millions of individuals and families confronting the full weight of conflict-driven adversity. As violence and instability grew more pronounced, the humanitarian needs surged in magnitude and complexity, posing a multidimensional dilemma for aid agencies, national governments, and global institutions. The toll on civilians has been layered, manifesting not only in physical wounds but also in lasting psychological injury, enforced migration, and the disintegration of social fabrics. Families have been separated, income-generating activities obliterated, and entire neighbourhoods dismantled. Beyond the fatalities directly inflicted by belligerent groups, uncounted civilians have been deprived of food, potable water, and essential health services, deepening existing vulnerabilities and undermining the core of human dignity. Children have borne an outsized share of the burden, with schooling suspended, increasing vulnerability to exploitation, and routine exposure to violence. Response mechanisms to the crisis have displayed uneven degrees of efficacy and coherence. Humanitarian agencies and national/international NGOs have mobilised to distribute life-sustaining aid, yet have confronted access denial, escalating security threats, and chronic underfunding. States and multilateral partners have pledged critical financial support, yet the pace of resource mobilization continues to lag the shifting and expanding needs of the population. Neighbouring countries—most notably Lebanon, Turkey, and Jordan—have prudently opened their borders but are themselves strained by the influx, shouldering the immediate economic and social costs of integration.The recent wave of people fleeing Syria has overtaxed already fragile services and infrastructure, creating conflated social, economic, and political contests that host communities can hardly absorb. Beyond their immediate borders, these pressures have heightened regional volatility, deepening pre-existing frictions and layering new complications onto the present geopolitical crises. Any effective way to deal with the humanitarian dimensions of the fallout must therefore be broad and indivisible, coupling urgent aid with the longer planning required for reconstruction and the durable support needed by displaced persons and host populations alike. Priorities must include working with local people, grounding responses in cultural realities, and strengthening the day-to-day capacities of communities. Simultaneously, diplomatic and policy responses must be of one piece with humanitarian principles, acknowledging that the consequences reach well beyond Syria and obligate a coordinated international effort.

Regional Ripple Effects: Spillover into Neighbouring Countries

The Syrian civil war has generated broad regional repercussions that reach well beyond its borders, embedding instability across Lebanon, Turkey, Jordan, and Iraq. These states have absorbed the conflict's shockwaves, each becoming a receipt of the political, economic, and security distortions that originate within Syrian territory. This section will untangle the intersecting currents of spillover and clarify the layered, asymmetric pressures exerted on each host state and on their collective order.

Lebanon's historically intertwined relationship with Syria—shaped by shared culture, politics, and demographics—has rendered it particularly vulnerable to the ongoing conflict. The surge of Syrian refugees has intensified Lebanon's brittle socio-economic structure, raising social tensions and overwhelming already deficient public services and infrastructure. Concurrently, the cross-border transmission of sectarian violence and militant activities has deepened Lebanon's internal security quandaries, undermining its precariously balanced sectarian order. Turkey, with its extended Syrian border, has faced parallel pressures, including refugee arrivals and the movement of extremist factions. The conflict has strained Turkish resources and tested national cohesion, compelling a series of intricate policy adaptations to align refugee management with counter-militant and border security imperatives. Economic disturbances from Syria have further reverberated within Turkey, undermining trade, deterring investment, and severely impacting macroeconomic stability. Jordan, positioned as a principal international ally in Syrian crisis mitigation, has nevertheless shouldered a heavy refugee load. The continued influx has strained Jordanian public finance, particularly within healthcare, education, and the socio-economic opportunities available to both Jordanian citizens and displaced Syrians.

Moreover, the war's drawn-out trajectory has heightened Jordan's border security anxieties, spurring the Kingdom to intensify surveillance, fortify crossings, and erect defences to guard against the destabilising currents that the Syrian conflict has sent rolling across the desert. Iraq, already contending with sectarian fragmentation and political paralysis, has not been insulated from the turbulence: the emergence of ISIS and the resurgence of militia activity, framed as spillovers from the war to the west, have deepened Baghdad's insecurity, unravelled the hard-won gains of the post-2006 surge, and deferred the timetable for economic and political recovery. The swirl of displaced Iraqis returning across the border, coupled with bazaars of small arms and the passage of veterans who fought on either side, has further frayed Iraq's already depleted societal fabric. The Syrian war's spillover has thus seeped into the geopolitical and socio-economic strata of its neighbours, generating interlocking crises that elude unilateral resolution. Grasping the intertwined and ever-shifting ripple effects will be essential for regional actors and external mediators if they are to fashion sequenced and context-sensitive policies that address the conflict's ethics, its security taxonomy, and, ultimately, the precarious coherence of the Levantine security order.

Economic Consequences: Destruction, Displacement, and Destitution

The economic fallout of the Syrian civil war has been devastating, reverberating well beyond the Syrian state to erode regional economies that previously intersected and complemented one another. Years of bombardment, urban warfare, and sieges have not only razed buildings but have shattered the electricity grids, transport arteries, and water networks that served as the regional hub for Arab trade. Export-led sectors, from agriculture to light manufacturing, have been hollowed out, and supply chains extending into Jordan, Lebanon, and Turkey have splintered, driving up the cost of basic goods and curtailing bilateral trade.

What was once a vibrant economy is now tasked with reconstructing itself from ruins. Millions of displaced Syrians have burdened neighbouring countries, intensifying competition for jobs, housing, and public services. This refugee surge has compounded the vulnerability of already precarious economies, heightening social tensions and fuelling political instability. The ripple effects on human capital are severe; many of the country's most skilled workers find themselves in jobs for which they possess neither training nor passion, or migrating further afield. Consequently, the pool of expertise necessary for reconstruction is shrinking. Scarcity of decent jobs and widening income gaps have driven poverty rates ever higher, endangering an entire generation of youth who are missing classrooms and vocational training. The collapse has also multiplied opportunities for corruption and informal economies, obstructing the emergence of a transparent, resilient financial order. Humanitarian and investment flows, meanwhile, have struggled to keep pace with the scale of need, leaving the economy saddled with unsustainable debt, runaway inflation, and stagnant output. The disintegration of economic order has delayed regional integration efforts and complicated diplomatic efforts, as neighbouring states recalibrate their allegiances and strategies in an increasingly unpredictable environment.

Diverting financial resources toward humanitarian assistance and security responses prevents the timely implementation of critical infrastructure development and the reliable delivery of basic services, thereby reinforcing the persistent cycle of economic distress. The ripple effects of this diversion reach well beyond budgetary deficits; they are entangled with the broader geopolitical order and shape the prospects for durable peace in the region.

Diplomatic Endeavours: Attempts at Peace and Reconciliation

The Syrian civil war has caused profound humanitarian distress and geopolitical upheaval, provoking a succession of diplomatic initiatives explicitly designed to secure ceasefires and promote a broader culture of reconciliation among warring parties. These initiatives have drawn participation from multilateral organisations, neighbouring states, major international powers, and various non-state stakeholders. Although each confrontation has generated a distinctive constellation of obstacles, sustained diplomatic engagement has remained a necessary instrument for disaggregating the war's intertwined humanitarian, security, and governance crises. Central to this diplomatic architecture has been the United Nations, which has consistently sponsored peace talks and facilitated Syrian interlocutors—state and non-state—within the UN-led Geneva process. This track has aimed to catalyse negotiated political transition while laying the groundwork for an inclusive and representative governance framework; the initiative has, however, remained stalled, repeatedly thwarted by rigid negotiating stances and the persistence of competing military campaigns. In parallel, regional organisations, particularly the Arab League, have advanced separate rounds of mediation and intermittently negotiated temporary ceasefires, thereby attempting to create spaces for dialogue and for incremental confidence-building. Meanwhile, Washington, Moscow, and the European Union have maintained iterative engagement through differing frameworks and multilateral summits, attempting to harmonise divergent strategic objectives while stabilising the conflict's ever-expanding spillover effects.

Engagement by influential regional and global actors illustrates the complex geopolitical backdrop of the Syrian civil war and the conflicting interests guiding each participant. In tandem, Syria's immediate neighbours—Turkey, Jordan, and Lebanon—have placed themselves at the centre of diplomatic efforts, convening refugee summits, extending humanitarian assistance, and championing mechanisms for lasting peace. Although these initiatives have repeatedly run aground, they have also prompted several critical achievements. The creation of de-escalation zones and humanitarian corridors, negotiated by external intermediaries, has delivered much-needed relief to encircled populations and ensured the transport of supplies. Concurrently, efforts to negotiate local ceasefires and reconciliation have highlighted the viability of community-based peace building, reinforcing local resilience and fostering intercommunal dialogue. Still, ongoing military campaigns and the continued fragmentation of the armed opposition continue to frustrate diplomatic continuity. Competing international agendas, combined with the unwillingness of pivotal actors to yield, have thwarted the drafting of comprehensive accords. This fact accentuates the urgency of fortifying multilateral mechanisms and deploying diplomatic clout to dismantle entrenched barriers to reconciliation. Future initiatives must reconstruct diplomacy on robust inclusivity, ensuring that the voices of marginalised constituencies, especially women and ethnic and sectarian minorities, are amplified and integrated into every negotiating table.

By placing a premium on inclusive stakeholder engagement and nurturing settings where dialogue can flourish, diplomatic efforts may deconstruct the labyrinthine dimensions of the Syrian war and chart trajectories that lead to durable peace and meaningful reconciliation.

Media Narratives: Perceptions Shaping Outcomes

A decisive variable in the shaping of the Syrian civil war and its regional ramifications has been the media environment. From the initial flare of hostilities, disparate outlets have crafted reports to serve circumscribed political, military, or ideological objectives. The result has been a dense thicket of contradicting accounts, half-truths, and overtly partisan disseminations, which have redirected public sensibilities and guided the calculus of governments, NGOs, and international institutions. Chief among the consequences of this fractured media ecology has been the international fracturing of opinion: rival factions have mobilised parallel support networks, each contesting the moral and strategic high ground. Western outlets, frequently privileging humanitarian frames, have foregrounded the surge of refugees and the toll on civilian life to mobilise popular sympathy and justify intervention. In concert, Syrian and allied state-controlled media have minimised evidence of abuses, characterising military offensives as the only bulwark against terror and thereby consolidating legitimacy for the regime's unyielding hold on power.

Social media platforms have fundamentally restructured the media environment, offering a conduit for the swift distribution of unverified information and extremist narratives, which, in turn, amplifies disinformation and entrenches societal divides. The depiction of core actors and events within the Syrian civil war has been profoundly mediated, circumscribing diplomatic messaging, moulding public sentiment, and guiding the allocation of military and humanitarian resources. Moreover, these constructs have permeated collective memory, determining how the conflict and its prospective legacies are envisaged within and beyond the region. The reach of mediated narratives transcends empirical reporting, interweaving with grand geopolitical calculus and power contestation, thereby elevating the centrality of narrative warfare in modern confrontations. Consequently, an in-depth analysis of the interrelation between media reproduction, public perception, and strategic outcome is indispensable for grasping the intricate realities of the Syrian civil war and for apprehending its protracted reverberations across the Middle East.

Long-term Implications: Shifting Geopolitical Balance

The Syrian civil war is now an axis upon which the future configuration of the Middle East is being redrawn. The most salient consequence resides in the redistribution of geopolitical power and regional authority. The conflict has unsettled longstanding diplomatic attachments, fostered emergent alignments, and exposed the brittle architecture of state institutions, thereby recalibrating the equilibrium of influence in and beyond the Levant.

This section assesses how the Syrian war has reshaped the geopolitical distribution of power in the Middle East and the wider global order. Shifting patterns of influence show themselves in the reappraisal of relations between principal regional actors. Long-standing alignments have come under strain, giving way to novel coalitions forged in the fires of the conflict. At the same time, the war has laid bare the internal contradictions of global partnerships, forcing capitals to revisit the underpinnings of their strategic calculations. The ascent and retreat of competing armed groups within Syrian territory have, in turn, redrawn the maps of the levies and projects commanded by distant powers. Continuing instability has loosened the grip of established conventions, leading to sharpened rivalry for geopolitical returns. Within that conversational theatre, older rivalries have widened into surrogate warfare and direct military forays that further fray regional coherence. Superpower engagement has layered yet more intricacy upon the already tangled terrain, magnifying Syria's role as an arena of contested authority. The race to project military and diplomatic weight raises the stakes of misjudgment and conflict escalation, the impacts of which could extend far beyond the Levant.

Beyond the immediate regional consequences, the Syrian conflict has produced global ramifications that testify to the diffuse nature of contemporary security interdependencies. The sheer scale of refugee migration, coupled with the transnational propagation of militant ideologies, has revealed the fragility of formerly insulated diplomatic and security interests. The conflict's protracted character has compelled governmental and scholarly communities to reevaluate the viability of inherited frameworks of geopolitical stability, collective security, and multilateral cooperation. The principal analytical task now is to interpret the durable uncertainty provoked by the evolving alliance patterns that the Syrian crisis has catalysed, and to formulate policies that remain resilient within that fluid context. As violence and governance voids continue, the conflict's capacity to reconfigure power relations—while simultaneously offering selective openings for influence—requires sustained attention from regional and extra-regional actors committed to differential ends of stability, deterrence, and crisis management.

4

Lebanon's Sectarian Balance

Political Fragility and Resilience

Lebanon's Sectarian Tapestry

Lebanon's rich sectarian plurality constitutes a defining trait that has shaped both its social fabric and its governance. This intricate mosaic has accumulated over centuries, sustained by a pattern of negotiated coexistence among numerous religious communities. Presently, its constituents embrace Sunni and Shia Muslims, Maronite and Eastern Orthodox Christians, and Druze, among smaller groups. Each community retains distinctive customs, ritual practices, and doctrinal commitments, collectively forming Lebanon's variegated civic identity. The reciprocal influence of these affiliations reaches every sector of public life, informing the constitutional distribution of authority and the subtler codes of everyday social conduct. The roots of Lebanon's sectarian dispersal originate in Ottoman administrative practices and the policies of the French mandate, both of which instituted systems of communal classification and subtly fortified communal frontiers. These legacies solidified into the confessional structure that continues to mediate both conflict and collaboration among the sects.

Lebanon's protracted civil conflict and the wider regional wars that surrounded it have woven a persistent communal fracture into the very fabric of Lebanese life, a fracture that the 1990 Taif Agreement merely papered over rather than healed. The façade of post-war tranquillity has concealed a deep reservoir of mutual suspicion and sectarian animosity that now underlies every electoral strategy and every clientelist nexus. Although the country's confessionally diverse population enriches its cultural and affective registers, the same plurality generates chronic instability concerning the design of governance and the distribution of power. The delicate confessional equilibrium that was painstakingly crafted after the war serves today as the sole measure of political legitimacy; any perceived deviation from the intricate balance of numbers or portfolios has repeatedly revived the spectre of civil strife or induced the political system's complete stasis. The overlap of sectarian loyalty and sovereign power further clarifies the dynamics of the Lebanese political arena; confessional tribunals govern matrimony and inheritance, while Waqf institutions (Endowments) and clerical hierarchies wield substantial leverage over the civil service, school curricula, and electoral turnout. This hierarchical fusion of sectarian belonging and legal-political order is a leviathan that subordinates both the judiciary and the security services, perpetuating Lebanon's chronic pattern of fragmentation between state and society.

Historical Roots of Sectarian Division

Lebanon's sectarian divisions are the product of long-running historical processes during which overlapping patterns of governance, migration, and economic competition coalesced into a durable and polarising social structure. Since the early Ottoman period, the millet system allowed communal leaders to exercise local authority in return for loyalty to the imperial state, reinforcing communal identities while also sowing the seeds for future competition over state resources. As mountain and coastal regions became integrated into regional and global trade networks, the resulting mobility encouraged the formation of heterogeneous settlements. Yet uneven economic development, punctuated by external intervention, nurtured the perception of zero-sum competition among the communal elites who mobilised their constituencies to capture the state apparatus. France's post-World War I mandate codified these rivalries in the National Covenant of 1943, which embedded sectarian quotas in government institutions, ostensibly as a temporary measure but effectively ossifying the sectarian frame of public life. Subsequent civil strife, foreign intervention, and post-war reconstruction programmes further crystallised sectarian identities, rendering them both a resource for political mobilisation and a barrier to social mobility and collective political action.

Lebanon's complex social structure—home to Maronite Christians, Sunni and Shi'a Muslims, Druze, and smaller communities—has been both the forge and the reflective surface of the country's political and social life. The Ottoman millet system, which granted semi-autonomous legal jurisdictions to the Empire's religious groups, deepened the sense of communal identity and the expectation of collective governance. Within this inherited scheme, loyalty to religious affiliation increasingly outpaced the nascent idea of civic belonging. The subsequent French Mandate intensified the practice of sectarian segmentation, entrenching administrative and electoral frameworks that incentivised communal middlemen. The 1943 National Pact, which restated this confessional calculus in an explicitly enumerated distribution of political offices, sought to mediate sectarian strife through the proportional sharing of state authority. Although its designers viewed the mechanism as a safeguard for minorities and a facilitator of equilibrium, it also crystallised sectarian demarcations, creating opportunities for external powers to leverage Lebanon's multilayered instability. The Lebanese civil war of 1975 to 1990 intensified these divisions, displacing communities and searing communal memories. Within that crucible, episodic sectarian violence became the signature of the Lebanese condition. Only by mapping the historical accretion of sectarian politics can one grasp the persistent and at times obdurate determinants that shape contemporary governance and social relations in Lebanon.

It illustrates the depth and complexity of Lebanon's political and social relations, as well as the persistent fragilities that threaten its institutional durability and social cohesion.

The persistence of such attachments exposes the multi-faceted obstacles that any endeavour to reform Lebanon's sect-centred governance must confront. A candid assessment of the resulting order enables scholars to pinpoint the variables that may mitigate sectarian discord and nurture a shared national solidarity. Therefore, a comprehensive exploration of the historical genesis of sectarian clustering provides a lens through which to discern the persistent fragilities that threaten Lebanon's institutional durability and social cohesion.

The Taif Accord: A Fractured Balance

Negotiated to end the prolonged civil conflict, the Taif Accord of 1989 embodies a precarious and intricate blueprint for recalibrating the national power constellation. The agreement altered the allocation of authority by recalibrating both the quotas and the leverage accorded to the country's myriad sectarian constituencies. Its architects framed the document as a formal plea for national reconciliation, explicitly aiming to transcend the deep-seated animosities that had unleashed the violence. In practice, the accord sought to mitigate the recurrent tensions among Lebanon's religious communities by formalising a power-sharing schema that tethered official appointments and public functions to sectarian affiliation.

The reorganisation of Lebanese state institutions and the meticulous distribution of competences were the twin foundations of the Taif Agreement, which aimed to equitably allocate power while simultaneously acknowledging the country's confessional pluralism. The accord delineated the respective jurisdictions of the presidency, the parliament, and the judiciary, striving for cumulative sectarian parity at every echelon of decision-making. Although Taif succeeded in averting a return to civil war and in imposing a tenuous veneer of order, it simultaneously bequeathed a series of adverse legacies. Analysts argue that the power-sharing formula entrenched sectarian boundaries and fostered a clientelist culture that stifled genuine democratic development. The architecture of the accord has furthermore hampered the emergence of a cohesive national identity, producing disjointed governance and recurrent legislative deadlock. Regardless, the Taif Framework retains a decisive grip on Lebanese statecraft, and its stipulations continue to shade every round of political negotiation. A nuanced understanding of Taif's design and its subsequent trajectories is therefore essential for analysing Lebanon's confessional equilibrium and for evaluating analogous regional experiments in power-sharing.

Political Institutions and Power-Sharing Mechanisms

The elaborate lattice of Lebanese political institutions and the corresponding power-sharing regimes reveal the persistent tensions embedded within the country's confessional fabric.

Lebanon's political system rests upon a fragile balance among its major religious communities, each assigned designated roles and offices. The 1989 Taif Accord adjusted this balance following the civil war, emerging as the framework for the present political order. Under Taif, the presidency remains reserved for a Maronite Christian, the premiership for a Sunni Muslim, and the speakership for a Shiite Muslim, the intention being to embody political coexistence and inclusive governance. The confessional distribution of parliamentary seats, structured to mirror the confessional balance of the population, reinforces the framework and aspires to guarantee plural representation. However, the very measures created to contain sectarian dominance precipitate dysfunction. The rigid allocation of state positions generates perennial stalemate, incapacitating legislative and executive bodies that repeatedly fail to implement pressing reforms. Clientelist networks, inseparable from the circulation of offices, foster patronage and perpetuate nepotism, eclipsing criteria of competence. While foreign powers profess allegiance to a sovereign Lebanon, they often overlay their strategic priorities, rendering the state's policy imperatives more difficult to pursue.

Against this backdrop, Lebanon's model of political power-sharing, long framed as both bulwark and bond, now confronts relentless challenge from popular protests and geopolitical intrigue alike. Addressing such pressures demands reform agendas that protect Lebanon's pluralistic fabric while forging an agile and accountable state. Reconciliation between these imperatives necessitates the redesign of political incentives so that participation and competence, rather than sectarian affiliation, become the preconditions of authority, thereby yielding a genuinely united national output. A reform path grounded in a methodical examination of the current institutional matrix can promote accountability, heighten transparency, and invite broader civic engagement. By deftly negotiating the complexities of existing consociational practices, the polity might nurture a governance structure alert both to inherited norms and to the imperatives of contemporary crises.

Impact of Syrian Civil War on Lebanese Sectarian Dynamics

The Syrian Civil War has unsettled Lebanon's sectarian equilibrium, reconfiguring risk and opportunity alike. Once the conflict spilt over the border, Lebanon emerged as the buffer and transit zone for its consequences, polarising long-dormant sectarian fault lines. The influx of refugees—albeit framed in humanitarian terms—tightened an already fragile sectarian compact, heightening fears of demographic transformation and intensifying competition for already scarce public goods.

The Sunni-Shia divide intensified during the Syrian crisis as each Lebanese community aligned with opposing foreign patrons, complicating Beirut's position in the regionalisation of rival power blocs. The conflict likewise destabilised Lebanon's internal security: an increase in cross-border militias and a steady stream of munitions across the leaky frontier elevated the frictional risks. Together, these dynamics reengineered the domestic political landscape, compelling sectarian parties to recalibrate both rhetoric and practice, while shifting the equilibrium of power within the formal state apparatus. The Syrian insurgency's call to arms further saturated public discourse with sectarian inflexion, poisoning inter-communal trust. Nonetheless, amidst these centrifugal forces, the Lebanese sectarian arrangement manifested a noteworthy, though conditional, durability. Fragmented civil society coalitions, select religious authorities, and grassroots reconciliation programmes worked to mitigate inflammatory discourse and to preserve informal channels of communication. Several political elites, in turn, pursued cross-communal alliances rooted in short-term calculations, thereby hinting at the emergence of a recalibrated sectarian compromise. The persisting crisis, however, has compelled Lebanese authorities to reassess the regulation of communal plurality and to script new modalities for genuinely participatory governance.

Across the Syrian war, the convergence of carefully calibrated humanitarian relief and support for indigenous peace-building activities has mitigated the risk of renewed sectarian violence spilling into Lebanon. The protracted conflict has laid bare the porous link between Lebanon's confessional divisions and external violence, encouraging analysts, decision-makers, and civic leaders to revisit the assumptions underpinning Lebanon's power-sharing system. Their response has been to channel resources into mechanisms that foster durable social cohesion and strengthen institutional resilience throughout the entirety of the Lebanese state.

Role of External Influences in Domestic Stability

Lebanon's domestic stability is therefore not solely a product of its own social and political adaptations, but rather a contested territory where external interventions reconfigure local balances. The historical entanglements of Lebanon with Syria and Iran have not only moulded its sectarian order but have perpetuated a circuit of stability and instability. When external powers intervene, even in pursuit of ostensibly neutral objectives, they amplify pre-existing divisions and re-energise competitive elites. Syria's influence, once evident in the bayonetted presence of troops until the 2005 withdrawal, outlasted its soldiers through a composite of political brokers, security services, and clandestine communications networks. While the Lebanese polity now formally rejects the Syrian imprint, the tacit acknowledgement of shared interests creates a paradox where loyalty and enmity coexist. Iran, conversely, has operationalised its leverage through Hezbollah, embedding a robust, militia-backed wing within the Lebanese state. Tehran's financial and military assistance has fortified Hezbollah's dual identity as a state-within-a-state and a parliamentary bloc, raising persistent fears of a parallel security architecture and political decisions being subordinated to external commands. The cumulative effect of these interventions is a polity that remains susceptible to perturbations from its peripheries, oscillating between precarious consensus and re-tribalised conflict.

The active involvement of regional powers—particularly Saudi Arabia, the Gulf monarchies, and Turkey—combined with the US-Russian superpower competition, significantly complicates the landscape of Lebanese politics at every tier. When these external players wield influence via military, economic, or diplomatic instruments, their priorities often dovetail with Lebanon's entrenched sectarian partitions. This congruence tends to harden factional allegiances and trigger cyclical escalations of violence. Lebanese leaders, therefore, are obliged to address chronic domestic governance deficits while simultaneously grappling with the consequences of foreign engagement. For governance to be genuinely effective and inclusive, interventions must be conceived with the twin aims of fostering internal harmony and mitigating external rivalries. Only with such deliberately orchestrated measures can Lebanon incrementally build strategic autonomy and diminish the disruptive leverage of both regional and transnational agendas.

Socio-Economic Challenges Within Sectarian Lines

Sectarian structures remain fundamental to the architecture of Lebanese society, shaping both the political sphere and the patterns by which socio-economic opportunities are allocated. Public resources—from state contracts to educational scholarships and formal employment—tend to be parcelled out in accordance with confessional affiliation. Such a distribution advantage particular sectarian groups while systematically excluding others, entrenching, normalising and reproducing disadvantage. Young people from marginalised communities, therefore, face structural impediments to upward mobility and wealth generation. The palpable, unequal treatment fuels social bitterness, limiting visions of national cohesion and crystallising a politics rooted in sectarian entitlement rather than in a vision of shared statehood. Effective remedying of these entrenched inequalities demands policy action that deliberately steps outside sectarian allocation, reallocating both resources and opportunities in a way that secures socio-economic integration and fosters collective social stability.

These processes have generated divergent regional trajectories, with certain regions and demographic groups experiencing intensified economic hardship and eroding opportunities for upward mobility. Activities shaped by sectarian identities have, in turn, fortified competing economic interests and perpetuated patronage networks. Such sectarian economic configurations have prevented the emergence of a cohesive, nationally integrated economic policy by mobilising rival interests along sectarian lines, thereby impeding the articulation of comprehensive social and institutional reform. The labour market itself illustrates these divides; recruitment norms and advancement routes routinely hinge upon sectarian affiliation, engineering a misallocation of talent that forecloses human-capital accumulation along rational rather than partisan lines. The result is a corrosive erosion of meritocratic principles, the inflating of collective grievances, and a reinforcement of communal oppositions, which together fracture social cohesion and obstruct the advance of a unified national agenda. Socio-economic disparities that track sectarian demarcations are further magnified in the domain of social welfare and public service delivery. Educational systems, healthcare networks, and infrastructure become unevenly distributed, entrenching variations in living conditions and quality of life. Lastly, while sectarianly motivated philanthropy and charitable initiatives may initially relieve specific pockets of hardship, they simultaneously fortify communal boundaries and undermine the broader endeavour of constructing a cohesive and inclusive national society.

Lebanon's ongoing socio-economic crises demand a carefully calibrated, pluralistic approach that respects and actively engages the country's sectarian mosaic. Addressing the long-standing gradients of economic opportunity that align with sectarian identity requires targeted policy measures that secure equitable resource allocation, promote wide-ranging economic participation, and reform the institutional apparatus that perpetuates sectarian bias in budgetary and regulatory practices. Concurrently, fostering regulatory and fiscal incentives for cross-sectarian partnerships and collaborative enterprises will be essential for bridging economic divides and reinforcing the foundation for a cohesive and prosperous future.

Pathways to Political Reform and Resilience

Lebanon's entrenched sectarian equilibrium continues to impede meaningful political reform and to challenge the state's long-term resilience. Paradoxically, the same equilibrium also harbours pathways toward a political order that could be both more durable and more widely representative. Effective reform depends on the ongoing revision and re-calibration of the power-sharing formulas that have shaped public governance since independence. Such a task necessitates a systematic, evidence-informed appraisal of the Taif Agreement, measuring its ability to adjust to the demographic and socio-economic shifts that have redefined the country since the accord's formulation. The overarching objective is to sustain equitable sectarian representation while nurturing an emergent sense of national cohesion. Attainment of this objective, however, is contingent upon a shared, genuine commitment from political elites to prioritise the state's endurance and the public good over the temporal advantages of sectarian advantage that have too frequently informed their decision-making.

The prevailing circumstances demand that Lebanon adopt a governance model which is both inclusive and participatory, one which credibly acknowledges and incorporates the diverse voices and aspirations of its citizens. Alongside this model, it is imperative to strengthen state institutions, enhancing their capacity to deliver essential services fairly across all regions. This comprehensive agenda must target meaningful reforms in the judiciary, security apparatus, and public administration, with each domain focused on cultivating accountability, transparency, and operational efficiency. Confronting corruption and deeply embedded nepotism in both the political and economic spheres is, of course, an essential prerequisite for the establishment of a governance framework that is both resilient and capable of earning public trust. A steadfast commitment to ethical leadership and to the principle of meritocracy will determine the state's capacity to represent and serve all citizens fairly. Ongoing collaboration among civil society organisations, grassroots movements, and international partners will remain crucial for political reform and systemic resilience. By promoting inclusive policies, pursuing dialogue that transcends sectarian divides, and diligently monitoring reform implementation, these constituencies can exert constructive pressure on the political elite and help convert reform pledges into a sustained, effective reality.

Ultimately, the development of a civic culture grounded in active citizenship and sustained civic engagement is essential for strengthening the democratic underpinnings upon which a durable political order in Lebanon must rest.

The promotion of interactive forums that invite thoughtful dialogue, the sustained involvement of younger generations, and the steadfast safeguarding of speech freedom are essential components of an informed, active citizenry. The durability of Lebanon's political reform and the fortification of national resilience rely on a holistic plan that addresses institutional shortfalls, nurtures social cohesion, and elevates the common interest above narrow sectarian claims. By embedding the principles of equity, justice, and pluralism within institutional practice, Lebanon can transcend its persistent fractures and lay the foundation for a robust and cohesive political future.

Case Studies: Sectarian Alliances and Ruptures

To grasp Lebanon's sectarian mosaic fully, one must turn to case studies that document both moments of inter-sectarian harmony and the ruptures that periodically disrupt them. A particularly revealing case emerges in areas where sustained coexistence and joint civic enterprises flourish. In those localised settings, diverse communities engage in daily inter-sectarian dialogue and mutual recognition, negotiating shared spaces and collective projects. Such examples underscore an enduring capacity for reconciliation and common purpose. Conversely, Lebanese political history illustrates that, when crises erupt, dormant grievances are reactivated, revealing the fragile equilibrium that earlier compromises had masked.

Tripoli, above all, has seen cycles of violent clashes, during which the revival of sectarian militias and the rekindling of street-level mobilisations have laid bare the weight of long-standing grievances and the considerable barriers to rebuilding civic trust that transcend communal divisions.

An instructive case study examines differential sectarian responses across Lebanon to economic decline in the wilderness and stark social stratification. Some political and civil groupings have temporarily allied to contest stratification, while others have retreated into sectarian rivalry, either contesting scarce economic spoils or re-enacting identity-based tropes. Field observations expose the variable structure of sectarianism itself, underscoring the combined agency of economic, political and social motives that decide conflictive versus conciliatory trajectories. They furthermore delineate the limits of elite power-sharing but also signal existing, realistic avenues for articulating sustained tolerance, structured dialogue, and a coexistence that integrates Lebanon's composite confessional network.

Conclusion: Navigating the Sectarian Landscape

Successful traversal of Lebanon's stratified sectarian landscape necessitates a systematic grasp of the overlapping historical, political and socio-economic vectors at play. This inquiry has interrogated the sectarian equilibrium, simultaneously marked by tenuousness and endurance. The cumulative observation is that navigation itself is impossible without attending to the co-constitution of religious, political and economic layers. Sectarian friction remains tightly linked to the external geopolitical calibrations that continually reconfigure Lebanon's domestic sovereignty.

Consequently, addressing these challenges requires us to scrutinise transnational influences, internal party dynamics, and the everyday livelihoods of citizens, all at once, while also nurturing societal norms that prioritise inclusivity and uphold respect for pluralism.

A thorough appraisal of Lebanon's internal and external contexts indicates that both regional and global forces periodically heighten the country's entrenched sectarian divisions. Nevertheless, any calculative engagement with Lebanon's confessional order must attend equally to the delicate interlocking arrangements that prop up its institutional viability. The risk of overt sectarian rupture, while salient, should not obscure the intermittent, frequently overlooked instances of cross-sectarian assembly and cooperation. These micro-histories, modest in scale but weighty in implication, attest to the persistent viability of civic collaboration and offer replicable instances for strengthening horizontal social bonds. The recurrent capacity of the Lebanese populace to regroup and recalibrate in the wake of sectarian reversals further affirms the latent social reservoirs that undergird coexistence within a plural polity. If Lebanon were to actively reaffirm and amplify its inter-sectarian dialogues and joint undertakings, its diversities could yet, be alchemised into a durable collective asset rather than a centrifugal burden. The future negotiation of sectarian terrain rests on unwavering commitment to the principles of inclusivity, empathy, and equilibrium in compromise. When governance instruments and policies uniformly shield and empower each community, the menace of sectarian volatility is attenuated, permitting the weaving of a more cohesive and resilient national tapestry.

The long-term overcoming of Lebanon's sectarian geography rests upon an abiding civic resolve that persistently transcends both confessional attachment and territorial boundaries.

Acknowledging the worth of pluralism and fostering mutual esteem are indispensable—not only for Lebanon's internal unity but for the broader stability and advancement of the Levantine region. The present examination has demonstrated that grasping the complexities of Lebanon's sectarian order and engaging with them productively does not rest with the ruling class alone; it constitutes the shared responsibility of every citizen. Through the deliberate nurturing of common belonging and reciprocal solidarity, Lebanon may embark upon a durable and just peace, overcoming the constraints that sectarian loyalty has for so long imposed upon its potential.

5
External Powers and Proxies
The International Arena of Syrian Soil

The Global Stakes in Syria

The Syrian conflict has crystallised into a principal theatre of global geopolitics, ensnaring a heterogeneous cast of external actors whose interests are both convergent and divergent. The country's geographic and geopolitical positioning—sandwiched between pivotal Middle Eastern, European, and Eurasian corridors—renders it indispensable in any larger tableau of regional and global strategy. The variegated objectives of the intervenors are therefore inextricably woven, each power calibrating its aims against the broader choreography of rival ambitions. For Washington, contemporary Syria has come to symbolise a front where the struggle for authority, the pursuit of regional stabilisation, and the safeguarding of global security intersect. US policy is animated by the dual imperatives of containing transnational extremist networks and countering the steadily encroaching tracts of influence that Moscow and Tehran are incrementally consolidating. Moscow, conversely, interprets the ongoing conflict as a rare opportunity to entrench a durable power projection platform, safeguarding access to southern maritime arteries and reasserting Russia's status as an indispensable architect of the regional balance.

Moreover, Russia's enduring backing for the Assad regime is a component of its wider strategy to prop up autocratic rule whenever such regimes confront mass dissent. Turkey's military engagement in Syria, conversely, is anchored in its resolve to neutralise Kurdish groups near its border while simultaneously seeking to reinforce its regional political clout. Iran's military, political, and logistical investment, meanwhile, is dual-purpose: it is designed to prevent the Assad regime's collapse and to extend Tehran's influence across the Levant, buffering Iranian territory from its arch-enemies. The European Union, for its part, wrestles with a humanitarian obligation to aid the millions of civilians suffering nearly a decade of violence while also safeguarding its own territory from the security repercussions of uncontrolled migration and the risk of radicalisation among the displaced. Israel, consistently, has taken a pre-emptive approach to confront any Iranian encroachment that could endanger its northern border, viewing military strikes and intelligence operations as necessary to sustain its deterrent posture. Within the

Arab League, the Syrian crisis has exposed the disunity of the membership, as varying degrees of political alignment and tactical engagement reflect each state's unique geopolitical calculus and prevailing factional loyalties.

With the participation of numerous global players now firmly entrenched in the Syrian theatre, the situation has become a litmus test not only for regional stability but for the evolving architecture of world power relations. Each actor calculates its moves against the backdrop of the enduring search for relative advantage on every continent, making Syria a crucible of geopolitical competition.

The United States: Strategic Interests and Involvements

The American engagement in the Syrian civil war has evolved in response to layered strategic calculations and the unpredictable behaviour of neighbouring states. Washington quickly appreciated that a prolonged civil war in Syria could destabilise the Levant, prompt refugee surges into Europe, and empower hostile non-state actors operating on its periphery. Thus, the US sought to protect its core interests by countering the Islamic State, supporting Jordan and Turkey, and sustaining the deterrent posture of Israel. Early on, the administration authorised small arms to a diversity of opposition brigades and air power to assist the Syrian Democratic Forces in the north, framing each action, however, against the stiff reality of the Assad-Russian-Iranian entente. President Obama's reluctance to escalate—even after the violation of the red line on chemical weapons—exposed the tension between deterrence and caution that has defined American policy. The pivot to a narrowly focused counter-ISIS campaign, while effective in territory denial, ultimately diluted Washington's influence in the political resolution, revealing the costs of an ambiguous, episodic approach to a multipolar civil war.

The policy recalibrations under the Trump administration—including the withdrawal of forces from select territories—revealed the persistent strategic fragmentation characterising US engagement in Syria. The resultant friction with Turkey, a member of NATO, over Kurdish militias deepened the operational dilemmas facing American leaders. In addition to its military footprint, the United States has sustained extensive diplomatic leverage and has injected considerable humanitarian relief, responding to the protracted humanitarian toll generated by the fighting. Through its position in multilateral forums, Washington has endeavoured to guide the narrative, galvanise diplomatic backing for a negotiated political settlement, and concurrently address the humanitarian exigencies. Moving forward, an evolving Syrian landscape and shifting great-power rivalries will prompt the United States to recalibrate its strategic calculus. Confronted with ambiguous rivalries, asymmetric alliances, and urgent humanitarian imperatives, US policy will remain committed to recalibrating military and diplomatic posture in ways that safeguard American interests while furthering collaborative, higher-order initiatives aimed at a durable resolution of the Syrian catastrophe and at the consolidation of a stable regional order.

Russian Influence: Objectives and Military Engagements

Russia's engagement in Syria has been a crucial factor in restructuring the regional balance of power.

Russia's enduring strategic preoccupation with the Eastern Mediterranean and the overwhelmingly important Middle East gives rise to a spectrum of interrelated goals in Syria, among which the reinforcement of geopolitical leverage, the safeguarding of military installations, and the projection of power to a wider audience stand out as key drivers. When the uprising erupted, Moscow's foremost aim crystallised in the rescue of the Assad administration, which it regards as a non-negotiable bulwark against a cascade of threats in the Levant. Supporting Damascus' promises, continued operational access to the naval facility at Tartus, thereby securing a critical strategic corridor through the Eastern Mediterranean that underpins both military-to-military engagement and maritime trade. Beyond the immediate naval interest, the Kremlin equates the survival of the Syrian state with a broader calculus of regional equilibria, convinced that the collapse of central authority invites centrifugal violence that could ultimately permeate the North Caucasus and beyond. To this end, Moscow has committed substantial military elements, deploying an array of fixed-wing and rotary-wing platforms, surface and undersea naval units, as well as mechanised brigades and state-of-the-art precision-guided munitions. The operational calculus extends beyond tactical assistance; the campaign furnishes the Russian armed forces with a live laboratory for doctrinal experimentation, enabling the Kremlin to refine both joint-force interoperability and broader regional engagement strategies.

The vacuum left by the United States' partial withdrawals from Syria has allowed Russia to emerge as a central actor in directing the trajectory of the Syrian conflict. By engaging in a network of diplomatic overtures and cultivating relationships with a broad spectrum of regional stakeholders, Moscow has worked to establish itself as the sole necessary arbitrator of Syrian affairs, using the dual leverage of its military footprint and diplomatic access to pursue its own interests and deepen its regional footprint. Russia's military operations have also recalibrated the regional power balance, notably in relation to Turkey, Iran, and Israel. This dynamic, characterised by a constant oscillation between collaboration and confrontation in light of Russia's pronounced posture, has intensified the intricacies of the Syrian crisis. Although the international community has repeatedly urged restraint and the stimulation of peace-building initiatives, Russia's persistent arms deployments and strategic diplomacy reveal its unwavering intention to steer the conflict in accordance with its long-term strategic calculus. A thorough examination of Russia's military and political footprint in Syria, therefore, proves indispensable for deciphering the overlapping geopolitical ambitions and shifting power relations that continue to mould the Syrian theatre and echo throughout the wider international system.

Turkey's Role: Between Security Concerns and Territorial Goals

Turkey's engagement in the Syrian conflict is anchored in a graduated calculus of pressing security imperatives and persistent territorial aspirations.

Turkey's northern border with Syria has become a crucible for security challenges since the onset of the Syrian civil war. An ever-increasing flow of refugees has strained the social contract within Turkey, while the ascendancy of Kurdish militias has revived Ankara's historical anxieties regarding its own Kurdish population. In response, the Turkish leadership has mounted a series of military campaigns, loosened its support for rebel factions, and intensified border security, all aimed at blunting what it perceives as an irredentist Kurdish consolidation parallel to its frontier. Preventing the emergence of an autonomous Kurdish administration remains the lodestar of Turkish grand strategy, as its leaders equate even nominal Kurdish self-rule with a potential dissolution of the national polity. These actions, including the establishment of swathes of security-forward buffer zones, Operation Euphrates Shield, and the subsequent Operation Olive Branch, reveal a remarkable persistence of Turkish arms and policy into the conflict's fragmented centre of gravity.

Turkey must also navigate a treacherous diplomatic corridor marked by simultaneous dealings with the United States, a putative ally conflicted over its support for Kurdish forces, and Russia, a competitor now entangled deeply within Syrian affairs. The interplay of Turkish military hardware, American sanctions, and tacit Russian coordination creates a fragile triad that Ankara has exploited to deepen its territorial keeps and protect its far-forward security architecture. By securing tacit American airlift during the Euphrates Shield and negotiating de-escalation corridors through Russian military police, Turkish commanders have rehearsed a competitive yet tactical entryism that is more survivalist than grand strategic. As the Syrian civil war matures into a stalemated multipolar phase, Turkey's policy of autonomous buffer statecraft and uneven supranational military presence will remain a decisive variable, redistributing regional power while committing Turkish lives and resources to a conflict that refuses closure.

Furthermore, the consequences of Turkey's military interventions in Syria reach further than the original security calculus, giving rise to complex diplomatic challenges and reverberations for the overall equilibrium of the Middle East. Analysing Turkey's conduct in the Syrian theatre reveals the layered contest of national security calculations, geopolitical competition, and alliance politics that has directed both the internal dynamics of the conflict and its multidimensional fallout.

Iranian Presence: Expanding Influence Through Proxies

Iranian involvement constitutes one of the most consequential external variables in the Syrian civil war, informed by the dual ambition of consolidating territorial and ideological influence while safeguarding the Assad regime. Leveraging a sprawling constellation of non-state militias, Tehran has managed to project military power well beyond its national frontiers, recalibrating the balance of forces and embedding itself into the fabric of the Levant. The forward deployment of the Islamic Revolutionary Guard Corps and the specialised Quds Force has manifested the Islamic Republic's willingness to sacrifice strategic depth for strategic depth, reinforcing the Syrian Army while simultaneously creating a durable military and political corridor to the Eastern Mediterranean. Iran's calculations are animated not only by a desire to assert deterrence against Israeli operations or Saudi regional hegemony, but also by the imperative of contesting what it perceives as a Western encirclement.

Iran has pursued a deliberate strategy of fostering Shiite militant formations and cultivating partnerships with diverse non-state actors to secure its objectives in Syria. Prominently, Hezbollah, the Lebanese Shiite militia with deep Iranian backing, has functioned as a pivotal proxy for Tehran, engaging directly in the Syrian civil war and acting as a conduit for the proliferation of Iranian authority across the Levant. In tandem, Iranian backing of formations such as the Popular Mobilisation Forces in Iraq and assorted contingents in Yemen illustrates the multidimensional character of its proxy apparatus and its cohesive regional design. The ramifications of Iran's ascendant footprint in Syria transcend its borders, indirectly reconfiguring the strategic landscape of Lebanon and the broader Middle East. This depth of influence bolsters Tehran's deterrent posture and augments its leverage in regional rivalries, thereby redrawing the balance of power in the Eastern Mediterranean and exacerbating pre-existing geopolitical fractures. The interpenetration of Iranian expansionism with an extensive lattice of cross-border affiliations highlights the multidimensional contours of the Syrian war, spotlighting the transnational repercussions of proxy warfare for both regional order and global diplomatic calculus.

With Iran's influence expanding and recalibrating the dynamics of the ongoing conflict, its role has become a decisive element on the overarching Middle Eastern geopolitical chessboard, generating consequences that propagate into Syria, Lebanon, and beyond.

European Union: Humanitarian Concerns and Diplomatic Efforts

The European Union has confronted the Syrian conflict through sustained humanitarian outreach and sustained diplomatic initiatives designed to forge viable political outcomes. As the world's preeminent donor of humanitarian assistance, the Union has been crucial in delivering essential support to refugees, internally displaced persons, and host communities in the region. The magnitude of the emergency has compelled EU institutions to coordinate the rapid deployment of funds, expert personnel, and logistical networks, ensuring that humanitarian aid aligns with the immediate and long-term needs of those affected by hostilities. Alongside this humanitarian mobilisation, the EU has maintained a rigorous diplomatic track, circumscribed by the conviction that only a negotiated political settlement will end the violence. In this regard, the Union has championed inclusive dialogue, marshalled multilateral forums, and underscored the indispensable primacy of international law. By integrating humanitarian and diplomatic action, the EU aims both to mitigate immediate suffering and to lay the groundwork for a sustainable political resolution.

The European Union has repeatedly affirmed its backing for the United Nations and broader multilateral mediation endeavours aimed at advancing a durable peace in Syria. Leveraging its diplomatic outreach and targeted funding, the EU has sought to augment the capacity and legitimacy of local peace building actors and civil society networks committed to reconciliation. Emphasising the imperatives of inclusive governance and respect for human rights, the EU has consistently highlighted that transitional justice and accountability processes must occupy a central place in any credible peace architecture. Beyond its diplomatic and humanitarian engagements, the EU has played a crucial role in confronting the enduring ramifications of the conflict, especially the imperatives of stabilisation and reconstruction. EU funding, together with its technical acumen in post-conflict recovery, has established an early foundation for resilience and recovery in Syria and its surrounding neighbourhood. In parallel, the Union has championed targeted interventions in education, job creation, and economic empowerment, thereby seeking to alleviate the socio-economic burdens of the war while nurturing the long-term prospects for peace and shared prosperity.

In facing the intricate interplay of global power interests and conflicting agendas pursued by third parties, the European Union has consistently reaffirmed its adherence to the multilateral legal order, its championing of universal human rights, and its harmonised strategy for resolving the Syrian crisis. Notwithstanding the persistent and formidable obstacles, the EU's continuous political, economic, and humanitarian investment evidences its conviction that a sustained, principled intervention can, over time, mitigate human suffering and advance the goal of a durable peace, not only in Syria but throughout the wider Middle Eastern region.

Israel's Calculations: Security at the Northern Border

Israel's defensive calculations along the northern front derive their urgency from the interplay of the Syrian civil war and a volatile regional security architecture. The war's geographic proximity, the proliferation of armed non-state entities, and the potential for armed spillover compel the Israeli leadership to formulate a comprehensive deterrent posture. Central to this posture is the persistent surveillance of and prompt response to Hezbollah's military entrenchment on Syrian territory, where the Iranian-backed Shiite militia has expanded its missile and logistics infrastructure in contravention of both Syrian and regional stability. Israel's operations in the theatre are calibrated not only to fortify the frontier, but also to constrain Hezbollah's strategic depth and compel its commanders to weigh the costs of escalation.

Israel regards Hezbollah as a potent rival and considers the militia's reinforced presence near the Syrian border a pressing security threat. The possible delivery of sophisticated armaments or sensitive technologies from Iran to Hezbollah across Syrian territory sharpens these worries. Consequently, Israeli intelligence scrutinises these transfers with particular intensity, and the Israel Defence Forces (IDF) have frequently resorted to precision airstrikes intended to thwart enhancements of Hezbollah's military infrastructure. Israel's security calculus, however, reaches beyond that group to the wider governance and stability dilemmas in Syria. The fragmentation of Syrian state authority in several sub-regions raises alarms that extremist factions might consolidate power or that advanced munitions could diffuse beyond control. Accordingly, Israel remains alert to any adversarial entities that might secure a long-lasting foothold in these contested zones and systematically reassesses how Syrian dynamics might reverberate across the frontier. At the same time, the intricate drift of the Syrian civil war has obliged Israeli strategists to recalibrate the nation's diplomatic posture across the region and beyond. Israel has therefore pursued measured consultations with pivotal states and multilateral actors, articulating its security necessities while seeking to harmonise overlapping interests in a more secure and stable border environment.

Moreover, Israel's engagement with the United States, Russia, and other key regional and global actors is intended to ensure that its security imperatives are explicitly acknowledged and incorporated into any comprehensive negotiations across the Levant. As the Syrian conflict continues to unfold, Israel's assessments of its northern periphery are both fluid and calibrated. The convergence of security imperatives, diplomatic outreach, and cross-border realities creates a complex framework within which Israel pursues the protection of its strategic interests along the northern boundary.

Arab League Dynamics: Varied Responses and Diplomatic Motions

The Arab League's handling of the Syrian crisis has comprised a succession of diplomatic initiatives and markedly divergent preferences among its 22 members. The League has confronted the Syrian conflict since its outbreak in 2011, initially suspending Syria's membership in direct response to the regime's lethal suppression of dissent. This suspension signalled a regional repudiation of the Assad government's tactics and a tentative Arab commitment to facilitating a conflict resolution. Yet as the violence metastasised into a protracted civil war entangled with multiple external stakes, the League's coherence eroded, exposing divergent national calculations and uneven strategies toward Syria.

Member states such as Saudi Arabia and Qatar supported anti-Assad rebel groups, while others, notably Iraq and Algeria, resisted external military involvement and championed dialogue as the means to a political settlement. These contrasting stances underscored the complex tapestry of geopolitical alliances and rivalries across the Arab world, thereby complicating the League's efforts to craft a coherent policy on the Syrian crisis. The Arab League has nevertheless positioned itself as a critical arena for diplomacy, convening successive rounds of peace talks and endorsing diplomatic intermediaries. Its endorsement of the Geneva Communiqué in June 2012 provided a blueprint for a negotiated political transition, and the organisation has intermittently hosted meetings designed to reconcile fractious opposition camps and edge them toward a lasting settlement. Yet, the impact of these diplomatic overtures has been blunted by persistent intra-League disputes, clashing national priorities, and the pervasive intervention of external actors, each of which has magnified the complexity of the Syrian war. The League has also struggled to translate its rhetorical commitment to humanitarian protection into effective, collective measures, facing particular obstacles in coordinating assistance for displaced populations and in confronting documented violations of international human rights law.

As the Syrian war persists, the Arab League remains central to the shifting patterns of regional power, confronting the overlapping political, military, and humanitarian challenges the crisis poses. Its success in harmonising the competing interests of its member states while engaging relevant international actors will determine both the immediate management of the Syrian situation and its long-term consequences for the wider Middle East.

The Proxy Landscape: Militias, Extremists, and External Patrons

The Syrian conflict has become a battleground for proxy forces, whose engagement has decisively tilted the balance of power. Militant groups and paramilitary brigades, backed by foreign governments and non-state sponsors, have militarised local grievances and frozen any prospect of a negotiated settlement. External patrons, in both their overt and covert dimensions, deepen the fragmentation by providing arms, finance, and strategic direction, complicating the already fragile ceasefire efforts.

Within the landscape, the militias fight for a spectrum of ambitions, including battlefield gains, sectarian retribution, and the re-mapping of political authority. Their proliferation has eroded state authority, splintered the opposition, and generated micro-conflicts that the original war no longer commands. The Syrian conflict has thus mutated from an insurrection against a dictatorial state into a distributive contest among competing power brokers, each leveraging violence to secure leverage over a negotiated future.

Some actors, notably the Kurdish-led Syrian Democratic Forces, have oriented themselves toward the international coalition, whereas others have sought partnerships with neighbouring states, thus eroding the clarity of allegiance and entrenching the obstacles to a durable peace and regional stability. Amid this fragmentation, extremist entities, particularly the self-styled Islamic State and al-Qaeda affiliates, have exploited the prevailing disorder to consolidate their presence and project authority, generating acute security threats far beyond Syrian territory. The survival of these groups highlights the persistent difficulty of dismantling radical ideologies while simultaneously ameliorating the social and political grievances that foster violent mobilisation. The active intervention of external patrons, who have armed and subsidised divergent militia networks, has further internationalised the fighting and forestalled any common political exit. State actors have delivered weaponry, fiscal resources, and operational direction to their selected proxies, thereby elongating hostilities and diluting the momentum toward reconciliation. Concurrently, non-state militants, regional financiers, and informal networks have reshaped the constellation of armed actors, complicating any coherent settlement. The Syrian proxy configuration thus functions as a compressed theatre of larger geopolitical contests, revealing the collision of multiple, often conflicting, ambitions and the associated competition for influence that both fracture Syria and reverberate across the broader international order.

The consequences of proxy engagement reach well beyond the borders of Syria, influencing both neighbour stability and the wider international order. Unless the spread of proxy forces is arrested and their disruptive consequences contained, durable progress toward a unified and secure Syria will remain unattainable.

Conclusions on International Involvement and Its Impact

Global engagement in Syria has decisively shaped both the trajectory of the war and its repercussions throughout the Levant and beyond. The proliferation of militias, extremist factions, and foreign backers has forged a dense mosaic of shared geostrategic interests and antagonistic rivalries, redrawing the conflict's internal balance. Outside powers, pursuing diverse, sometimes competing objectives, have produced effects that reverberate from the humanitarian theatre to power redistribution among states. Perhaps the clearest manifestation of this international imprint has been the dramatic expansion and consolidation of non-state armed formations, which have substituted for, and sometimes eclipsed, the state's monopoly on violence. The result has been a conflict that is both prolonged and increasingly resistant to stabilisation, creating ongoing peril for governance and security in neighbouring states.

The dispersion of authority and the uneven distribution of power have rendered the pursuit of substantial diplomatic remedies increasingly elusive and have entrenched oscillating cycles of violence and revenge. Furthermore, the foreign backers who have fortified the various proxies have injected their separate objectives into the Syrian theatre, amplifying both the geographical reach and the political complexity of the crisis. These interventions have strained relations between global and regional powers and transformed local grievances into instruments for external manipulation and escalation. As a result, the contest for dominance and territory has erected persistent barriers against a durable settlement. The repercussions of this global involvement transcend the front lines, reconfiguring the political map of the wider region. Divergent objectives, articulated by the United States, Russia, Turkey, and Iran, have propagated interstate rivalries and recalibrated long-standing alliances throughout the Middle East. The resulting rise in regional friction and the looming risk of wider conflagration have elevated the stakes for bordering states and for the global order alike, intensifying the imperative of a coherent resolution. Therefore, any plausible trajectory for the future must confront the layered influences of foreign powers and the ways these influences have reshaped the conflict in Syria.

Achieving this outcome necessitates a sophisticated grasp of the overlapping interests, aims, and tactical frameworks of every relevant actor, fortified by a persistent dedication to meaningful communication and collaboration among all parties. It is only through a united and broadly participatory endeavour that the historical record of external engagement may be transformed from a source of fragmentation into a foundation for authentic concord and enduring stability.

6
Hezbollah and Iran
Complications in Lebanon's Political Landscape

Historical Overview: The Formation of a Strategic Alliance

The alliance between Hezbollah and the Islamic Republic of Iran originated in the early 1980s, contemporaneously with the emergence of Hezbollah amid Lebanon's multifaceted civil conflict. The group was drawn to Iran's revolutionary discourse and its avowedly anti-Western posture, both of which dovetailed with Hezbollah's own imperatives of repelling Israeli incursions and advancing Shi'a communal objectives. That convergence matured into a formal alliance as both parties engaged in coordinated efforts spanning operational training, doctrinal indoctrination, and fiscal subsidisation. Symptomatic of this trajectory was Hezbollah's initial absorption of counsel and material from the Islamic Revolutionary Guard Corps, which was instrumental in refining the organisation's combat doctrine and enhancing its tactical arsenal. The bombings of the U.S. embassy and Marine barracks in 1983 epitomised the juncture at which Hezbollah demonstrated its capacity to project Iranian policy, registering a pronounced escalation in coordinated hostilities against Western interlocutors. The cessation of the Iran-Iraq War in 1988 further remedied the partnership's profundity, as the reconstitution of Iranian strength released surplus Iranian assets for propagation and consolidated Hezbollah's role as a forward Iranian proxy in the Levant.

During this period, there arose a transnational Shia identity, bolstered by Iran's active spread of revolutionary ideology and by the deliberate dissemination of its core revolutionary principles beyond national borders.

Ideological Foundations: Shared Objectives and Divergent Tactics

The ideological framework that binds Hezbollah and Iran is indispensable for understanding their intricate alliance and the subsequent effects on Lebanon's political order. The two actors are anchored by a common Shia Islamist vision that frames resistance to Western imperialism and Israeli expansionism as both a religious duty and a strategic imperative. This convergent outlook undergirds their strategic partnership and furnishes a rationale for reciprocal assistance. United by the objective of shielding the Shia polity from external encroachment, they interpret every foreign intervention through a lens of communal defence. Central to their collaboration is a shared conviction that hegemonic powers, chiefly the United States and its regional clients, must be confronted on every front. Nevertheless, the history of the alliance reveals a gradual divergence in tactical execution and operational prioritisation. While the resistance doctrine is the common thread, Hezbollah's execution of that doctrine is conditioned by the peculiarities of Lebanese terrain and governance. Inside Lebanon, the Party has refined its capabilities to fuse military, political, and social instruments, thereby embedding itself in the national fabric as both a paramilitary entity and a governing force.

In contrast, Iran has adopted a comprehensive regional

strategy, leveraging fiscal networks, diplomatic channels, and clandestine support to influence developments across the Middle East. The differing modalities of these approaches bear the signature of the asymmetrical power structure governing their alliance: Iran exerting expansive geopolitical reach, while Hezbollah concentrates formidable firepower on a concentrated theatre. A systematic inquiry into their ideological underpinnings reveals how congruent objectives coexist with differentiated operational doctrines, illuminating the delicate calibration of their partnership and its consequential effects on the intra-Lebanese balance of power and broader regional geopolitics.

Hezbollah's Role in Lebanese Politics: A Power Beyond the State

An examination of Hezbollah's function within the Lebanese political system reveals an organism that, while nominally embedded in state structures, exercises authority that regularly eclipses the state's institutional capacity. Rooted in a synthesis of Shia religious dogma and an unremitting commitment to armed resistance against Israel, Hezbollah has matured into a synthetic body in which parliamentary representation, social welfare delivery, and elite military training coalesce. This tripartite configuration allows Hezbollah to dictate political outcomes, govern local economies, and project military deterrence simultaneously, situating the organisation beyond the classical sovereignty of the Lebanese state apparatus.

Hezbollah's direct penetration of Lebanese state institutions has afforded the group decisive influence over policymaking arenas affecting both domestic and extraterritorial matters. This confluence of military might and institutional authority has elevated the group to the status of a decisive arbiter in the overall governance and geopolitical orientation of the nation.

Iran's Influence: Financial, Military, and Political Support

Iran's imprint on Lebanese politics, articulated chiefly through its commitment to Hezbollah, manifests in a triad of support: economic, tactical, and diplomatic. Cash transfers from Tehran furnish the group with a steady flow of funds that underwrite its social services, repair and construction projects, and armament procurement. Such financial undergirding enables Hezbollah to embed itself more deeply in Lebanese civil society, reinforcing its claim to legitimacy and its wider political negotiating power. Tactical assistance, encompassing sophisticated ordnance, cadre training, and operational advice, has further refined Hezbollah's military profile, recalibrating the regional balance of power and affecting the wider geopolitical tableau. Finally, Iran's diplomatic sponsorship provides Hezbollah with the international legitimacy and political cover necessary to act autonomously within Lebanon, while simultaneously shaping the country's foreign policy orientation and its interactions with neighbouring states.

Tehran's consistent backing of Hezbollah decisively directs the group's operational calculus, thereby conditioning Beirut's diplomatic tactics, internal governance, and interactions with regional neighbours. This sponsorship is so deeply embedded that it complicates Lebanon's internal political fabric and generates a spectrum of ramifications for both regional equilibrium and global diplomatic calculations. A thorough grasp of the extent and mechanisms of Iranian involvement is therefore indispensable for analysing the multifactorial interactions that animate Lebanon's evolving geopolitical environment, as well as the wider Middle Eastern strategic landscape.

Domestic Challenges: Balancing Shia Interests with National Unity

Lebanon's domestic environment is profoundly constellated, characterised by a careful negotiation between sectarian loyalties and the drive for national cohesion. Within this constellation, the Shia community—chiefly articulated by Hezbollah—complicates policy calculations by insisting that its communal aspirations be integrated into the larger national project. Lebanese politicians, therefore, confront the persistent dilemma of accommodating Shia demands while safeguarding the appearance and substance of national solidarity. This dilemma is rooted in historically layered socio-political developments that have crystallised the Shia community's identity and formulated its aspirations in ways that both enrich and fracture the national ecosystem.

The rise of Hezbollah, rooted in the socioeconomic dislocations of the historically marginalised Shia population, catalysed the articulation of Shia rights, identity, and agency within Lebanese public life. By framing the struggle against external adversaries as the cornerstone of its political and military posture, the organisation has successfully rallied much of the Shia community behind its banner, thereby entrenching itself as a central actor in Lebanese governance. Yet, the prioritisation of Shia collective agency sometimes collides with the exigencies of a fragile national consensus, generating friction that risks fragmenting the Lebanese body politic. Hezbollah's alignment with the Iranian leadership, its invocation of asymmetric military strength, and its infrastructural parallelism to state institutions have catalysed apprehensions regarding Lebanon's territorial integrity, public order, and diplomatic credibility. Such a setting obliges policymakers to craft a graduated and synchronised approach that reconciles the aspirations of the Shia population with the imperatives of national solidarity and the integrity of state sovereignty. Intrinsic to this reconciliatory effort are the variegated and occasionally antagonistic currents within the Shia community itself. Although Hezbollah exerts a monopolistic influence on discourse and resources, it cannot suppress the spectrum of elite and popular positions advocating alternative trajectories for the country. Synthesising these domestic divergences while institutionalising inclusive mechanisms of representation is indispensable for the cultivation of a national identity that decisively transcends confessional cleavages.

Such a balancing act necessitates discerning leadership, transparent governance, and a broad dialogue that listens to the genuine grievances and ambitions of the Shia community, while simultaneously fostering a collective sense of ownership and identity among every Lebanese citizen. Programmes that strengthen historically marginalised groups, advance fair socio-economic development, and reinforce the integrity of the legal system will advance a prospective common future that honours the country's pluralism. Mastering these internal issues will consequently create a durable framework that anchors Lebanon in sustainable stability, thereby recognising and weaving the contributions of each community into the cohesive tapestry of the nation.

International Perception: Hezbollah as a "Terrorist" Entity versus Freedom Fighter

The international understanding of Hezbollah is not just a matter of academic debate, but a strategic imperative. It navigates a web of conflicting discourses, designating the group variously as a terrorist body or as a legitimate liberation force. This ambiguity arises not only from Hezbollah's own actions, but also from the divergent lenses through which state and non-state actors interpret those actions. In the United States and Europe, the group is categorically branded a terrorist organisation, a label grounded in its purportedly coordinated assaults on civilians, its anti-Western rhetoric, and its strategic alliance with the Islamic Republic of Iran. Conversely, Arab publics and many Shiite constituencies champion Hezbollah as a bulwark against Israeli expansion and a guardian of marginalised peoples, framing its military confrontations with Israeli forces not as aggression but as justified defence. The gulf between these interpretive frames creates polarised understandings of Hezbollah's strategies and moral standing. Proponents of its liberation ethos argue that the organisation's battlefield successes, notably in the campaigns of 2000 and 2006, exposed the vulnerabilities of the Israeli Defence Forces and earned Hezbollah a reputation as a credible deterrent against state violence.

Critics assert that Hezbollah's strategy, featuring asymmetrical warfare and rocket fire directed against civilian zones, illustrates a readiness to violate international legal and humanitarian standards, thus sanctioning its classification as a terrorist entity. Moreover, the group's commitment to the Syrian civil war, whether depicted as imperialist meddling or as a defensive measure against Sunni militancy, further obscures its international standing. Placing Hezbollah's behaviour against the backdrop of shifting Middle Eastern power relations is critical to understanding the divergent global interpretations of its identity and mission. The contemporary fluidity of global alignments, compounded by intra-Arab rivalries and great power recalibrations, further blurs the lines between legitimate resistance and terrorist practice. Analysts and decision-makers must, therefore, account for these layered perceptions when crafting interventions and gauging Hezbollah's influence on the delicate regional order. The resonance of Hezbollah's name abroad is thus less a reflection of its actions in isolation than the outcome of intersecting geopolitical rivalries, contested historical memories, and abiding ideological loyalties (such as anti-Israel sentiment and anti-Western rhetoric), cementing the organisation's place in ongoing international discord.

Policy Dilemmas: Navigating Sanctions and Diplomatic Pressures

Lebanon's governance landscape is presently entangled in the ramifications of Hezbollah's political manoeuvring and the cascade of Western sanctions that follow its every expansion.

Hezbollah's designation as a terrorist organisation by multiple Western states imposes acute constraints on its operational latitude and its interactions with the global arena. Targeted sanctions that encompass both financial systems and trade channels curtail the group's access to capital and materials, while simultaneously constraining its capacity to project influence within the Lebanese political fabric. These coercive measures seek to engineer the group's diplomatic isolation and to erode its perceived legitimacy on the world stage. The repercussions for Lebanese governance and political stability are considerable, obliging Beirut to balance the assertion of national sovereignty with a pragmatic commitment to evolving international norms. The layering of diplomatic coercion further complicates Lebanon's posture, as the state attempts to sustain constructive engagements with major powers while confronting Hezbollah's fusion with the country's political and security structures. Such a dynamic renders Lebanese governance a continuous exercise in managing multilayered policy contradictions. Diplomatically, the Lebanese manoeuvring requires refined calibration among the divergent preferences of external states, internal political realities, and the wider regional consequences of Hezbollah's strategic choices. The complex trade-offs between adherence to foreign regulatory frameworks and pressing domestic imperatives thus manifest as persistent and multilayered quandaries for Lebanese decision-makers.

Consequently, Lebanon's diplomatic effectiveness and its strategic capacity to buffer against adverse consequences stemming from external actions remain critically important. A thorough examination of these policy challenges illuminates both Hezbollah's entrenchment within the Lebanese polity and its evolving engagement with the international order. The long-term outcome of this complex interaction hinges on Lebanon's ability to reconcile the safeguarding of core national imperatives with the imperatives of multilateral cooperation. Operating at the intersection of punitive sanctions and diplomatic subtleties has thus become a signature feature of Lebanon's current political reality, wherein the political elite persistently negotiate domestic imperatives alongside shifting international prerequisites.

Impact on Lebanese Institutions: Parallel Structures and Governance

Hezbollah's multidimensional influence has irreversibly altered Lebanon's institutional landscape and modes of governance. The group has forged enduring parallel infrastructures across the social, security, and economic domains, thereby recalibrating the parameters within which the state apparatus operates. Hezbollah's expansive constellation of social welfare initiatives and community-based aid has filled critical gaps in Lebanese public service delivery, particularly in regions persistently marginalised by official policy. While such interventions have engendered a reservoir of popular legitimacy for the organisation, they simultaneously provoke anxiety regarding the incremental dilution of state sovereignty and the long-term stamina of the central governing authority.

In security terms, Hezbollah operates autonomously from the Lebanese Armed Forces, cultivating extensive military assets and maintaining a disciplined militia. This alternate apparatus challenges the state's exclusive authority to wield force and complicates efforts to enhance central sovereignty. It also generates concern regarding the structure and oversight of national security planning, particularly regarding the potential rapid escalation of conflict and the consequent international repercussions. The simultaneous presence of Hezbollah's military apparatus and official state agencies has thus indexed a hybrid governance environment in which allocation of resources and policy formulation is mediated by a conjuncture of recognised and emergent power brokers. Such duality has impeded the formulation of coherent national strategies because divergent interests exert friction on the pursuit of unified governance. Moreover, the intertwining of Hezbollah's political, military, and socio-economic clout complicates accountability and transparency in state processes. The indistinct boundary separating party agendas from state functions undermines democratic accountability, the rule of law, and the safeguarding of individual rights throughout Lebanon. Consequently, Hezbollah's penetration of institutional life exceeds mere electoral presence; it has reconfigured the very architecture of governance, obliging analysts and policymakers alike to engage with institutional realities that now embody a persistent and multidimensional complexity.

Understanding these dynamics is crucial for effectively engaging with Lebanon's complex political landscape and for confronting the challenges created by competing governance structures that operate outside state authority.

Public Opinion: The Dual-Edged Sword of Support and Criticism

Attitudes toward the nexus of Hezbollah, Iran, and Lebanon reveal the layered nature of Lebanese political life. The perception of Hezbollah's alliance with Iran triggers distinctly different responses across society, illuminating the broad spectrum of political, sectarian, and identity-based calculations. Within the Shi'a community, and especially in districts governed by Hezbollah, the party is commonly regarded as an indispensable guardian. Supporters cite its military achievements, particularly in the confrontations with Israel, and its extensive network of health, education, and infrastructure services in regions long abandoned by the state. These endorsements are informed by historical traumas—including the 1980s Israeli invasions, the subsequent occupation, and the pervasive absence of the Lebanese state in Shi'a-majority areas—that have anchored loyalty in concrete, lived experience. In contrast, segments of Lebanon's Sunni and Christian populations interpret Hezbollah's Iran-oriented trajectory as an erosion of national sovereignty. For these observers, the party's military autonomy, its weapons stockpile, and its regional activities—framed as services to Iran—reward external agendas at the cost of the Lebanese state's authority and stability. Critics of Hezbollah draw attention to the group's active participation in conflicts beyond Lebanon's borders, especially in Syria, and warn that this engagement deepens sectarian divisions within Lebanon itself. When several Western nations classified Hezbollah as a terrorist organisation, the resultant framing of the group did not remain external but infiltrated Lebanon's political culture, fostering cleavages in domestic opinion. For policymakers, the divergence of views on Hezbollah thus becomes a strategic hurdle, as their capacity to construct a cohesive civic framework hinges on bridging these separations. Crafting a viable response to the apprehensions of the Shi'a constituency without endangering the state's autonomy from outside entanglements demands a dexterous policy that respects the mosaic of loyalties and fears embedded in Lebanese society. The accelerated circulation of opposing narratives through social media adds another layer of contestation to public opinion, revealing the inadequacy of monologic state communications. Dialogue must, therefore, be intentionally inclusive, inviting voices from all segments, recognising the fears and aspirations that sectarian histories have generated, but also strengthening the civic identity that binds the population. Concurrently, policy must advance social and economic interventions—expanded public services and transparent judicial and administrative practices—connected to systemic reform, so that the grievances fuelling polarisation are addressed at their roots.

Simultaneously, fostering openness regarding Hezbollah's ties to Iran and their repercussions for Lebanon is vital for nurturing a well-informed and productive public dialogue. The gradual shifts in public sentiment will, in turn, exert a decisive influence on the future of Lebanese-Iranian ties and on the wider geopolitical currents affecting the Eastern Mediterranean. Grasping the intricacies and layered dimensions of public attitudes is therefore indispensable for operating within the dense lattice of loyalties and anxieties that characterise Lebanon's political order.

Future Trajectories: Potential Pathways for Lebanese-Iranian Relations

Looking forward, the trajectory of Lebanese-Iranian relations will bear directly on the stability and strategic configuration of the Eastern Mediterranean. When mapping the prospective courses, it is imperative to factor in the diverse and interlinked forces that will steer these ties, spanning domestic political shifts and the wider contests of regional power. Chiefly, the changing geopolitical landscape across the Middle East will exert a non-negotiable influence on Lebanese-Iranian interactions. As conflicts persist and alliances mutate, Beirut and Tehran will inevitably adjust their policies to contend with the new realities. The continuing

Syrian civil war, the Israeli-Palestinian dispute, and the over-arching Sunni-Shi'i rivalry will each leave a distinctive mark on the evolution of the relationship between Lebanon and Iran.

The influence of extra-regional powers, specifically the United States, Russia, and major European states, remains a decisive variable in the Lebanese-Iranian relationship. Their evolving policies, diplomatic manoeuvres, and sanctions regimes towards Beirut and Tehran will inject additional layers of uncertainty. On the economic front, Iran's ongoing military and financial pressures compel its leadership to explore new channels of economic collaboration, a calculus that will necessarily include Lebanon. Commercial exchanges and investment projects will become focal points of bilateral diplomacy, and the depth of these economic entanglements will in turn condition the political rapport between the two capitals. Domestic variables will be equally consequential. In Lebanon, the fragile equilibrium among sectarian parties, the partial integrity of governmental bodies, and the operational autonomy of militant networks, notably Hezbollah, will jointly steer Beirut's degree of reliance on Iranian patronage. Across the border, Iranian politics—marked by electoral cycles, institutional rivalries, and broader strategic calculations—will dictate Tehran's level of engagement. Ideological, religious, and cultural dimensions will continue to operate alongside these political and economic calculations. Historical legacies, sectarian solidarities, and religious networks will either reinforce avenues for cooperation or expose points of friction, thereby framing the range of cooperative and confrontational postures that will characterise Lebanese-Iranian relations in the evolving regional landscape.

Policymakers and analysts, while projecting future trajectories for Lebanese-Iranian relations, must incorporate a range of possible outcomes, including diplomatic advances, escalated hostilities, or the spectre of limited warfare. The intricate architecture of the bilateral relationship compels a granular examination of the differentiated yet interconnected drivers shaping its evolution. Accordingly, the effort to discern and evaluate probable trajectories must transcend single-issue frameworks, integrating geopolitical, economic, domestic, and sociocultural variables. Only such a multidimensional approach will yield a sufficiently layered and empirically grounded understanding of Lebanese-Iranian ties, thereby enriching strategic deliberation regarding one of the Eastern Mediterranean's decisive geopolitical axes.

7
The Israel-Hezbollah Dynamic
Balancing on the Brink

Historical Context: Origins of the Israel-Hezbollah Tension

The animosity between Israel and Hezbollah has its origins in the early 1980s. The militant group, along with its political branch, arose in the aftermath of Israel's 1982 invasion of Lebanon, a military campaign designed to displace the Palestine Liberation Organization from the country's south. The invasion, framed by Israel as a means of securing its northern border, instead galvanised the Lebanese Shia community, many of whom came to see Hezbollah as the vanguard of national and communal resistance. The organisation's early tactics merged asymmetric warfare with intricate social mobilisation, portraying every Israeli soldier in the south as

a legitimate target and every military casualty as a vindi-
cation of its cause. The Israeli Defence Forces withdrew in
2000, a partial and contested victory for Hezbollah, which
asserted that its campaigns of attrition had forced the enemy
to retreat. Nevertheless, the absence of a formal peace, the
Iranian-supported group's efforts to re-arm, the quagmire
of Shebaa Farms, and the frequently contested border spark
continual volatility that never quite dies. In 2006, Hezbollah's
pre-emptive capture of two Israeli reservists escalated into a
month-long conflagration, with extensive Lebanese civilian
casualties and destruction of infrastructure that is still visible today. The cycle of retaliation, mixed with deep ideological divergences and external patronage—Tehran's backing of
Hezbollah, and Israel's reliance on immediate US military and
political support—ensures that animosity, now articulated
through missile stockpiles and electronic warfare, remains
a theatre of the unresolved.

Israel characterises Hezbollah as a terrorist group that operates under Tehran's directional aegis, whereas Hezbollah
presents its operations as a legitimate response to Israeli
occupation and encroachments. The resulting divergence
in self-definition reinforces a recursive cycle of retaliatory
escalation and ideological entrenchment, thereby colouring
the present contours of Israel-Hezbollah relations.

Military Engagements: The Conflict Landscape

The enduring confrontation between Israel and Hezbol-

lah has systematically shaped the regional conflict landscape through successive military encounters and evolving
military doctrines. Each side has persisted in a dense and
multilayered regimen of hostilities, where isolated incidents
reverberate through the wider Middle Eastern geopolitics.
The 2006 Lebanon War, a turning point in the modern confrontation, inflicted heavy losses and devastated civilian and
military infrastructure on both sides, entrenching mutual
animosity and raising the spectre of a wider regional conflict. The military doctrines underlying Israeli and Hezbollah
operations—fortified by deterrent and pre-emptive imperatives on the Israeli side and by resistance and asymmetric
deterrence on the Hezbollah side—have evolved in concert
with successive conflicts and ceasefires. The asymmetric
character of the struggle has compelled both sides to fuse
conventional and irregular tactics, employing urban con-
cealment, surface-to-surface missiles, and precision strike
capabilities, animating a conflict of densely interwoven escalatory mechanisms. Differentiated military objectives—Israeli security in depth against missile fire and Hezbollah's deterrent and operational depth through missile threats—have
rendered the operational theatre both intricate and prone
to miscalibration. The situation is further complicated by
regional proxy imperatives, where actors such as Iran finan-
cially and logistically empower Hezbollah, while covert Israeli activities against Iranian entrenchment afford deniabili-
ty and operational depth, sustaining a condition of enduring,
yet delicately suspended, confrontation.

The involvement of external states compounds the volatility of the contested terrain, layering diplomatic rivalries
on top of the local antagonisms. Each external actor in-

jects specific interests and tools—military, financial, and political—heightening the fragility of existing ceasefire lines
and increasing the risk of unintended escalation. Territorial skirmishes, proxy pathways, and the competition for
sphere-of-influence ports and airspace now intersect, demanding that policy planners adopt a layered, adaptable
conflict-management framework. A robust appraisal of past
confrontations and the cascading vulnerabilities they expose is therefore indispensable for discerning how the Israel-Hezbollah balance-point affects wider Middle Eastern
order and for identifying minimally disruptive pathways to
durable stability.

The Role of Deterrence: Strategies and Implications

Central to the Israel-Hezbollah equilibrium is the practice
of deterrence, which exerts considerable influence on the
security fabric of the Levant. Deterrent credibility—rooted
in the certainty of punitive second-strike capabilities—compels both sides to temper their operational calculations. The
execution of deterrence is less a matter of pure firepower
than the synthesis of tangible arsenals, symbolic signalling,
and psychological conditioning, each component calibrated to diminish the appeal of escalation. For Hezbollah, the
deterrent calculus is complex, leveraging its asymmetrical
advantages as a non-state formation while mustering increasingly sophisticated missile production lines, cyber capabilities, and a deep ideological conviction to complicate
Israel's risk assessment.

The organisation has, over time, calibrated its capacity and posture to function as an influential actor not only within Lebanese territory but across the adjoining regional theatre, using its military branch to manifest an image of durability and strength. Through the procurement of an elaborate missile inventory and the intentional cultivation of partnerships with both sovereign and sub-sovereign entities, Hezbollah aspires to a deterrent equilibrium that, in its calculus, would frustrate any would-be military interlocutor, with Israel prominently identified as a principal target. The submerged, yet unmistakable, signal accompanying this strategy is that any act of aggression directed at Hezbollah or the Lebanese State would confront an immediate and disproportionate riposte, an eventuality ostensibly choreographed to negate any incentive to act first.

Israeli policy, conversely, has traditionally rested on a layered deterrent architecture that is, at its core, political yet materially bolstered by advanced technology and a tradition of decisive military action. Through the coordination of preventive air operations and calibrated displays of manoeuvre warfare, the Israel Defence Forces strive to engrave the impression that the price exacted on aggressors would outweigh any conceivable gain. The narrative is complemented by diplomatic engagements and the maintenance of strategic partnerships that project a consensus whereby any hostile act would invoke a domino effect of operational and political costs extending far beyond the origin of the aggression. The reach of deterrent logic is not confined to fielded forces; it reaches into political calculation, economic sanction architecture, and the civilian psyche on both sides of the frontier. A deterrence that resonates across these spectra can conceivably dampen the likelihood of misjudgment and dampen the chances that an incident might spiral into an uncontrolled escalation.

Yet reliance on deterrence is fraught with risk, resting as it does on shared perceptions of resolve, rationality, and capability. Misreads, erroneous assumptions, and calculational errors can quickly diminish deterrent credibility, raising the spectre of inadvertent escalation. The changing character of warfare compounds these dangers; the diffusion of asymmetric capabilities means that even states possessing substantial conventional power may face destabilising responses. Cyber operations, irregular military methods, and hybrid campaigns create gaps in traditional deterrent postures, demanding both agile recalibration and imaginative design. Therefore, recalibrating deterrent doctrines to the demands of the current security milieu is essential for managing the fraught nexus between Israel and Hezbollah. Deterrence, in this richer view, reveals the delicate interdependence of power, perception, and readiness. A diligent analysis of these doctrines and their ramifications is therefore indispensable for assessing the geopolitical environment, for constructing feasible avenues of restraint, and for fostering durable regional equilibrium.

Border Security: Danger Zones and Buffer Zones

Border security between Israel and Lebanon remains a

decisive variable within the Israel-Hezbollah calculus, profoundly influencing the likelihood of both conflict escalation and its mitigation. The delineation is marked by both danger zones and buffer zones, each of which exerts a unique gravitational pull on tactical and strategic calculations.

Danger zones delineate geographic theatres where the risk of military confrontation is markedly heightened, typically overlapping with contested territories, disputed delimitations, and historically charged flashpoint locales. Their presence alone imposes multilayered complications that exacerbate the already fragile equilibrium. The entanglement of state and non-state armed elements within these strata further erodes the efficacy of conventional border-security paradigms, multiplying the obstacles to sustained stability and the suppression of cross-frontier aggression. By contrast, buffer zones are structured to institute tangible separation and diminish the likelihood of head-on engagement. Such strata may combine demilitarised corridors, the deployment of multinational peacekeeping contingents, or specialised diplomatic lanes, each calibrated to lower friction and foster negotiation. The operational legitimacy of these buffer configurations, however, is inseparable from the mutual commitment of the concerned parties to uphold the prescribed demarcations and procedural strictures. Even with the continued deployment of the United Nations Interim Force in Lebanon and auxiliary peacekeeping initiatives, the guardianship of the border area evolves into a persistent operational theatre, further complicated by the spectre of asymmetric warfare and the possibility of abrupt escalation. The coexisting geometry of danger and buffer zones thus reveals the tenuous equilibrium that characterises the Israel-Hezbollah interaction, underscoring the imperative for resilient institutional mechanisms that can avert unintended encounters and discipline crisis dynamics.

Any infraction of border integrity can catalyse a wider regional explosion, highlighting the necessity for sustained vigilance and anticipatory engagement by all pertinent actors. Consequently, a granular comprehension of the operant dynamics within these peripheries is vital for policymakers and military strategists committed to untangling the intricate border security dilemmas endemic to the Israel-Lebanon theatre, where the equilibrium of regional and, by extension, global security is manifestly imperilled.

Intelligence and Surveillance: Behind the Scenes Operations

The Israel-Hezbollah relationship has been profoundly sculpted by clandestine intelligence and surveillance campaigns waged by each side. The secretive character of these undertakings perpetuates a low-grade, simmering confrontation that regularly recalibrates the deliberations of the highest political and military echelons. Both actors have channelled vast resources into expanding and modernising their intelligence apparatus, deploying sophisticated technologies alongside layered human and technical networks to harvest data and scrutinise each other's movements. These operations transcend conventional spying, interfacing electronic eavesdropping, sophisticated cyber operations, and aerial reconnaissance. In such an environment, the critical importance of accurate and temporally precise intelligence emerges not merely as an advantage but as an existential requirement, informing military posturing, preemptive calculations, and escalatory deterrence.

Furthermore, the introduction of unmanned aerial vehicles and other advanced surveillance systems has enabled continuous observation of vulnerable border regions and prospective targets. Their covert employment complicates an already fractious relationship, since any erroneous interpretation or inadvertent misstep could trigger a shift to full-blown hostilities. An ongoing cat-and-mouse contest of data collection and countermeasures has thus become fundamental to the Israel-Hezbollah relationship, reinforcing a perpetual atmosphere of distrust and maximum readiness. The technical layers involved also underscore the wider geopolitical context, as regional and external actors scrutinise each shift and attempt to translate the intelligence flow into strategic advantage. Consequently, the impact of surveillance and reconnaissance reaches well beyond the direct Israel-Hezbollah encounter, interweaving with larger balances of power and security calculus. In a period marked by the swift maturation of dual-use technologies and adaptive threat conditions, the persuasive power of intelligence over this rivalry continues to reshape, generating novel dilemmas and openings for the parties involved as well as for the wider international system.

International Influence: The Impact of Global Powers

The Israel-Hezbollah nexus cannot be understood solely through the national boundaries of Israel and Lebanon. Global powers have infused the conflict with dimensions that compel attention far beyond the Levant. The United States, Russia, European states, and regional actors—most notably Turkey—have all injected competing priorities, altering both the conflict's immediate configuration and its long-term horizon. International intervention has applied multiple levers, including tactical military aid, diplomatic mediation, and force deployments, each calibrated to produce a specific outcome. Washington and Moscow, through rival bloc allegiances and arms supplies, have long recalibrated the regional balance of power; their competing brokerages have consequently hardened the parties' maximal demands. European capitals, for their part, have underwritten initiatives that couple pressure with humanitarian discourse, while also maintaining observer roles in multilateral ministerial meetings designed to contain escalatory spillover. Turkey, evoking both past Ottoman influence and contemporary regional ambitions, has sought to reinforce maritime claims and humanitarian outreach, thus reframing its own deterrent posture in the Eastern Mediterranean. Collectively, these pressures render the Israel-Hezbollah stand-off less a bilateral confrontation and more a multidimensional chess match ordered by the strategic calculations of the world's principal powers.

Global powers have made the crisis more intricate, elevating the stakes and widening possible fallout. Their postures and interventions have altered the clash not only on the battlefield but also in the framing and myths that surround the Israel-Hezbollah rivalry. News outlets and public discourse often mirror the priorities of the great powers, selectively spotlighting episodes that reinforce their official positions and thus colour the international community's understanding of the hostilities. This fusion of statecraft, media framing, and civic dialogue reveals the interwoven character of the Israel-Hezbollah contest and illustrates how global influence radiates in multiple directions. As the clash advances, the capacity of outside capitals to either ignite further discord or guide events toward détente remains a decisive factor in the overall script. To chart a plausible avenue for de-escalation and eventual regional stability, analysts must disentangle and weigh the international imprints that form the background against which Israel and Hezbollah confront each other.

Public Perception: National Narratives and Media Influence

Public sentiment is far more than a mirror; it is an active agent that reinforces the Israel-Hezbollah rivalry and settles preferences for policy. Each side cultivates a historical legend that describes self and other, casting itself as a rightful defender and the opponent as a fixture of existential menace. Domestic media, often subsidised or choreographed by the state, amplify these myths, favouring imagery and language that resonate with national memory and tribal loyalty. International reporting, meanwhile, frequently privileges the lens of great powers, replicating their biases and assumptions. Within this space, leaders frequently invoke public outrage to legitimise military preparedness or retaliatory strikes, framing each action as a necessary and popular mandate. Communities on both sides recognise these rituals: a civilian casualty on either side crystallises into a talking point that fuels the cycle. Perceptions are thus not passive by-products; they are the currency by which fighters, journalists, and politicians transact and reinforce a volatile equilibrium. For analysts, probing these mediated realities is indispensable for anticipating shifts in behaviour, calculating thresholds of tolerance, and, ultimately, identifying fragile openings for restraint.

Both sides have deployed media platforms and nationalistic rhetoric to reinforce their arguments, each casting itself as the guarantor of national survival against encroaching peril. In Israel, the traumatic resonance of past wars and the collective memory of violence and displacement have solidified the perception of an enduring existential menace from Hezbollah, which is depicted as an assailant whose campaign of rocket fire, infiltrations, and abductions knows no limit. This view, amplified by television, print, and official commentary, cultivates public anxiety and consensus around rigorous deterrent policies. Hezbollah, for its part, has exploited satellite networks, social media, and local press to frame its militant posture as a legitimate, heroic defiance of the Israeli state, depicting incursions and air strikes as provocations to which the Party of God responds with calibrated resistance.

Through slick video montages of rocket launches, martial funerals, and parades, the movement projects an image of invulnerability and popular legitimacy that resonates with its domestic constituency and sympathetic audiences across the region. The mutual reinforcement of these historical and media-driven portrayals perpetuates a cycle of enmity that obstructs compromise and durable peace. When the enemy is represented as a lethal, annihilating force, public and elite perceptions harden, dialogue is bracketed as treason, and conciliatory gestures are read as weakness. Thus, the cycle of distrust is institutionalised and the political appetite for negotiation systematically eroded.

The amplification of nationalist narratives through various media platforms has intensified animosities and reinforced the perception of a zero-sum confrontation, obstructing avenues for collaborative interaction and sustainable coexistence. Biased reporting and selective framing have further entrenched prejudicial beliefs and distortive stereotypes, thus replicating a cycle of mutual demonisation and polarisation. Public attitudes, informed by these dominant discourses, have decisively shaped domestic agendas, altered regional alignments, and coloured international perceptions. Accordingly, disentangling the relationship between national self-representations and media-driven influence is essential to the effort of fostering de-escalation and achieving lasting peace within the area.

Political Manoeuvring: Diplomatic Channels and Stalemates

Political manoeuvring surrounding the Israel-Hezbollah confrontation embodies an intricate calculus of diplomacy, factional rivalry, and entrenched institutional interests. Diplomatic channels remain critical instruments for reducing tensions and for pursuing remedies to this enduring confrontation. Both regional and external stakeholders have repeatedly engaged in diverse initiatives designed to curb violence and to promote dialogue. Yet, the recurrent impasses that mark these initiatives expose the persistent obstacles that any effort to normalise this highly volatile relationship must confront.

Within the regional context, Lebanon, Syria, and Iran have consistently influenced the political order through material and strategic support for Hezbollah. Their diplomatic initiatives have included publicly articulated commitments as well as discreet back-channel discussions, illuminating the complex lattice of partnerships and antagonisms that characterise the Middle East. Intervention by great powers such as the United States and Russia has further layered the diplomatic environment, embedding the situation within a broader global rivalry that complicates every mediation. Specialised agencies, notably the United Nations, have sought to inject neutrality by sponsoring ceasefire talks, verifying frontiers, and coordinating humanitarian access. Yet, these mechanisms have repeatedly floundered, spurred by hereditary ideological predispositions, the absence of a common negotiating baseline, and the reciprocal siege mentality exhibited by both Tel Aviv and Beirut. Diplomatic stalls manifest predominantly from historic resentments, divergent strategic visions, and the calculated bargaining of both sides. Redressing these impasses mandates a calibrated combination of pressure and diplomatic finesse, alongside a sustained, reciprocal willingness to entertain concessions.

The interlocking nature of domestic, regional, and global pressures perpetuates an environment in which constructive negotiation remains difficult. Within each participant state, internal political calculations can override—or, conversely, justify—strategic moves intended to craft shared security. This iterative logic of escalation and restraint obscures the margins in which diplomats typically operate, leaving them to champion incremental gestures whose offsetting symbolic and substantive dividends can be quickly annulled. Consequently, while a diplomatic aperture may occasionally widen, the anchored legacy of mutually constitutive grievances and the weight of any proposed compromise keep the risk of renewed hostilities unusually high. Engaging the Israel-Hezbollah equation, therefore, demands an elaborately calibrated policy that is sensitive to collective historical memories, shifting microbalances of deterrent capability, and the centrifugal pressures exerted by neighbouring actors. Within this careful choreography, political diplomacy remains both the first and final order of business, even as each move across the negotiation table reinforces the perception of a protracted, transactional rivalry.

Economic Impacts: Regional Stability at Stake

The conflict's reverberations extend decisively into the regional economy, threatening any prospect of stability and long-term growth. Persistent hostilities translate into a pervasive risk premium that discourages both domestic entrepreneurs and foreign investors. Ports, supply chains, and telecommunications face intermittent disruptions, while energy infrastructure is doubly vulnerable: supply lines drawn across the Levant and the broader Eastern Mediterranean become the focal point for both kinetic strikes and speculative undersupply. Consequently, tourism-centric economies that stretch along the Mediterranean arc, along with the nascent interconnection projects across the Gulf and Eastern Mediterranean, confront a protracted wait-and-see dependency that defers otherwise promising integration dividends. Economic recovery, therefore, hinges on a decisively calmer security environment, one that diplomatic actors can only, for the moment, influence rather than guarantee.

The prospect of military escalation and the accompanying risks to critical infrastructure and maritime corridors represent an immediate and growing threat to the economic stability of Israel and Lebanon, and of the broader Eastern Mediterranean. Even the possibility of hostilities acts as a deterrent to foreign direct investment and hampers the growth of key industries, notably tourism and trade. The financial strain of ongoing military readiness consumes public budgets, siphoning funds away from programmes aimed at long-term social and economic advancement. In addition, an enduring risk of hostilities produces a climate of perpetual uncertainty, which erodes investor confidence across the region. Businesses are compelled to adjust to an environment of elevated geopolitical risk, discouraging capital commitments and fostering pricing volatility. The repetitive sequence of conflict and subsequent reconstruction locks the economy into a fragile equilibrium characterised by instability rather than growth. Consequently, the ramifications extend well beyond the immediate theatres of fighting, disrupting trade flows, joint investment initiatives, and multilateral economic dialogue. The Israel-Hezbollah confrontation also compounds pre-existing vulnerabilities, amplifying unemployment, widening poverty gaps, and deepening inequalities that the region can least afford.

The reallocation of fiscal resources toward military and security expenditures circumscribes the ability of governments to confront socio-economic obstacles and to nurture human capital. The resultant shortfall underpins a repetitive loop of economic volatility and popular discontent, which further heightens the prospect of regional destabilisation. Financial pressures on public budgets, when compounded by the depletion of human and material capital, engineer conditions under which durable economic viability recedes further from reach. The fallout from such fragility is not contained by borders; it radiates outward, dislocating the global economy. Disruption within the Eastern Mediterranean jeopardises energy supply chains, unsettles maritime corridors, and invites amplifying geopolitical discord. Given the intertwined character of contemporary markets, contraction in a single area reverberates globally, heightening the imperative for coordinated, preventive diplomatic and economic measures. The conflict between Israel and Hezbollah thus presents economic risks of a magnitude that demands immediate strategic redress to preserve the region's stability and its broader prosperity.

Future Prospects: Pathways Towards De-escalation

Within the intricate realities of the Israel-Hezbollah confrontation, identifying and nurturing prospective pathways to de-escalation is a fundamental condition for any durable regional stability.

The prospects for reducing tensions and advancing a durable peace depend on a holistic strategy that embraces the political, military, economic, and social dimensions of conflict. Central to this strategy are sustained diplomatic initiatives that create opportunities for dialogue, negotiation, and mediation. Such initiatives ought to include regional and global actors, working together to forge consensus and to design durable frameworks for dispute resolution. Concurrently, confidence-building measures—exemplified by joint humanitarian corridors, co-managed environmental projects, or shared water-resource agreements—can yield concrete, visible benefits that diminish mistrust and deter escalatory behaviour. Multilateral dialogue fora and long-term peace building initiatives offer settings in which parties can acknowledge and address the conflict's underlying drivers—territorial claims, security dilemmas, and historical grievances—within a structured, supervised environment.

Reinforcing the authority of international law, including pertinent Security Council resolutions, provides a normative foundation for a rules-based resolution of differences and for curtailing the likelihood of violence. Equally critical is the need to confront the socio-economic dimensions that sustain and amplify tensions. Targeted investments in sustainable development, vocational training, and resilient infrastructure in fragile and marginalised communities can tackle the grievances that feed recruitment by violent extremists and that breed recurring violence. Such measures not only stabilise the immediate environment but also cultivate the long-term social and economic resilience essential for enduring peace.

Engaging the military dimension of the Israel-Hezbollah conflict requires, first and foremost, the establishment of resolute lines of communication and deconfliction protocols among the relevant parties. These instruments can contain miscalculations and accidental escalations, thereby lowering the probability of immediate confrontation. Concurrently, the articulation of demilitarised zones, supplemented by precise arms-control arrangements, can cultivate reciprocal trust and diminish the frequency of military confrontations. It is vital, however, that de-escalation measures expand beyond the operational realm to incorporate confidence-building practices directed at the wider public. Educational programmes, cultural exchanges, and structured dialogues among ordinary citizens can promote mutual comprehension, empathy, and the slow, yet critical, process of reconciliation. Such initiatives cultivate the socio-political soil in which sustainable peace and coexistence can take root. Thus, the future of the region's stability hinges on the adoption of a comprehensive and inclusive strategy that attends to the conflict's varied dimensions, thereby opening credible avenues toward de-escalation and the enduring establishment of peace and stability.

8
Refugees as Catalysts
Demographic Pressures and Regional Implications

Refugee Dynamics in Syria and Lebanon

The protracted conflict in Syria produced a refugee crisis whose reverberations are felt well beyond Syria's borders, most acutely in neighbouring Lebanon. Displacement trends in the region began in earnest with the outbreak of civil war, when escalating violence obliged civilians to flee in search of security. Lebanon's reception of approximately 1.5 million registered Syrian refugees has created overlapping challenges: rapid demographic change, overstretched social services, fiscal strains, and the reactivation of sectarian and political rifts. The scale and interrelated nature of these pressures require scholarly analysis of the push factors that sustain mass exodus as well as the longer-term consequences for both origin and host states.

Syria's war, marked by relentless fighting and systematic violations of human rights, has generated one of the largest refugee movements in contemporary history. The relentless bombardment of urban centres, the destruction of livelihoods, and the pervasive threat of detention and torture destroyed the infrastructures of survival. Lebanon, hemmed in by a rigid border, historical ties to Syria, and a long record of informal movement, quickly emerged as the first safe, if temporary, destination for families seeking to escape the immediate perils of the conflict.

The rapid arrival of large numbers of Syrian refugees has markedly transformed Lebanon's demographic composition while imposing profound socio-economic burdens that have tested the limits of the country's infrastructure and institutional capacity. The escalation in refugee populations has overwhelmed Lebanon's already vulnerable social services—namely, healthcare, education, and housing—intensifying competition for already limited resources and fuelling friction between host communities and displaced groups. The sheer scale of the refugee presence has, in turn, heightened demand for critical public services and narrowed employment opportunities, widening existing socio-economic stratification and breeding dissatisfaction among Lebanese citizens and refugees alike. The ramifications of this displacement extend well beyond immediate welfare concerns, shaping the political landscape in both Lebanon and Syria. The refugee surge has revived historical sectarian divisions, provoked political disputes, and complicated the governance reform agenda. Furthermore, the temporary hosting of such numbers has provoked security anxieties and strained the fragile equilibrium of power and stability within Lebanon itself. In this context, a rigorous examination of the refugee dynamics operating between Syria and Lebanon is essential for grasping the comprehensive ramifications of large-scale displacement in both states.

Strategically tracing the evolution of the crisis alongside its multifaceted repercussions across different societal domains cultivates a comprehensive perspective necessary for the formulation of timely humanitarian initiatives and the calibration of evidence-based policymaking regarding the escalating refugee demographic.

Historical Overview of Displacement Trends

The chronological examination of the displacement of populations between Syria and Lebanon accentuates the sustained mechanisms of coerced migration, revealing how deeply entrenched these processes have become for both nation-states. Both have intermittently confronted large-scale dislocation, triggered by civil disturbances, regional confrontations, and persistent macroeconomic stresses. These recurrent movements have continuously redrawn the demographic contours, interspersing communities of varying ethnic and sectarian identities and hence complicating the already intricate social texture. Such recurrent upheaval has inscribed long-lasting changes upon the social order, governance structures, and livelihoods of both Syria and Lebanon. Syria, traditionally celebrated for its archaeological and architectural heritage, has confronted successive surges of outward and internal displacement since Ottoman rule, with pressures markedly escalating during pivotal twentieth-century episodes, including the dispossession of Armenian populations, World War II, and a succession of unstable regimes.

In Lebanon, the historical pattern of displacement is inseparable from the country's internal conflicts and the pressures exerted by the broader region, resulting in persistent waves of Palestinian refugees and more recent arrivals from Syria and other crises. This trajectory reveals the remarkable resilience of both Syrian and Lebanese societies confronted by constantly shifting demographics. A historical perspective on displacement reveals the extent of the challenge while indicating the necessity of durable solutions that confront the underlying drivers of forced migration and facilitate safe, dignified return or resettlement. Careful analysis of earlier trends and motivators enables policymakers, researchers, and humanitarian actors to appreciate the complex and interlinked dimensions of the refugee phenomenon, thereby informing more precise and effective responses that promote long-term regional stability.

Sociopolitical Impact of Refugees on Host Communities

The arrival of a substantial refugee population has produced demographic shifts that, while humanitarian in origin, have strained the capacities and solidarity of Lebanese host communities and recalibrated the country's political dynamics. Escalating competition over jobs, rental accommodation, and the bandwidth of public services has bred heightened grievances and a pervasive sense of exclusion among long-standing residents. Equally, the demographic weight of the refugee population has magnified pre-existing anxieties regarding security and systemic fragility, revealing the limited resilience of political and social institutions. Such pressures have, in turn, guided policymaking at every administrative echelon, where the reflex to triage scarce resources has often superseded integrative approaches. Concomitantly, the refugee crisis has set in motion a layered social milieu where Lebanese and Syrian newcomers interweave their lives. The result has been a terrain where solidarity networks and economic cooperation coexist with moments of tension produced by differing cultural codes, competing livelihood imperatives, and the perception of zero-sum resource distribution. Within this intermingled space, questions of identity, belonging, and the compact of national citizenship have been brought to the forefront, recalibrating public debates on rights and social compact while leaving the political field in continual re-negotiation.

Moreover, the arrival of refugees has prompted a thorough reassessment of social inclusion mechanisms, humanitarian assistance frameworks, and the strategies employed for community involvement. Consequently, a number of innovative programmes and collaborative ventures have emerged, oriented toward the shifting priorities and interactive complexities that now characterise host municipalities. The sociopolitical ramifications of the refugee wave, however, transcend immediate logistical hurdles and raise larger, more systemic inquiries regarding governance structures, representational equity, and the durability of social concord. The resulting discussions have centred on public-policy design, the distribution of finite resources, and the crafting of durable strategies that merge integration imperatives with sustainable development goals. Importantly, these debates have illuminated the inextricably linked social and political terrains of the region, compelling all actors to evaluate how the refugee situation refracts onto continental governance stability and on inter-state diplomacy. Consequently, a comprehensive grasp of the sociopolitical reverberations of forced migration for host societies is imperative not only for cultivating resilience and preventing marginal exclusion but also for reducing the probabilities of social fragmentation and escalating conflict. Surmounting these layered sociopolitical realities will, therefore, demand rigorous analytic inquiry, synchronised cross-sectoral action, and frameworks that fully account for the interwoven complexities of the refugee-host community nexus.

Economic Strains: Challenges and Opportunities

The Syrian refugee arrival in Lebanon has had a measurable effect on national economic conditions, presenting the polity with simultaneous burdens and strategic openings.

On the one hand, the surge in the number of refugees has placed heavy demands on Lebanon's already overburdened infrastructure, labour market, and social services. Enhanced competition for limited jobs and housing stock has exacerbated existing economic inequalities and stoked social friction within host communities. The strain on public utilities and services, already fragile, has forced the national government to grapple with the challenge of delivering effective and equitable support to both Lebanese citizens and refugees. At the same time, the informal labour market has faced shockwaves, with the arrival of low-wage workers creating downward pressure on wages in the agriculture, construction, and domestic-work sectors. On the other hand, the refugee presence has opened a range of economic avenues. The entrepreneurial drive and skill sets many Syrian refugees bring have enriched Lebanon's economic fabric, stimulating a more varied and dynamic landscape within small enterprises, crafts, and informal trading networks. Rising demand for food, housing, and services has, in turn, opened new markets, creating jobs particularly in the northern Beqaa Valley and the southern suburbs, areas where refugee concentrations are highest. Several enterprises have pivoted to meet the distinct needs of refugee customers, generating innovative business models and fostering cross-cultural partnerships. Balancing the economic pressures with the latent opportunities thus demands both targeted policymaking and a willingness to leverage the refugee presence as a catalyst for inclusive growth.

Policy interventions should be directed towards integrated development frameworks that create synergies between host communities and refugee populations, capitalising on their pooled human capital to fortify local economies. Streamlining and regulating the informal labour sector is critical, as it can safeguard decent working conditions while neutralising potential downward pressures on wages and employment opportunities for both refugee and domestic workers. Humanitarian financing remains indispensable in alleviating the economic pressures associated with sudden population displacement; consequently, donors should channel resources towards infrastructure, public employment opportunities, skills training, and educational services that lay the foundation for durable resilience. Pursuing partnerships with the private sector to design inclusive value chains and to incubate joint enterprises that involve both refugees and host community members can yield development dividends that extend beyond relief. Effective alignment among public agencies, civil society organisations, and multilateral institutions is also necessary to amplify the efficacy of assistance and to eliminate unnecessary overlap. In sum, reframing refugee settlement as a catalyst for economic and social advancement demands a holistic blueprint that reconciles immediate assistance with proactive measures of inclusion and empowerment for the foreseeable future.

Lebanon can transform the pressures of refugee integration into avenues for renewal by confronting immediate economic challenges while capitalising on the skills, entrepreneurial spirit, and cultural dynamism that refugees can bring. If the state, civil society, and international partners pursue inclusive and adaptive strategies, the country can emerge from this crisis with an expanded social and economic base that proves resilient against future shocks.

Policy Responses and International Aid Efforts

Lebanon's policy landscape and the constellation of international assistance structures have evolved since the initial wave of refugees. Governments and multilaterals, alongside an array of civil and humanitarian actors, have architected a coordinated web of interventions designed to shield the most vulnerable while fostering shared social and economic dividends. As a result, premium attention has been paid to integrating refugees into the public healthcare and education systems, formalising labour rights, and expanding legal pathways that protect the dignity and agency of displaced populations. Continuous assessment has animated these measures, enabling local authorities, civil society partners, and international agencies to offset tensions that might otherwise amplify the fragility of both host and displaced communities. In parallel, bilateral and multilateral financial instruments, technical missions, and capacity-building programmes have supplemented national capacities, translating donor pledges into on-the-ground improvements that reinforce local governance and civil society responsiveness.

These initiatives have been designed to ease the strain on Lebanese public institutions while strengthening their capacity to respond to the multidimensional pressures generated by the refugee influx. Aid modalities have consequently shifted to include longer-term development goals in recognition that the refugee situation is likely to remain protracted and that interventions must therefore overcome systemic obstacles. This integrative framework insists that refugee concerns be situated within broader development blueprints so that underlying drivers can be addressed and affected host communities can be fortified against future shocks. Accordingly, an intentional focus on expanding livelihood prospects, nurturing social cohesion, and reinforcing governance systems has gained primacy on the aid agenda. Nevertheless, obstacles endure, including persistent financing gaps, divergent coordination practices, and political dynamics that influence the ordering and operationalisation of programmes. Therefore, robust coordination among donor states, Lebanese authorities, and civil-society implementing organisations is crucial to amplifying the efficacy of external assistance. Ultimately, the convergence of policy formulation and humanitarian support delineates an adaptive environment continually recalibrated by changing operational realities, altered political currents, and the necessity of harmonising time-sensitive humanitarian actions with enduring developmental imperatives.

Identity and Integration: Cultural Bridging or Division?

The Syrian refugee crisis and its reverberations throughout Lebanon foreground the intricate interplay between identity and integration as a pressing societal concern. The steady arrival of Syrian refugees has itself generated a flux of cultural energy that challenges, and at times invigorates, the host communities. Displaced populations arrive with patterned traditions, social practices, and worldviews, com-pelling host societies to confront the terms of assimilation, coexistence, and the risk of segmentation. An informed ex-ploration of the sociocultural consequences of refugee set-tlement demands a nuanced and layered analytical lens. Cen-tral to this reflection is the fragile imperative of safeguarding the distinctive identities of both Lebanese communities and refugee groups, on one hand, and, on the other, of cultivat-ing an integrated civic space wherein common values may gradually converge. The analytical lens must illuminate the reciprocal processes through which host and refugee popu-lations exchange and adapt, thereby enriching the collective social fabric without eroding foundational heritages. The question of cultural bridging or division must therefore be placed beyond the registers of exchange and diffusion; it must also be situated within the evolving practices of accep-tance, tolerance, and an ethical respect for pluralism. When Lebanese and Syrian communities embrace this pluralism, they initiate a set of interactions that are, in principle, mutu-ally rewarding, cultivating new perspectives and dynamically reconfiguring the societal landscape.

Nevertheless, without sustained engagement and in-formed policy frameworks, the danger of cultural fragmen-tation and social isolation remains palpable. Efforts—both domestic and international—geared toward the cultural as-pects of refugee inclusion must therefore prioritise the creation of environments that deliberately invite intercul-tural exchange and collective endeavour. Programmes that support language acquisition, intercommunity festivals, and joint social or economic projects function as pivotal instru-ments for cultivating reciprocal understanding and shared empathy across varied populations. Moreover, the story-line of identity negotiation and settlement must be broadened beyond the refugee population alone; it must equally acknowledge how uprooting influences the host society's own conception of self and communal belonging. Attending to host-community anxieties—whether rooted in economic, cultural, or psychological dimensions—is thus an essential step in nurturing a social climate in which mutual honour and accommodation can flourish. Cultural integration, far from being a remedial exercise, harbours the transformative potential to convert the ruptures of displacement into collective channels of enrichment and solidarity. By confronting the layered realities of identity and by foregrounding our shared humanity, societies can yet translate the pressures of large-scale migration into a durable, harmonious co-existence that cherishes and amplifies diversity.

Security Concerns: Realities and Perceptions

Within the refugee wave provoked by the Syrian civil war, security anxieties have surfaced as a centre-stage concern.

Host countries and the wider international community continue to confront the multifaceted security challenges associated with large refugee outflows. A clear distinction must be drawn between the actual security risks and the narratives that often amplify public anxiety. Security dimensions range from the threat of terrorism to everyday crime and broader social frictions. While responsible authorities must address these risks, the analysis must remain evidence-driven and unclouded by bias. Statistically, the predominant profile of refugees is that of non-combatant civilians escaping violence and repression. Yet isolated incidents of crime and the occasional identification of extremist individuals travelling with refugee flows cannot be dismissed. Furthermore, limited infrastructure, constrained job markets, and pressures on housing can exacerbate tensions between displaced populations and host communities, feeding into historic societal fault lines. When these socioeconomic tensions become politicised, they can trigger violence. On a larger scale, the acceptance of significant refugee populations can recalibrate regional security equations; states bordering the conflict region might perceive the inflows as a security liability, prompting them to recalibrate border controls and military postures.

Diplomatic tensions often follow security-focused refugee policy choices, inhibiting multilateral cooperation needed for sustainable management of forced displacement. To overcome this, policymakers must reconcile verifiable threat levels with the beliefs that drive public and official narratives. Misinformation, amplified by political rhetoric, magnifies suspicion of refugees and positions entire groups as security liabilities, thereby complicating their socio-economic integration. Consequently, security frameworks should rely on multi-layered threat analyses and intelligence derived from empirical evidence, distinguishing between extremist networks and the broader asylum seeker population. This evidence-based approach can provide policymakers with the reassurance and confidence they need to make informed decisions. Tactical responses must target verified risks while concurrently avoiding the stigmatisation of innocent civilians.

In parallel, ongoing, structured dialogue between refugee communities and the resident populace proves essential for normalising coexistence. Regular, facilitated inter-group exchanges weaken stereotypes and humanise the aid-recipient population, thereby mitigating the affective dimensions of threat perception. A balanced policy acknowledges the host state's right to security while countering unfounded fears with transparent and participatory information-sharing. This emphasis on balance can make policymakers feel the need for fairness and equity in their decision-making. Such dual recognition empowers public institutions and civil society to forge responses that are both protective and compassionate, ultimately enhancing the resilience of host societies as well as the well-being of displaced persons.

Demographic Shifts: Long-term Regional Consequences

The influx of Syrian refugees has induced deep demographic shifts whose long-term consequences for the region are profound. As waves of displaced individuals and families have crossed the border into Lebanon, the demographic profiles of both Lebanon and Syria have been irrevocably altered, creating effects that reach far beyond numerical change alone. The implications for population size and distribution are inextricably linked to the reconfiguration of social structures, political configurations, economic resource allocation, and cultural identities. The seriousness of these consequences can be grasped only by examining how demographic redistribution interacts with the larger regional context.

At the most elementary level, the refugee crisis has modified the ethnic, religious, and linguistic composition of both Lebanon and Syria. Such transformation can provoke or intensify pre-existing social and political fractures, particularly within Lebanon, where the fragile equilibrium of sectarian representation and power-sharing has long been the foundation of political stability. The geographical clustering of refugees in particular governorates or districts risks overburdening local resources and services, undermining traditional livelihoods, and eroding community cohesion that had evolved over decades.

From an economic standpoint, these demographic shifts exert further pressure on already overstressed infrastructural systems, public goods, and labour markets in both Lebanon and Syria. The absorption of refugees into housing, education, and health systems that were already strained before the crisis compounds existing vulnerabilities, while simultaneously creating new pressure points in regional supply chains and bilateral economic relations. However, it's important to note that refugee integration can also bring economic benefits, such as increased labour supply and consumer demand, which can help to stimulate economic growth and development in the host communities. By highlighting these potential benefits, a more balanced and positive narrative about the economic impact of large refugee populations can be promoted.

Competition for scarce jobs and the strain on public services increasingly jeopardise the region's economic resilience. At the same time, managed long-term incorporation of refugees into local labour markets and communities could drive inclusive economic diversification and growth. Conversely, neglecting the interrelated demographic and economic pressures risks producing entrenched inequality, widening social divides, and threatening stability and transformative development. Beyond socioeconomic repercussions, demographic redistribution also carries regional security implications. Concentrated settlements of displaced populations can recalibrate power distributions, expose fragile border zones, and complicate geopolitical agendas, thus aggravating pre-existing rivalries. Changes in population size and location also recalibrate voting bases and formal representation, reshaping political fissures and the future of regional governance. Understanding these dynamics demands disciplined, multi-scalar analysis and forethought. By synthesising historical analogues, case-based evidence, and rigorous quantitative modelling, government and civil society actors can identify vulnerabilities and craft anticipatory, integrated responses to the enduring repercussions of population redistribution.

In addition, robust policy frameworks, evidence-based intervention measures, and strengthened cross-border partnerships must be designed with the dual purpose of mitigating demographic stresses and leveraging diversity as a catalyst for cohesive, adaptive, and peaceful regional societies.

Case Studies: Successes, Failures, and Lessons Learned

A rigorous examination of refugee integration and its regional fallout mandates a focus on empirically grounded case studies that illuminate both constructive and counterproductive methods. Lebanon's hosting of more than a million Syrian refugees, for instance, presents a pivotal context for unpacking the logistical and social dimensions of mass displacement. Confronted with the sheer number of arrivals, Lebanese authorities and civil society actors developed a spectrum of interventions, from livelihood and vocational programmes to catch-up education and psychosocial support. These programmes delivered selective benefits to both refugees and host communities but also revealed coordination gaps, resource constraints, and, at times, political fatigue. Systematic scrutiny of these interventions permits identification of critical enablers—such as inclusive local governance—alongside recurrent bottlenecks like fragmented donor support. Evolving into Syrian territory, the plight of internally displaced persons (IDPs) further complicates the integration calculus, as regional actors must navigate protection concerns, the resilience of host households, and the uncertainty of return in a conflict-scarred environment.

In this study, we draw upon the coordinated efforts of national authorities, multilateral agencies, and community-based movements to expose both the possibilities and the limits of protection for civilians caught in zones of sustained,

violent conflict. Certain operations have succeeded in alleviating immediate hardship while establishing preliminary
pathways toward durable peace; nevertheless, others expose
the dangers of neglecting coherent strategic design and
sectoral collaboration. Expanding our inquiry beyond the
Levant, we examine parallel situations across several prolonged refugee contexts. Jordan's pioneering integration of
displaced workers into national labour sectors and Turkey's
adaptive safety-net revisions exemplify how policy choices,
social perceptions, and observable field conditions interact
in complex ways. A blended review of these instances allows
us to extract adaptable policy heuristics that anticipate both
the needs of refugees and their potential contributions to
host societies. The compiled testimony not only enriches
the quantitative database of forced migration studies but
also reanimates the human stories that underscore both the
resilience and the vulnerability of displaced populations.

They embody both the steadfastness of individuals displaced by violence and the imperatives that compel informed
and humane action against one of the paramount humanitarian crises of our era.

Conclusion: The Path Forward for Incorporating Refugee Populations

Reflecting on the effects of refugee inflows on Syria and
Lebanon, we discern that constructive long-term incorporation of displaced persons into receiving societies entails

a multi-pronged strategy. A dense interlacing of economic, social, and political dynamics must be disentangled with care to promote durable settlement and regional peace. Governments, international bodies, non-governmental organisations, and citizen networks must align their efforts to mitigate obstacles while harnessing the latent possibilities that accompany demographic change. Central to this strategy is the commitment to policies that advance the socio-economic agency of both refugees and receiving communities. While humanitarian support remains vital for immediate safeguarding, programmes must evolve toward avenues that foster autonomy and long-term robustness. Such reorientation not only uplifts displaced individuals and households but also strengthens the national economies and social fabrics of the host states, yielding benefits that extend far beyond the refugee population itself.

Above all, cultivating a pervasive sense of shared identity and belonging stands as a critical countermeasure to social tension and as a precondition for enduring peaceful coexistence. Cultural and educational programmes expressly designed to nurture dialogue, foster mutual understanding, and cultivate reciprocal respect among heterogeneous groups can establish, over time, the bedrock of a truly inclusive society. Viewing diversity as the wellspring of social strength, rather than as a fissure, is indispensable for reframing the prevailing narrative into one of unity and proactive collaboration. Concurrently, joint efforts to address security imperatives remain crucial for the stability not only of host communities but of the region overall. Comprehensive, transparent mechanisms for the orderly management of refugee movements, together with rigorous yet humane border governance, directly address the genuine security concerns articulated by host populations. At the same time, concerted campaigns against xenophobia and discrimination must be sustained through legal safeguards, public education, and advocacy designed to uphold the full corpus of human rights norms. The longer-term regional ramifications of demographic transformation call for a foresighted, integrated vision that transcends mere reactive measures. Host states are therefore encouraged to adopt policies that recognise refugees as potential catalysts of economic dynamism and cultural enrichment. By tapping the expertise, creative capacities, and entrepreneurial zeal within refugee populations, societies can create synergistic outcomes that confer significant advantages upon every stakeholder within the regional tableau.

To conclude, the future of refugee integration within Syrian and Lebanese societies hinges on a multidimensional and interconnected strategy. Central to this approach must be the empowerment of displaced citizens, the cultivation of inclusive local environments, the responsible navigation of security imperatives, and the recognition of diversity as a shared asset. By applying these interconnected principles, the region can traverse this critical juncture with sustained resilience and measured hope. While the road ahead is bound to test both systems and spirits, a united affirmation of shared humanity can transform present challenges into the foundations of a different and better shared future—one in which refugees are perceived not as liabilities but as essential agents of renewal and communal flourishing.

9
Water Security
Resource Scarcity Meets Geopolitical Tension

Regional Water Resources

The interplay between regional geology and climate governs the quantity and reliability of water supplies throughout the Levantine corridor. Throughout the Middle East, including Syria and Lebanon, the dominance of aridity is underscored by relatively sparse annual rainfall and elevated rates of evaporation. Conditions of pronounced water deficit are magnified by extensive desert landscapes, such as the Syrian Desert and Lebanon's Bekaa Valley, where the year-round shortage directly constrains human and ecological subsistence. Structural relief further modulates the spatial distribution of hydrological resources, as localised orographic lift can yield enhanced precipitation on windward slopes, thereby enlarging available surface and subsurface supplies, while adjacent leeward zones encounter acute deficiency. The gradation from coastal lowlands to elevated plateaus determines the depth, recharge, and hydraulic connectivity of aquifer systems, thereby influencing the rate of extractable groundwater and the vulnerability of these stocks to overuse. Long, hot summers and sporadic winter rainfall associated with interannual climatic variability inject an element of unpredictability into hydrological planning. When combined with anthropogenic pressures from irrigated agriculture and expanding urban settlement, these climatic and geomorphic variables amplify risks of systemic water stress.

Consequently, deciphering the intricate relationships between geography and climate becomes indispensable to overcoming regional water security challenges and to devising viable, long-term management interventions.

Historical Overview: Water as a Strategic Asset

The historical record reveals that water has long been recognised as a geostrategic resource, a fact that has governed the behaviour of states and communities. Whether assessing the hydraulic civilisations of the Tigris and Euphrates, the Nile, or the present-day water politics of the Eastern Mediterranean, one sees a near-unbroken pattern: the availability and control of surface and subsurface water have shaped borders, alliances, and conflicts. The strategic calibration of rivers, lakes, and aquifers has provided rulers with the means to exercise dominion over territory and peoples. That connection between water and territorial integrity has often crystallised into legal, customary, or martial forms of authority, embedding water scarcity and abundance into the very definition of state capacity. Decision-makers of the past recorded, and often broadcast, their understanding of water as a central factor of power. The architectural and administrative legacies—irrigation networks, Qanawats (canals), and fortified settlements near springs and aquifers—attest to the long-standing recognition that water security underpins political survival and expansion.

The strategic significance of water thus goes well beyond immediate needs for consumption and irrigation, influencing commerce, navigation, and the sustenance of biological networks. Alongside major river arteries and littoral zones, ancient mercantile paths took shape, underscoring the dual economic and strategic incentives of navigable water. Civilisations across eras further discerned the potent effect of restricting maritime or fluvial access, wielding water as a deliberate instrument of geopolitical pressure. Over centuries, records of both strife and partnership regarding water demonstrate a persistent human tendency to engage in calculation and diplomacy concerning this vital medium. Such a historical lens is essential for interpreting today's geopolitical struggles linked to water shortages in the Eastern Mediterranean. By illuminating how societies have consistently reframed water as a question of power, one appreciates the layered complexity underlying current water governance disputes and the pronounced consequences for regional stability and strategic security.

Current State of Water Scarcity

Across the Eastern Mediterranean, water scarcity has assumed critical significance, most acutely for Syria and Lebanon. Growing urban populations, intensifying agricultural demands, and the persistent impact of climate change are exerting unprecedented pressure on the limited and unevenly distributed freshwater resources of these states. Urban expansion compounds the existing inequalities in supply, while demand for irrigation intensifies in response to shifting agricultural practices and climate variability.

In Syria, recurrent droughts compounded by ineffective governance of water resources have resulted in overdrawn aquifers, reduced flow in the Euphrates, and a declining ability of communities to gain access to potable water. In Lebanon, the influx of refugees from Syria and other conflict-affected areas has further strained a water sector already operating under significant limitations, raising the pressure on ageing pumps, distribution networks, and treatment plants. Combined, these forces have rendered the sustainable delivery of water for households, irrigation, and manufacturing increasingly uncertain. The impacts of diminishing water supplies, however, are not confined to human welfare; they are also compromising aquifers, wetlands, and the fragile ecosystems that underpin regional biodiversity and the reserve of goods and services upon which the affected states depend. Diminishing natural flows have led to intensifying disputes over the Orontes and the Litani, fostering political rivalries and raising the spectre of confrontational hydro-diplomacy. The scramble for diminishing water supplies is also likely to exacerbate already-fragile governance, as communities and elites contest access in a climate of shrinking budgets and clientelist management. To mitigate these symptoms and, more critically, to avert escalating conflict, responses must therefore transcend emergency repairs and regulatory coordination, advancing basin-wide, multinational frameworks that encompass environmental, socio-economic, and security dimensions of the water cycle.

Policymakers, civil society, and international organisations must urgently forge collaborative frameworks that integrate sustainable resource management, emerging technologies, and fair risk-sharing arrangements to alleviate the escalating risks linked to water scarcity in the Levant and to reinforce regional stability. The imperative to act is multidimensional: water shortages are inextricably tied to food security, public health crises, and economic stagnation. For Syria and Lebanon, the persisting deficits in water availability are not merely technical failings but systemic vulnerabilities that necessitate coordinated cross-border strategies capable of safeguarding infrastructure integrity and protecting human well-being over the generational horizon.

Transboundary Water Management Challenges

The geopolitics of transboundary waterways compounds these vulnerabilities. The equitable allocation of shared basins remains a diplomatic quagmire, encumbered by competing national priorities, hybrid legal regimes, and variable hydrological data. When states prioritise their immediate demand, dialogue over fair distribution risks degenerating into zero-sum posturing. In the Syria-Lebanon context, the absence of ratified, basin-focused accords prolongs historical grievances and leaves critical aquifers and surface flows subject to unilateral abstraction and neglect. The interplay of historical grievances and fluid geopolitics consequently renders water governance not only a technical necessity but a vital, yet contested, dimension of regional security.

Competing national interests and the inertia of enduring rivalries continue to frustrate moves toward effective joint management of transboundary watercourses. Divergent hydrological realities—such as differing flood and drought patterns—combined with uneven commitments to conservation and extraction, deepen the chasm. Disputes thus escalate from narrow issues of allocation to broader threats to regional security, to economic viability, and to the integrity of common ecosystems. Resolving these challenges requires a layered policy framework that binds diplomatic finesse, empirical hydrology, and equitable governance. Central to that framework are instruments for real-time data exchange, transparent basin-wide monitoring, and joint, evidence-based decision processes. In tandem, the purposeful engagement of global river-basin experts and sustained, impartial dialogue among riparian states can yield solutions that balance interests rather than merely settling quarrels. By acknowledging the reciprocal dependency undergirding water security and cultivating a collaborative ethic, contiguous states can progress toward management regimes that are both sustainable and parsimonious, defusing the spectre of conflict while reinforcing regional stability.

Political Manoeuvring: Water as Leverage

In the dense fabric of geopolitics, water is increasingly weaponised as a diplomatic lever, intensifying and prolonging hostilities already under strain. Sovereign authorities, as well as influential non-state groups, calibrate the flow, quality, or availability of shared waterways to advance their strategic, economic, or territorial agendas. In so doing, they deepen the entanglements that define the regional order.

Political manoeuvres concerning shared water resources encompass a range of deliberate actions, including dam building, river diversion, and control of transboundary aquifers, each of which jeopardises the water security of affected riparian states. Such interventions can upset ecological balances, disrupt irrigated agriculture, and threaten the livelihoods of populations reliant on predictable water availability. The deliberate leverage of water in diplomatic bargaining compounds these risks, introducing a volatile variable into already delicate international relations. The regional geopolitics of water, as scholars and practitioners increasingly recognise, functions as both a trigger and a cordon for violence—its history and present-day exertions both portraying its dual capacity to inflame and to pacify. The entwined fabric of sovereign imperatives, national prestige, and shifting power hierarchies renders cooperative management of shared river basins exceptionally complicated, resulting in protracted negotiations punctuated by overt and whispered confrontations. Consequently, the hydropolitics of the region commands analytical lenses that equally weigh hydrological data, territorial maps, economic viability, and diplomatic histories. Remedial actions must build on transparent and inclusive dialogue, rigorous adherence to prevailing international legal frameworks, and the early entrenchment of fair and sustainable allocation regimes. Neglecting these imperatives raises the spectre of worsened rivalries and regional volatility, magnifying systemic vulnerabilities that no single riparian actor can surmount in isolation.

For policymakers, diplomats, and all stakeholders, acknowledging the political dimensions embedded in water management processes is essential. Moving beyond mere technical fixes, they should pursue collaborative strategies that transcend sectional gains, fostering mutual benefit and constructive cooperation even in the face of diverging national or regional interests.

Urgent Impact on Local Communities and Livelihoods

The intersection of water scarcity and geopolitical tensions is proving disastrous for local communities and their livelihoods across the conflict-affected regions of Syria and Lebanon. Eroding access to reliable potable and irrigation water is disrupting the agricultural calendar upon which rural families depend. With irrigation networks already aged and poorly maintained, the cumulative pressure of reduced rainfall and military interventions has driven yields down and pushed crop failure upward, intensifying both nutritional deficits and the collapse of farm-based incomes. Smallholder and tenant farmers, already encumbered by conflict-related debt, find their capacity for seasonal credit and crop rotations dwindling, deepening rural poverty.

At the same time, shortages of treated water for drinking and sanitation are aggravating public health crises. Hospitals in both countries, already in distress mode, report surges in cholera and leptospirosis, driven by overburdened water management and refugee resettlements. Women and girls, who constitute the majority of caregivers, are frequently absent from schools or income-earning opportunities as they traverse longer distances for water. This domestic burden, combined with food shortages, is reinforcing restrictive gender norms in both agricultural cooperatives and the more precarious informal economy.

Competition over the few remaining diesel pumps and surface streams is further undermining cross-community trust. Municipalities that once negotiated seasonal water sharing are now fortifying legal and military barriers to pipelines, and local councils in northern Lebanon report increased threats of violence over access to shared wells. These fractures are deepening sectarian stratification and marginalising younger leaders who have sought innovative, cross-border resource agreements. In such a polarised atmosphere, the prospect of collective resilience appears increasingly tethered to the onset of broader political agreements, rather

than to the adaptive capacities of local farmers and municipalities.

Potential of Technological Innovations in Water Conservation

The cascading effects of water scarcity ripple through
human societies and penetrate ecological systems, thereby
destabilising biodiversity and jeopardising the integrity of
natural balances. When water stress intersects with geopolitical conflict, entire populations may be uprooted, pursuing the elemental need for hydration and sanitation. Such
mass mobility further burdens the already overstretched
infrastructural and social services of host cities, amplifying
the complexities of governing rising, heterogeneous populations. Addressing these interconnected problems, therefore,
necessitates comprehensive policies that transcend emergency water distribution and embed the broader ramifications for community structures and economic stability. Any
enduring remedy must embed participatory governance,
prioritise previously marginalised groups, and institutionalise equitable allocation practices, thereby cushioning the
adverse effects of dwindling water supplies and geopolitical
strife and fortifying the livelihoods and adaptive capacity of
vulnerable populations.

The enduring depletion of water assets in the Middle East
has catalysed a trajectory of technological ingenuity focused
on conservation and the optimisation of the water–ener-

gy–food nexus. Smart metering, membrane-based desalination, and information systems for irrigation scheduling have already begun to reshape water governance, paralleling the accelerating pressures of demographic expansion, rapid urban growth, and climate variability.

Within the current climate of growing water scarcity, a variety of advanced strategies have begun to reshape the management of this vital resource. Among the most effective is the implementation of drip irrigation, which channels water precisely to the plant root zone, thereby reducing evaporation and runoff. This approach not only cuts overall water demand but also improves the nutritional quality and overall yield of crops, aligning economic viability with environmental stewardship. Complementing this, smart irrigation networks integrate soil moisture sensors and automated valves to fine-tune watering schedules according to microclimatic data, enhancing water-use efficiency in agricultural fields, landscaped spaces, and municipal systems alike. On a broader scale, desalination has emerged as a critical mechanism for augmenting freshwater supplies in low-lying coastal areas. Through membrane-based reverse osmosis paired with energy-recovery technologies, these systems convert ocean or brackish water into water of drinking quality. Despite the high capital costs and energy requirements these plants entail, advances in membrane design and renewable energy coupling are steadily lowering their carbon and economic footprints, strengthening their role as a resilient, supplementary source of water for communities facing diminishing conventional supplies.

In wastewater treatment, techniques like membrane

bioreactors and advanced oxidation processes are being adopted to reclaim and purify effluent for non-potable reuse, thereby alleviating the pressure on dwindling freshwater supplies. Such decentralised treatment technologies enable the sustainable recycling of water resources, ultimately supporting broader conservation and sustainability goals. Complementing these efforts, the deployment of intelligent water grid systems, which leverage digital sensors and analytic platforms, optimises distribution networks while minimising leaks, thereby elevating the resilience and efficiency of urban water systems. Continued technological advancement, however, requires the cohesive efforts of academia, the private sector, and public authorities. Within this context, fostering innovation ecosystems and facilitating multi-stakeholder partnerships are critical for expediting the deployment of cutting-edge conservation technologies. By strategically aligning these resources, the Middle East can effectively confront water scarcity and create an adaptive, long-term framework for water governance amid evolving socioeconomic and climatic pressures.

Crucial Role of International Organisations and Treaties in Water Resource Management

Effective governance of shared aquifers, rivers, and lakes depends on sustained dialogue and legally binding arrangements among all riparian nations.

In this regard, intergovernmental institutions and normative treaties are indispensable to the formulation and consolidation of sustainable water governance. Central to these efforts is the United Nations, which, through the Economic Commission for Europe and the Economic and Social Council, promotes the cooperative exchange of best practices and the articulation of guidelines for the equitable and efficient management of shared water resources. Complementary to the UN's global orientation, regional organisations—most notably the European Union and the Arab League—supply critical platforms for the discussion, negotiation, and consolidation of transboundary water policies. Legal instruments further underpin these governance efforts. The 1997 United Nations Convention on the Law of the Non-Navigational Uses of International Watercourses articulates binding norms for the equitable utilisation and protection of international water systems. Parallel to these global commitments, detailed bilateral accords—exemplified by the 1994 Water Management Agreement between Jordan and Israel—illustrate how targeted diplomatic engagement can yield durable, mutually advantageous solutions. Collectively, these normative and institutional arrangements supply the procedural and substantive tools necessary for equitable water allocation, pollution control, and the peaceful settlement of disputes.

Guidelines for fair resource-sharing, ventures into environmental stewardship, and detailed protocols for settling disputes permit neighbouring nations to deepen their collaboration and enhance regional stability. Complementing these efforts, key international financial actors, notably the World Bank and the European Bank for Reconstruction and Development, play a decisive role by backing investments in water supply and management systems. Through a combination of capital injections, technical guidance, and policy advice, these institutions strengthen both individual nations and cross-border frameworks in their quest for water conservation and rational use. When international conventions and organisations promote uniform benchmarks and joint oversight, they not only ensure equitable access and safeguarding of the resource, but they also cultivate the openness and responsibility needed to resolve conflicts without recourse to force. In this framework, shared watercourses cease to be sources of friction and instead become instruments of durable development and heightened security for the populations that depend on them.

Future Scenarios: Adapting to Changing Climates

As long-term climate trajectories point toward greater variability and tighter water availability, proactive scenario development assumes urgent priority. Evidence already points to altered precipitation distributions, dwindling snow reserves, and heightened evaporative losses. To counter these trends, policy planners must therefore construct and test adaptive pathways that protect both supply stability and ecological integrity. Options may include advanced forecasting, strengthened aquifer recharge, and the phased introduction of demand-side efficiency measures. Sound decisions in the coming years will determine whether social and economic systems can thrive, despite the constraints imposed by a warming planet.

Projecting future water security necessitates careful examination of demographic dynamics, ongoing urban expansion, and innovations in hydrological stewardship. One credible outcome involves enhanced financial backing for desalination infrastructure, translating into increased freshwater availability in chronically water-deficient areas. Concurrently, refined techniques in recycling and reclaimed water distribution can significantly reduce demands on conventional aquifers and rivers. Simultaneously, nature-based interventions—such as the rehabilitation of coastal wetlands and strategic upland watershed protection—further expand the suite of risk-mitigating options. The coupling of climate-adaptive agronomic techniques with precision irrigation innovations can simultaneously minimise withdrawal rates and sustain agricultural yields. Nevertheless, translating these long-term possibilities into practice will depend on cohesive engagement among legislators, private-sector actors, civil society, and affected populations. Such collaboration must prioritise transboundary dialogue, enact anticipatory regulatory frameworks, and embed sustainability into every decision. Effective anticipation also requires a paradigm shift towards integrated management, one that openly recognises and addresses the interdependence of societal, ecological, and economic systems. Complementary outreach through formal education and community campaigns can instil a pervasive ethic of conservation, encouraging incremental yet cumulative reductions in per-capita water use. By embedding anticipatory policy with proactive, evidence-based strategies, societies can reduce vulnerability and enhance their adaptive capacity in a future of variable and uncertain climate particulars.

Envisioning plausible futures is more than a sterile intellectual endeavour; it is an urgent invitation to design and
cultivate adaptive water systems capable of enduring the
uncertainties awaiting the coming generations.

Pathways to Sustainable Water Security

Achieving enduring water security is a complex, layered
project demanding integrated measures and collaborative
resolve across all tiers of governance. To make this aspiration
a reality, several decisive routes require sustained attention
and ambition. First, systematic investment in the complete
water cycle—storage, treatment, and conveyance—remains
non-negotiable for moderating the adverse effects of scarcity. The design and construction of reservoirs, distribution
networks, and advanced treatment plants must be matched
by enduring maintenance regimes to guarantee a reliable
supply of potable water for households, crops, and industries. Simultaneously, the modernisation of irrigation systems and the promotion of moisture-conserving agronomic
practices can substantially lower water withdrawals, thereby relieving overstressed aquifers and surface sources. In
parallel, the deployment of emerging technologies—ranging from solar-powered desalination to membrane-driven
wastewater reuse—offers robust supplements to depleted
freshwater reserves, especially in semi-arid and coastal regions. These integrated investments do more than close current deficits; they fortify the water sector against the com-

pounded stresses posed by climate extremes and shifting population patterns.

Furthermore, advancing cooperative transboundary governance is essential for resolving disputes over water resources shared by multiple states. Effective joint basin authorities, early-warning and arbitration mechanisms, and transparent data-sharing arrangements promote shared understanding and reinforce the equitable, sustainable allocation of river and aquifer systems. Multilateral institutions and diplomatic networks can catalyse these partnerships, yet successful implementation also relies on local empowerment—capacity-building, participatory planning, and inclusive legislative design must enable communities to steward their water commons. Water security must, in parallel, be woven into broader policy landscapes that link ecosystem integrity, economic opportunity, and social cohesion. Countries should harmonise national water policies with global sustainability commitments, strengthen legal enforcement, and reward conservation-oriented practices. Lasting water security will therefore require a systemic shift towards integrated, forward-looking governance that balances justice, ecological integrity, and consolidated partnerships. By embracing these strategies, all stakeholders can forge the foundation for a future in which clean, dependable water is guaranteed for both current and future populations.

10
Economic Interdependencies
Ripples Across the Eastern Mediterranean

Eastern Mediterranean Economies

The economies of Syria and Lebanon, positioned within the dynamic and historically layered Eastern Mediterranean, are woven into a longstanding fabric of shared histories, cultures, and commercial ties. Each economy possesses its own governing logic, yet both are continuously reshaped by the legacies of Ottoman rule, colonial legacies, and post-independence state-building. Syria, endowed with energy resources and the remnants of the ancient caravan routes, has long been a nexus of trade, agriculture, and light industry. The tertiary sector that flourished around the major cities complemented these, creating a complex economic web. However, the recent civil war has deeply disrupted this economic web, fragmenting supply chains and undermining the fabric of formal and informal enterprises. Lebanon, by contrast, has leveraged its geographic location and lax regulatory environment to become a regional centre for finance, tourism, and, more recently, a burgeoning knowledge economy. Its banking sector has historically mediated not only domestic but also regional liquidity flows. However, Lebanon faces recurring cycles of political paralysis, currency depreciation, and external sanctions, diluting the robustness of its growth model. The economic landscapes of both nations are thus not only products of their own domestic reforms and crises but also of the porous boundaries between them. Cross-border trade corridors, remittance flows through Lebanon to Syrian households, and the movement of Syrian seasonal labour into Lebanese agriculture and construction underline a dependence that economic policy alone cannot decouple.

Cross-border trade, investment, and labour mobility have long created mutually reinforcing dynamics, intertwining the economies of Syria and Lebanon. Despite the vulnerabilities introduced by conflict and regional turbulence, concerted attempts to preserve economic collaboration have continued, motivated by overlapping interests and long-standing social ties. Diaspora networks, dispersed internationally, augment these efforts by transmitting trade, remittances, and capital. Each state confronts its own economic trials and prospects, yet their mutual reliance emphasises the need to situate their trajectories within the larger mosaic of Eastern Mediterranean economies. A rigorous examination of Syria's and Lebanon's disparate yet overlapping economic configurations illuminates the dense fabric of trade, investment, and resource allocation that resonates throughout the region. Appreciating the divergent conditions and complementary opportunities of the two polities is essential for deciphering the complexities and latent complementarities that characterise their economic interdependence.

Trade Routes and Economic Corridors: Historical Continuities and Changes

The Eastern Mediterranean possesses an enduring cartography of trade routes and economic corridors that has sculpted its commercial topography for millennia.

Across the Eastern Mediterranean, the intersection of cultures, civilisations, and empires has historically guided the circulation of commodities, capital, and intellectual currents. The timeless Silk Road and the maritime lanes forged by Phoenician and Venetian merchants together established the region's enduring stature as a centre of exchange. Although these arteries of trade have evolved over centuries, their structural persistence lends continuity to the present economic corridors. Contemporary Eastern Mediterranean trade manifests as both bilateral and multilateral alignment. Agreements among proximate states—such as Cyprus, Greece, Turkey, and Lebanon—have streamlined the movement of goods and services, cultivating shared economic welfare and mutual dependency. Concurrently, multi-lateral linkages nurtured by international organisations and regional blocs magnify the spread and effectiveness of the networks. These cooperative arrangements not only generate economic advancement but also consolidate diplomatic and geopolitical relations. A thorough exploration of present trade routes and economic corridors must therefore incorporate a careful examination of the historical transformations that forged the region's interconnected economic fabric.

Changes in global trading patterns, breakthroughs in transportation and digital technologies, and shifting geopolitical alliances have collectively redrawn the map of trade routes and economic corridors in the Eastern Mediterranean. Conflicts and competing power interests have, however, rerouted goods and capital, requiring states and enterprises to develop adaptive and resilient strategies in the face of persistent unpredictability. A thorough investigation of the historical continuities and mutations in these corridors is therefore essential for a full understanding of the current economic forces at play and for credible projections of future trajectories. Against this methodological backdrop, the following analysis will trace the interwoven trade relations and economic dependencies whose cumulative effects have rippled throughout the Eastern Mediterranean, defining the contours of its contemporary economic order.

Bilateral and Multilateral Trade Relations

The region's bilateral and multilateral trade frameworks have undergone a marked transformation, rooted in historical, cultural, and geopolitical realities. Interwoven trade networks have, in turn, cemented economic dependency among states, nurtured cooperative alliances, and, at times, ignited points of friction. Lebanon and Syria serve as a salient case: their trade relations, underpinned by customs and informal cross-border exchanges, have proven remarkably resilient even as political crises and armed confrontations have intermittently erupted.

Bilateral accords and trade agreements among the Eastern Mediterranean states have generally lowered barriers to the movement of goods, services, and capital, yet such gains have been periodically undermined by episodes of regional turbulence. These episodes can disrupt trade agreements, leading to increased barriers and reduced economic cooperation. Multilateral arrangements that bring Turkey, Israel, Cyprus, and Greece to the table have illustrated, by contrast, the extent to which national economies on the periphery are interwoven, revealing room for joint ventures that transcend single-issue, single-border scenarios. The Eastern Mediterranean's geographical positioning among Europe, Asia, and Africa intensifies each country's commercial imperative, prompting extra-regional powers to seek terminal and maritime rights that augment their market access. Concurrently, the reconfiguration of transit corridors and the injection of new transport networks are reshaping the routing of goods, fostering sectors that were peripheral to earlier models of exchange. While geopolitical contestation and domestic pressures persist, the persistence of both bilateral and multilateral channels is indispensable for mapping the region's collective economic future. The path ahead will thus demand rigour in the crafting of equitable arrangements and in the identification of common stakeholders whose vested interests can anchor a stability that, in turn, underwrites sustainable communal prosperity.

Impact of Regional Conflicts on Trade and Investment

Regional conflicts have nonetheless been a decisive, if perverse, variable in the trade and investment calculus of the Eastern Mediterranean. Each episode of violence or diplomatic rupture reroutes capital, redirects shipping lanes, and recalibrates the reputational risk that investors assign to the entire theatre. Products that once crossed borders ordinarily are entangled in new countermeasure tariffs, and supply chains that rested on predictable crossings are forced to seek alternative crossings, increasing administrative and transport costs. Sites once earmarked for foreign plants or joint-energy concessions may remain dormant for the duration of uncertainty, compressing both short-term revenues and long-term growth trajectories. The incremental yet cumulative gravity of these disruptions is thus on the ledger, arresting regional agglomeration and highlighting the inter-dependence whereby the fallout of one political crisis rever-berates, with diminishing elasticities, through the economic fabric of all. In the wake of each flare-up, the recovery of trade and investment flows is therefore contingent not on national recovery plans alone, but on the re-establishment of the regional legal and operational architecture that gov-erns the movement of goods, capital, and the certainty of jurisdiction.

A web of ongoing hostilities, notably the Syrian Civil War alongside broader geopolitical rivalries, has intensified risk and uncertainty for companies operating across the Eastern Mediterranean. The conflicts have propagated spillover con-sequences that now compromise entire corridors of trade and tarnish the outlook for future investments. One promi-nent effect has been the fragmentation of supply chains and the unravelling of formerly coherent trade networks. Con-tinued violence and security volatility have obstructed the timely movement of goods and services, generating logistical delays and pushing operating costs higher for firms engaged in cross-border commerce. The same environment of insta-bility has made foreign direct investment less attractive, as prospective backers baulk at the volatile and unpredictable macroeconomic frameworks typical of the most affected ar-eas. The result has been subdued growth rates and an ongo-ing shortfall in the capacity of the region to realise breadbas-ket economic promise. In addition, the layered uncertainties produced by the conflicts have deepened risk aversion with-in banks and multinational firms alike. Expanded geopolitical friction and the persistent risk of escalation have sapped raw investor confidence, with decision-makers increasingly adopting caution by postponing long-term commitments until clearer, stabilising signals emerge.

Consequently, the Eastern Mediterranean has encountered persistent difficulty in securing the capital inflows required for both infrastructural enhancement and meaningful economic diversification. Regional conflicts, intently entangled with energy assets, compound the difficulties confronting trade and investment. Territories abundant in hydrocarbons turn into magnets for geopolitical contestation, magnifying the intricacies of exploration, extraction, and transportation. When disputes arise, the immediate disruption of energy flows occurs alongside a deeper, lingering distrust that prevents the formulation of cooperative frameworks capable of delivering mutual gain across the entire region. Yet, in the midst of these headwinds, several Eastern Mediterranean economies have displayed resilience and adaptive ingenuity. A number of countries have attempted to exploit their geographic location and latent natural advantages to create alternative trade routes and to engage with newly emerging markets. In tandem, a broadening recognition has taken root that economic diversification and a diminished dependence on historically dominant trade partners are necessary to strengthen defences against the instability generated by surrounding conflicts. Navigating the enduring turbulence requires, above all, the cultivation of regional dialogue, effective collaboration, and enduring conflict-resolution mechanisms. The establishment of lasting peace and political stability, therefore, emerges not merely as a humanitarian necessity but as the precondition for realising the full economic promise of the Eastern Mediterranean.

Nurturing shared prosperity and addressing foundational conflict drivers are prerequisites for the Eastern Mediterranean nations to achieve lasting prosperity and create a favourable trading and investment climate.

Energy Resources: Strategic Partnerships and Geopolitical Rivalries

The Eastern Mediterranean is poised to become a prominent energy corridor, underpinned by sizeable hydrocarbon reserves across its sub-basins. Their discovery and ensuing development have catalysed both cooperative ventures and geopolitical friction between littoral states and major Powers. Notably, the Levantine Basin's offshore gas accumulations have triggered rival claims and strategic manoeuvres. Israel, Cyprus and Lebanon have initiated drilling and licensing programmes, while triangulated interest from Turkey and Egypt complicates the regulatory and security environment. As a result, a multifaceted geopolitical terrain is emerging, characterised by both contest and limited collaboration. States are recalibrating foreign policies, incentivising bilateral and multilateral accords that govern exploration, pipeline infrastructure and export routes. Such frameworks aim to convert hydrocarbons into instruments of economic advancement and diplomatic leverage, simultaneously knitting the Neo-Levantine littoral into a lattice of mutual, albeit precarious, dependence.

At the same time, geopolitical rivalries have sharpened as the principal regional and global actors seek both primacy and the safeguarding of national interests. These rivalries have crystallised in tensions over maritime boundaries, exclusive economic zones, and rights to hydrocarbon exploration, thus entangling regional politics in a dense matrix of overlapping assertions. The interventions of outside powers have further thickened the underbrush of the Eastern Mediterranean energy theatre. Russia, the United States, and the European Union have each sought to manipulate pre-existing alliances and emerging disputes in pursuit of their respective strategic objectives, mindful of the stakes surrounding European energy security and supply diversification. The intersection of these interests has drawn a widening circle of international actors into the Eastern Mediterranean, aligning energy imperatives with broader geopolitical calculations. Likewise, the basin's hydrocarbon potential has refracted into the domestic politics of the littoral states. The prospect of revenue has catalysed fierce debate over ownership, fiscal sharing, and regulatory governance, thereby reshaping institutions and the social contract within each polity. As exploration, development, and export schemes mature, it is clear that the politics of partnership and of rivalry will remain inseparable from the Sub-Mediterranean strategic architecture, deterring stability, refracting into global diplomacy, and influencing energy pricing and supply structure far beyond the Levant basin.

Infrastructure Projects: Cooperation and Competition

The infrastructure development in the Eastern Mediterranean is not just a local affair, but a global stage where both cooperative and competitive dynamics are actively played out. The investments in transport corridors, energy grids, and digital pathways are more than technical achievements; they are strategic tools that shape pathways for economic expansion, political leverage, and geopolitical calibration. These strategic undertakings, ranging from deep-water ports and international airports to highways, rail links, gas conduits, and high-capacity fibre-optic arteries, are collectively designed to tighten regional and intercontinental links. The endorsement of the Belt and Road Initiative by Beijing has added a global dimension, substituting the regional chessboard for a wider arena of influence. The Mediterranean itself, as a pivotal maritime nexus uniting Europe, Asia, and Africa, has drawn capital to upgrade and enlarge port facilities, simultaneously catalysing collaborative constructs, such as pooled terminal facilities, and zero-sum contests for gateway ascendancy. Energy narratives are equally pronounced; megaproject pipelines are on the drawing boards to ferry the Eastern Mediterranean's hydrocarbon bounty to European processor markets and world consumers, the undertakings reifying the duality of interstate partnership and bandwidth for rivalry. The most recent layer of the grid—submarine cable links and data landing stations—underscores that economic security now converges with digital sovereignty as states compete for data latency, bandwidth, and protected enclaves within the unstructured global information landscape.

Efforts to construct high-speed internet networks and digital hubs are designed not only to stimulate innovation and entrepreneurship but also to function as theatres of geopolitical influence and competition. Yet these projects confront a tripartite set of challenges—financing mechanisms, regulatory convergence, and the imperatives of environmental and social sustainability. In spite of these obstacles, new partnership models are emerging that cut across formerly rigid geopolitical lines, offering a glimmer of hope for the future. Furthermore, infrastructure diplomacy provides neutral arenas for dialogue that can attenuate conflicts and identify shared strategic priorities. In this light, the future of Eastern Mediterranean infrastructure initiatives depends on a sophisticated appreciation of how cooperation and competition coalesce, thereby reaffirming the region as a critical fulcrum in the reconfiguration of both global economic and strategic equilibria.

The Role of the European Union and Its Economic Policies

For several decades, the European Union has functioned as a cornerstone architect of economic order in the Eastern Mediterranean, providing a sense of stability and direction. Its influence is exerted through complementary programmes that govern trade relations, mobilise investment capital, and catalyse broad-based socioeconomic advancement, both within the Union's external neighbourhood and in partner states further afield. The Union's methodology is anchored in a tripartite set of instruments: binding regulatory acquis, grant and loan facilities mobilised through its neighbourhood and development programmes, and diversified strategic partnerships that align sectoral priorities across a wider circle of neighbours.

At the core of the EU's engagement with the Eastern Mediterranean lies the European Neighbourhood Policy (ENP), designed to nurture prosperity, stability, and accountable governance in the EU's immediate periphery. The policy grants participating countries conditional access to the EU's single market, accompanied by financial backing and technical expertise, thereby operating as a catalyst for economic integration and sustainable advancement. Complementing these economic incentives, the EU promotes infrastructure and connectivity initiatives designed to upgrade transport, energy, and digital corridors across the region. Access to the European Neighbourhood Instrument (ENI) and the Connecting Europe Facility (CEF) enables EU funding for strategic projects that streamline trade routes and deepen economic collaboration. Beyond bricks and mortar, the Union's trade policy—and a network of bilateral association agreements reinforced by the Generalised Scheme of Preferences (GSP)—shapes growing economic interdependence, permitting developing countries in the region preferential access to the EU market.

The European Union's economic policy architecture is designed to address critical areas, including competition policy, consumer safeguards, and the streamlined regulatory environment. These elements work together to ensure an equitable commercial environment and reinforce macroeconomic stability. The Union also champions sustainable growth and rigorous environmental safeguards, highlighting the importance of embedding these priorities in economic engagement with Eastern Mediterranean partners. The EU's continued influence in the Eastern Mediterranean will depend on its ability to manage complex geopolitical variables, bolster economic strength, and foster growth that is both broad-based and inclusive. Against a backdrop of simultaneous opportunity and risk, EU economic policy can act as a dynamic force, generating reciprocal gains and fortifying a more integrated and flourishing Eastern Mediterranean.

Economic Challenges: Inflation, Debt, and Growth Disparities

Geopolitical turbulence and intra-regional conflicts have compounded macroeconomic vulnerabilities, thrusting the Eastern Mediterranean into a precarious cycle of inflation, elevated public debt, and stark growth asymmetries. Inflation remains elevated across the region, steadily eroding consumer purchasing power and corroding the trust necessary for sustained private investment. The inflationary pulse is most acutely felt in staple commodities—food, energy, and transport—where price hikes disproportionately burden the lowest income households, thereby widening the existing socio-economic fault lines. National debt burdens continue to undermine the fiscal viability of the region's states, forcing governments to truncate expenditures on critical public services while squeezing investment in infrastructure and human capital. Each rise in public liabilities accentuates doubts about fiscal sustainability and sovereign creditworthiness, possibly narrowing access to external financing and disrupting longer-range economic trajectories. Divergent growth patterns, in turn, translate into uneven wealth distribution and pronounced socioeconomic fractures. A multi-faceted response is thus imperative: sound fiscal frameworks, strategic outlays on education, skills, and innovation, and deepened institutionalised regional dialogue. Containing inflationary impulses requires both vigilant monetary policy and calibrated price-control interventions to protect real incomes. Management of public debt, in turn, hinges on transparent and accountable governance, prudent borrowing, and broad-based revenue reforms anchored in economic diversification. Finally, fostering enduring, inclusive growth calls for synchronised, cross-sector strategies that dismantle lasting structural impediments and distribute opportunities equitably across the population.

By confronting these economic challenges directly, countries in the Eastern Mediterranean can build the institutional resilience needed to strengthen their economic underpinnings and lay the groundwork for sustainable prosperity, even in a context shaped by ongoing geopolitical tensions.

Socioeconomic Effects on Population Dynamics

The Eastern Mediterranean is marked by a complex relationship between economic variables, social structures, and changing demographic patterns, a relationship that carries decisive implications for regional stability and sustainable development. Historically, opportunities for employment, social stratification, and periodic political upheaval have jointly shaped migration flows, fertility behaviour, and patterns of urban growth. Over the past forty years, the Syrian conflict has been the most disruptive factor, generating both internal displacement and the largest refugee flows the region has ever experienced, notably into Lebanon and surrounding countries. This sudden increase in population has placed acute pressure on local infrastructure, stretching health, education, and housing systems that were already fragile, and intensifying political and social inequalities. Host communities have confronted a prolonged surge in labour supply that, coupled with slack demand, has led to heightened informality, downward pressure on wages, and deteriorating working conditions. At the same time, limited and often overstretched public services have resulted in stark disparities in educational attainment and healthcare access for both displaced and resident populations, threatening the long-term social cohesion that is essential for recovery and growth.

The demographic shifts precipitated by the refugee crisis have interlaced with pre-existing socio-economic fault lines, thereby amplifying communal and sectarian frictions. A rigorous analysis must appreciate the reflexive dynamics among economic conditions, changing population structures, and the integrity of social capital, since these remain the decisive determinants of the region's trajectory. Policy responses designed to counteract the resultant demographic strains must therefore be anchored in integrated socio-economic frameworks that advance inclusive and resilient growth, judiciously allocate scarce resources, and consciously cultivate social cohesion. By mapping the socio-economic repercussions on population behaviour and settlement patterns, the Eastern Mediterranean can endeavour to converge on resilient communities, sustain viable livelihoods, and nurture a demographic order that, taken together, underwrites long-term prosperity.

Future Prospects: Toward Collaborative Economic Growth

Prospects moving forward suggest a pathway of collaborative economic integration. As the Eastern Mediterranean contends with geopolitical volatility and persistent economic stress, concerted growth becomes not only desirable but essential. Acknowledging the region's interdependence, national strategies must converge on cooperative modalities that sustain and amplify developmental gains. Several interrelated dimensions offer viable pathways to elevated economic co-operation. Primarily, the judicious exploitation of shared natural resources and complementary human capital can catalyse joint enterprises and cross-frontier projects, thereby distributing both risks and rewards in ways that reinforce inter-state collaborative legitimacy.

The advancement of regional transport and energy infrastructure can catalyse heightened economic dynamism and expanded trade flows across the Eastern Mediterranean. The collective investment in research, innovation, and technological advancement—particularly in renewable energy, agritech, and digital services—further amplifies competitiveness and accelerates the diversification of national economies. In tandem, the alignment of regulatory regimes and trade provisions among the participating states can create a more hospitable climate for cross-border investment and commerce. Simplifying customs protocols, curtailing non-tariff impediments, and harmonising standards and accreditation mechanisms will deepen economic interdependence and enhance the appeal of the region to global investors. The institutionalisation of regular platforms for ministerial and technical dialogue on economic matters will institutionalise trust and cooperation, reinforcing economies against external shocks. In a complementary vein, cooperative instruments to confront shared socioeconomic challenges can yield collective gains. Joint action on youth unemployment, poverty mitigation, and income inequality—through coordinated policy initiatives and programme exchange—will enhance social cohesion and human capital. By prioritising education, vocational improvement, and responsive skills training across national frontiers, the regional labour force can be equipped to meet the dynamism and evolving needs of the integrated economy.

Developing strategic partnerships with external stake-holders—including multilateral institutions and proximate regions—can significantly enhance the effectiveness of co-operative economic maturation initiatives. Engagement with the European Union, the United Nations, and established regional configurations yields critical technical capacities, financial resources, and policy-coherent support. Collaboration with neighbouring areas, particularly the Gulf Cooperation Council and North African economies, can facilitate the emergence of novel trade arteries and capital flows, broadening the economic landscape. A deliberate commitment to a vision of shared prosperity and mutual advancement can generate the durable foundations for continued economic advancement across the Eastern Mediterranean. By elevating collaboration and mutual dependence above unilateral initiatives, regional states can move beyond historically rooted tensions and capitalise on their complementary economic capacities to construct resilient and adaptive markets. While obstacles remain, the trajectory toward a future anchored in cooperative economic expansion constitutes a persuasive and attainable route to collective prosperity.

11
Sectarian Fault Lines
Sunni-Shia Divisions and Their Broader Impact

Historical Roots of Sectarianism in the Middle East

The historical evolution of sectarian divisions within the Middle East is characterised by a converging series of religious, political, and socio-economic processes that have continuously reformulated the region's identity across the centuries. The roots of sectarianism extend to the early Islamic community, when the question of succession after the Prophet Muhammad's death crystallised the Sunni and Shia divide. This formative rupture established a backdrop of rival identities and grievances that continues to shape the area's contemporary geopolitical landscape. The subsequent expansion and adaptation of the Islamic empires further codified the Sunni-Shia divide, intertwining it with ethnolinguistic, tribal, and territorial rivalries. Under the

Abbasid and Umayyad caliphates, phases of Sunni and Shia collaboration alternated with violent rupture, embedding a stratified sectarian memory that has outlasted those polities. The Safavid Empire's promotion of Twelver Shia doctrine as a state ideology aggravated these fractures, inciting military and ideological challenges from Sunni neighbours and producing a sedimented legacy of mistrust that endures in current sectarian rhetoric and behaviour.

Histories of conquest and colonial intervention have repeatedly deepened sectarian cleavages, as rulers across eras have wielded religious difference as a tool of legitimation and control. Under the Ottoman millet system, the state acknowledged religious communities as distinct units of law, a move that formalised sectarian identities and converted difference into a bounded social fact. Communal boundaries hardened, and the politics of difference nurtured mutual perceptions of alterity. Later, the European partition of the Middle East mandated by the Versailles settlement redrew maps without cultural regard, shuttered communities together, and left arbitrary borders that fractured local allegiances. The subsequent installation of nation-states privileged some identities while marginalising others, thereby igniting sectarian violence that continues to inflect the region's politics. Such legacies reveal that the Sunni-Shi'i divide cannot be disentangled from a longer history where religious, political, and imperial motives have continually reframed and reactivated communal difference. A comprehensive comprehension of these processes is therefore requisite for any serious analysis of today's sectarian conflicts and their jeopardising of the region's wider stability.

The Role of Religion in Political Identity

Within the broader formation of political life in the Middle East, religion has consistently animated the cartographies of communal belonging, with the Sunni-Shi'i distinction emerging as a pivotal axis of definition.

In the Middle East, the long-documented interaction of religion and politics has forged the region's developmental trajectory, affecting hierarchies of authority, administrative functions, and patterns of social cohesion. Sunni and Shia Islam, each within its own civilisational boundaries, have habitually moulded the collective consciousness of their followers, supplying the instruments of social structuring, ethical orientation, and political fidelity. Embedded within this overarching condition is the historical consolidation of divergent doctrinal currents and ideological trajectories, which have fostered the crystallisation of distinct communal identities and political loyalties. Such divergence has extended beyond liturgical observance to penetrate the state, shaping legislation, institutional configurations, and foreign policy orientations. Numerous Middle Eastern polities have, accordingly, institutionalised a fusion of statecraft and ecclesiastical hierarchy, deriving administrative efficacy and fragile boasts of legitimacy from sponsorship of a designated sect. The resultant consolidation of sectarianised authority has, in turn, rigidified communal boundaries and relegated certain minorities to a quasi-permanent condition of socio-political subordination, thereby magnifying perceptions of exclusion and systemic bias. Moreover, the authority of religious jurists and clerical elites as political entrepreneurs has proved considerable. Their aptitude for eliciting collective consent, orchestrating communal mobilisation, and refracting public sentiment has decisively shaped the region's political calculus. Be it through sustained oratory, authoritative legal opinions, or the expanded circuitry of information technology, ecclesiastical leaders have habitually commanded instruments of persuasion that decisively orient public discourse and institutional decision-making.

Political and religious identities in the Middle East have increasingly been manipulated by disparate actors seeking immediate advantage, resulting in the deliberate exploitation of sectarian loyalty to achieve narrow objectives. This exploitation has fermented distrust, intensified societal fractures, and prolonged violence, thereby stalling genuine attempts to construct inclusive, pluralistic polities. The reflexive bond between sectarian identification and political allegiance has further complicated the capacity of contemporary states to govern heterogeneous societies animated by clashing religious discourses. States have struggled to reconcile constitutional commitments to religious pluralism with the exigencies of sovereignty and administrative cohesion, frequently leading to divisive legislation and public turbulence. Thus, religion remains woven into the structural DNA of Middle Eastern politics, shaping institutional choices, affecting intercommunal relations, and informing the geopolitical manoeuvres of both regional and external powers.

Key Events: Unravelling Sectarian Dynamics

The chronicles of the Middle East comprise decisive junctures that have ceaselessly reconstituted and, at times, destabilised the sectarian relation between Sunni and Shia communities. From the formative confrontations of the seventh century to the emergence of modern sovereign states, each episode has sedimented distinct social hierarchies, juridical precedents, and political alignments, thereby producing a layered and often contradictory inheritance that continues to influence contemporary governance and intergroup interaction.

The split within Islam that followed Prophet Muhammad's death, primarily over the rightful succession of leadership, created the enduring divide between Sunni and Shia Islam and positioned these communities for centuries of reciprocal antagonism. Subsequent caliphates saw power contests between Sunni and Shia elites become the primary theatre of political legitimacy, reinforcing communal boundaries. The martyrdom of Husayn ibn Ali at Karbala in 680 CE crystallised this animus, transforming a leadership dispute into a symbolically charged motif for Shia identity and perpetual mourning. In the contemporary era, the 1979 Iranian Revolution represented a decisive inflexion point. The establishment of a Shia theocracy under Ayatollah Khomeini galvanised Shia political mobilisation while alarming Sunni rulers, especially in the Saudi-dominated Gulf. Shortly before the Revolution, the Soviet invasion of Afghanistan mobilised a pan-Sunni jihadist bracket that drew volunteers from Egypt to Pakistan and gave rise to a paramilitary fraternity and doctrine that would reverberate throughout later intra-Islamic and transnational conflicts.

The 2003 U.S.-led invasion of Iraq further aggravated sectarian fissures by toppling Saddam Hussein's Sunni-centric regime. The ensuing power vacuum triggered confrontations among contending Sunni and Shia blocs, unleashing a wave of retaliatory violence. When ISIS emerged shortly thereafter, it systematically manipulated these sectarian animosities, unleashing brutal campaigns of genocide against Shia civilians and signalling a new, perilous phase of intra-Muslim conflict. Together, these developments have deepened and accelerated sectarian fragmentation, resurrecting ancient grudges while introducing novel violence patterns. A thorough comprehension of these pivotal historical moments is thus essential for accounting for the continuing volatility of sectarian fault lines across the contemporary Middle East.

Sunni-Shia Alliances and Rivalries

The Sunni-Shia division now operates as a grand, enduring framework on which regional politics are superimposed. The foundational sectarian schism, crystallised almost fourteen centuries ago, has since steered states and sub-state actors toward durable, albeit contingent, configurations of solidarity and enmity. Sunni powers, notably Saudi Arabia, the United Arab Emirates, and Turkey, have cultivated overlapping networks and institutions—primarily the Gulf Cooperation Council and NATO—to resist, contain, and undercut the imperial ambitions of Shia-majority Iran and its directed militias, which rally diverse Shia populations from Iraq to Lebanon under a shared, exclusionary political theology. The articulation of these rival blocs thus mediates not only the calculus of local conflicts but also the diplomacy of external interveners.

Conversely, Tehran has cultivated strategic partnerships with Shia populations and governments throughout Iraq, Lebanon, and Syria, thereby extending its regional footprint and enhancing its geopolitical leverage. These relationships are animated by overlapping religious and political motivations, each party promoting a distinct vision for the future of the Middle East while striving to enlarge its respective sphere of hegemony. The sharpening of Sunni-Shia antagonisms has been aggravated by proxy wars and foreign interventions, intensifying sectarian mobilisation and sustaining a cycle of instability that transcends national borders. The rivalry is manifest not merely among formal governments, but also through a lattice of non-state actors, including sectarian militias and entrenched militant organisations. The outcome is a dense and fluid matrix of allegiances and rivalries that thwarts concerted efforts to broker long-term peace and restore equitable governance. The persistent animosity between Sunni and Shia powers intensifies pre-existing societal fractures, magnifying the humanitarian and political calamities unleashed by the Syrian civil war and the protracted crises in Iraq. Furthermore, the contest for primacy between Sunni and Shia camps continues to resonate beyond the Levant, steering the internal discourse of

Muslim communities around the globe and shaping external perceptions of the region's enduring volatility.

The contest for ideological and political dominance has not only intensified the polarisation among Middle Eastern states but has also entangled the wider international system as major powers have been compelled to engage through arms transfers, diplomatic mediation, and, in some cases, military intervention. The resulting pattern of alliance and hostility disseminates beyond the Levant and Gulf, perturbing global supply chains, migration flows, and collective security arrangements, thus reinforcing rifts that the maps of the region alone cannot capture. A sober appraisal of the contemporary Arab-Persian confrontation cannot ignore the sectarian undercurrents, for these identities remain prisms through which governments, parties, and militant groups frame their strategies, justify military campaigns, and rally popular support. Only through a dispassionate analysis of these interwoven loyalties, animosities, and institutional inheritances can outside observers devise policies that acknowledge the political weight of the sectarian phenomenon while channelling its energies, wherever possible, into dialogue and incremental confidence-building, rather than reinforcing a zero-sum mentality.

Impact on Regional Power Structures

The Sunni-Shia schism has thus become a structuring force for the region's security architecture and political hierarchy. Over the decades, the rivalry has crystallised into a network of state and non-state actors whose mutual antagonism produces a perpetual contest for influence over contested territories and ideological legacies. Major capitals—some historically neutral, others with longstanding ties—have been compelled to select sides, both in public and in the shadowy arenas of proxy conflict, thereby hardening sectarian identities among populations whose lives had previously negotiated diverse confessional backgrounds. The result is a regional landscape in which strategic decision-making is as concerned with the presumed loyalties of military units, intelligence agencies, and civilian constituencies as with conventional measures of terrain, demography, or economic interest.

The consolidation of particular sects in pivotal states has produced an uneven allocation of authority, conditioning both intra-national governance and interstate interactions. In Saudi Arabia, the ruling strata lean decisively towards institutionalised Sunni Islam, while in Iran, the civil and clerical establishment remains permanently under Shia majority control. In both cases, sectarian dissociation has migrated from popular sentiment into the constitutional and bureaucratic nuclei of governance. These layers of contestation radiate outward, imprinting on bilateral and multilateral relations, so that the Sunni-Shia cleavage now furnishes the centrifugal and centripetal forces in interstate rivalry. The rise of proxy engagements, in which peripheral actors on both sectarian nodes contest spheres of influence, further liberalises the schism from an intra-national question to an international irritant. The Cartesian product of such politics is the consolidation of sectary coloured blocs—Sunni states manoeuvre to offset Iranian ascendancy, while Shia capitals reciprocate through asymmetric deterrence. These overlapping circuits of trust and enmity render the regional power topology both thinner in diplomatic degree and thicker in kinetic consequence, cementing geopolitical entrenchments that sidestep traditional balancing toward an equilibrium of fortified enmity.

In addition, the Sunni-Shia rivalry has consistently informed the calculations of external actors, who, guided by their own strategic imperatives, have sought to manipulate the region's sectarian fissures to consolidate their influence. This rivalry has generated not only direct military confrontations but also a subtler, protracted contest over ideological hegemony, as diverse and often antithetical interpretations of Islam are championed to sway global Muslim opinion. The struggle over the transmission of religious authority and legitimacy has provoked intra-Muslim sectarian fracturing, giving rise to a hierarchical competition among clerical and political elites that refracts onto the international stage. The consequences of this rivalry are thus both immediate—manifest in proxy conflicts and asymmetric intervention—and cumulative, having reconfigured the balance of power across the region. This sectarian prism becomes indispensable for any rigorous analysis of contemporary Middle Eastern politics, as it interlaces with, and often intensifies, contestations of statehood, nationalism, and transnational ideologies that continue to disrupt the region's stability.

Internal Conflicts and External Influences

The overlapping dynamics of internal disputes and external interventions in the Middle East have decisively determined the evolution of the region's sectarian fractures. Domestic tensions are rooted in enduring historical animosities, struggles over political authority, and uneven economic development among diverse sectarian constituencies. Yet, these internal fissures are heightened by foreign interventions—geopolitical manoeuvring, proxy confrontations, and the policy choices of both neighbouring and distant powers motivated by their strategic calculations. The resultant density and permanence of these internal disputes, when coupled with external pressures, have entrenched the region's persistent volatility. Troubles typically surface as armed revolts, protests, or insurgent campaigns, recursively reproducing violence and reinforcing sectarian cleavages. Such disturbances cannot be understood as isolated phenomena; they are shaped by and in turn influence the larger regional order. The overlapping of external forces—be they military aid, financial resources, or symbolic political endorsements—has further escalated and prolonged domestic conflicts, converting confined confrontations into region-wide crises. To comprehend the full dimensions of the Middle East's sectarian landscape, one must analyse the converging pathways of internal discord and external imposition.

By situating internal conflicts within their historical dimensions and contemporary expressions, one reveals the manner in which such struggles intertwine with external pressures to intensify sectarian divides and reinforce oppositional discourses. The impact of external agents on the aggravation of internal strife is significant, as their interventions magnify latent cleavages and thwart the pathways toward genuine reconciliation and enduring stability. The resulting multidirectional friction between domestic dissent and foreign interference highlights an imperative for comprehensive strategies that engage both the inherited grievances at the community level and the external dynamics that sustain violence. Future initiatives designed to cultivate lasting peace must therefore integrate internal and external variables, recognising their mutual reinforcement and pursuing diplomatic avenues that lower tensions and harmonise competing sectarian narratives.

Case Studies: Sectarian Tensions in Syria and Lebanon

To comprehend the overarching patterns of sectarian friction in the Levant, one must engage with illustrative country studies, primarily Syria and Lebanon. The historical and political trajectories of these two states illuminate the ways in which inherited divisions have crystallised into formalised political structures and everyday communal politics.

The Syrian civil war that ignited in 2011 thrust longstanding Sunni-Shia animosities to the forefront, merging the humanitarian cataclysm with a protracted sectarian struggle. The

Assad government, anchored in the largely Alawite sect, enlisted Iran and Hezbollah—both Shia-heavy actors—as crucial pillars of military and economic lifelines, while the opposition, largely framed through a Sunni lens, fractured into diverse militias, each claiming sectarian loyalty. This domestic polarisation, already deepened by two decades of neoliberal marginalisation, blended with a region-wide competition among the Iran-led axis and its Gulf Arab rivals, transforming villages and urban neighbourhoods into a geographically dispersed theatre of proxy violence and geopolitical signalling. Lebanon, meanwhile, has long been marked by its own sectarian architecture, whose equilibrium—codified in the 1989 Taif Agreement—remains fragile. The 1975-1990 civil war, the 1990 Syrian military occupation, and the subsequent 2005 Syrian withdrawal each reconfigured sectarian loyalties. Hezbollah's metamorphosis from resistance movement to state fixture has redefined the Shia political imagination while provoking Sunni-led countermobilisations that oscillate between electoral candidacies and military posturing. The porous border, marked by smugglers, labourers, and fighters, ensures that Syrian offensives, refugee surges, and Iranian arms shipments ricochet into Lebanese districts, complicating the already precarious coexistence of communalities across the Levant.

These case studies highlight the complex interaction between domestic conditions and external determinants, illustrating how sectarianism verges on becoming the primary impediment to lasting regional stability.

Sectarian Narratives in Media and Propaganda

Media and propaganda vehicles have been decisive in disseminating sectarian tropes that skew public perception and heighten communal strife across the Middle East. Established outlets and digital forums alike have been repurposed to serve sectarian agendas, magnifying historical wounds and cementing reductive stereotypes. When reports, editorials, and public debates are routinely framed to spotlight sectarian difference, the cumulative effect is to entrench the binaries that ultimately fracture societies. The advent of social media, with its capacity for instantaneous circulation, magnifies the danger; misleading or falsified material travels faster than correction, allowing rumours to crystallise into conventional wisdom. Both overt state campaigns and clandestine operations leverage such platforms to reinforce sectarian binaries, underscoring the political, ideological, and confessional objectives at stake. In some jurisdictions, state media have served as megaphones for dehumanising portrayals of rival sects, cultivating environments in which suspicion hardens into animosity.

Similarly, non-state militants and extremist networks have exploited communication platforms to disseminate incendiary discourse, validate sectarian loyalty, and attract recruits to their enterprises. In tandem, the politicisation of collective historical grievances and traumas through digital and broadcast networks has transmitted animosities across generations and deepened sectarian cleavages. Iconography, imagery, and crafted narratives are employed to trigger visceral reactions and solidify collective identity, thereby lengthening hostilities and hindering reconciliation. Within this framework, cultural forms—music, literature, and visual creations—have occasionally been put to service to promulgate sectarian doctrine and perpetuate societal fractures. The transnational dimension of contemporary media and propaganda must also be acknowledged; external entities have sought to alter regional dynamics by controlling narratives and shaping audience perceptions. Foreign states, proxy militias, and transnational movements have crafted media campaigns to strengthen local allies, delegitimise opposing factions, and rebalance power distributions. Concurrently, strategic calculations and interventionist designs have been legitimised through selective representation and the choreographed manipulation of public discourse, thereby perpetuating regional turbulence. In the final analysis, the influence of sectarian narratives and propaganda extends beyond mere transmission of information; it reconfigures social attitudes, shapes policymaking processes, and ensures the recurrence of violent conflict.

Overcoming these obstacles requires an integrated strategy emphasising responsible journalism, robust media education, the decisive confrontation of misinformation, and the construction of inclusive narratives that rise above sectarian divides. By recognising how media can fuel sectarian discord and undertaking sustained efforts to amend these representations, policy-makers and civil society can reduce communal tensions and nurture a more cohesive social fabric.

Cross-border Implications and Instability

The sectarian divides in the Middle East carry pronounced cross-border consequences that heighten regional instability and complicate geopolitical rivalries. The Sunni-Shia schisms are so interwoven that they routinely breach national borders, drawing in adjacent states and resonating throughout the broader geopolitical theatre. An appreciation of these cross-border dynamics is therefore indispensable for an accurate reading of contemporary Middle Eastern politics. The most direct evidence of their dangers is the capacity of sectarian tensions to migrate from one national setting to another. Each communal crisis can ignite localised disputes in its neighbours, magnifying and prolonging instability. The Syrian civil war exemplifies this spiral, as its collapse of governance allowed multiple regional actors to project sectarian rivalries, converting the conflict zone into a theatre for competing narratives and further inflaming tensions throughout the wider region. The intervention of foreign states and the mobilisation of sectarian proxies have deepened and internationalised these cross-border sectarian dynamics, increasing the fragility of all states caught in the vicinity.

The engagement of Iran and Saudi Arabia in backing their sectarian affiliates has intensified friction both domestically and in surrounding nations, sustaining a recurrent spiral of regional turmoil. Such sectarian polarisation has likewise shaped refugee movements, imposing demographic strains and igniting social frictions across frontiers. People fleeing sectarian violence have overloaded the capacities and resilience of their hosts, imposing social, economic, and political strains that reach well beyond the zones of initial violence. States receiving refugees are compelled to absorb the displaced while also confronting the risk that imported sectarian antagonisms might resurface within their own borders, thus complicating the already fragile equilibrium of the host society. Furthermore, sectarian rhetoric transmitted through various media and propaganda channels has intruded across borders, sharpening communal hostilities. Misinformation amplifies pre-existing divides and entrenches animosity between sectarian groups, complicating the pursuit of dialogue and reconciliation. The intertwined and cross-boundary nature of these sectarian repercussions therefore mandates approaches that are both nuanced and comprehensive to quell regional instability.

Any initiatives intended to foster regional stability and effective conflict resolution must account for the wider ramifications of sectarian rifts, attending to the intricate liaison among domestic, bilateral, and multilateral factors. A sophisticated comprehension of these cross-border factors creates enhanced prospects for attenuating regional volatility and instituting durable peace across the Middle East.

Towards Reconciliation: Bridging the Sectarian Divide

Mending the entrenched sectarian rift throughout the Middle East necessitates a comprehensive strategy that recognises cumulative historical grievances, encourages broad-based dialogue, and nurtures enduring reconciliation. Such an effort must transcend win-lose political rivalries and embrace collective, society-wide healing. At its nucleus, authentic reconciliation depends upon the active inclusion of diverse religious authorities, community leaders, and locally driven initiatives. Elevating these interlocutors allows for the cultivation of mutual comprehension and esteem, on which tangible advancement can rest. Equally critical is the acknowledgement of the distinctive cultural and religious patrimony of each community, recasting apparent differences as complementary assets rather than divisive liabilities. Concurrently, robust institutional mechanisms must be crafted to guarantee equal political representation and active participation for every sect across the region.

Whether they take the form of power-sharing accords, institutional reforms, or targeted affirmative action, the ultimate objective is to elevate marginalised groups and embed their voices within the corridors of power. By confronting the legacies of past injustices and embedding inclusive governance frameworks, polities can gradually restore confidence and cultivate an atmosphere wherein durable peace can take root. Concurrently, curricula reform and interfaith dialogue remain vital for eradicating deep-seated prejudices and nurturing intercommunal solidarity. Beyond domestic endeavours, regional and international stakeholders bear an indispensable responsibility for facilitating durable reconciliation. Diplomatic outreach, structured mediation, and confidence-building protocols can dampen the flashpoints of discord and span the divides that sectarian politics exploit. Shared cross-border economic initiatives and cooperative development ventures can erode the win-lose logic that frequently governs sectarian arenas, delivering concrete, mutual incentives for partnership. Continued, sensitive dialogue and negotiation, tempered by a respect for local autonomy and agency, is crucial for sustaining the momentum of reconciliation. At the same time, transitional justice instruments—including truth-seeking commissions and reparative programmes—can confront the legacy of violence while offering pathways to individual and collective closure, ensuring that societies progress without erasing the memory of their past wounds.

International endorsement of these programmes can reinforce the global obligation to safeguard human rights and to nurture shared recovery, thereby enhancing the credibility of the reconciliation process. Overcoming sectarian rifts, however, necessitates ongoing dedication, time, and compassionate listening. The required transformation is from exclusionary mindsets to one that recognises and celebrates diversity as fundamental to strength, discovery, and communal flourishing. Achieving lasting change will depend on comprehensive, cooperative, and uninterrupted actions that together disrupt the recurrence of sectarian conflict, fostering the conditions for a quieter, more integrated Middle East.

12
Governance Failures
Root Causes of Regional Turmoil

Historical Overview: Urgent Need for Addressing Dysfunction

The historical course of the region has indelibly shaped the governance frameworks that now define its realities. From the disintegration of the Ottoman Empire through the colonial mandates and on to the troubled quest for the post-colonial state, the Middle East has endured successive upheavals that created enduring governance deficits. The collapse of established authority patterns and the arbitrary delimitation of frontiers after the First World War planted enduring fractures in social and political cohesion. As the resultant states attempted to forge national identities, the residual patterns of colonial administration narrowed the political arena, privileging coercive institutions. The consolidation of authoritarian rule, often directed or sustained by external powers pursuing narrower geopolitical objectives, entrenched a logic in which stability was pursued through repression rather than through civic engagement or political contestation. The cumulative result has been a political environment in which governance is frequently conceived as the management of social order rather than as a legitimate expression of collective sovereignty.

The convergence of long-standing grievances, rival nationalist goals, and foreign interventions has produced widespread feelings of exclusion and anger, exacerbating the governance breakdown that still besets the region. An examination of this trajectory reveals that present governance failures are not temporary aberrations, but the inevitable product of sustained geopolitical turbulence and enduring structural weaknesses.

The Role of Authoritarianism: Power over Stability

Authoritarianism has been a decisive force, carving the political contour of the region by delivering a harsh brand of control that supplants democratic practices in the name of order. Over the years, authoritarian systems have asserted themselves by penetrating the fabric of the state apparatus and suppressing any organised challenge. They typically favour a rigid pyramid in which a sovereign leader—or a narrow caucus—exercises overriding sway. The fusion of authority not only constricts avenues for popular participation, but also births a perpetual atmosphere of intimidation and violence. The deleterious nexus between autocracy and instability reveals itself as institutions meant to restrain power, either under subservience to the sovereign will. Legal safeguards, independent agencies, and civil avenues of recourse are hollowed out or instrumentalised, breeding a permissive context for illicit enrichment, selective patronage, and entrenched networks of clientelism.

Such conditions erode the credibility of governing institutions and cultivate widespread alienation, leading the citizenry to regard the state as a mechanism of oppression rather than a promoter of social advancement. The preoccupation with coercion and censorship inflicts serious damage on civil society, stifling the emergence of pluralistic perspectives and rigorous critique that every adaptive political order requires. With pluralism and deliberation absent, political stasis ensues, obstructing adaptive solutions and inflating the very grievances the regime professes to contain. When authoritarianism takes root amid regional upheaval, it magnifies, rather than mollifies, the underlying social fractures, escalating disenchantment and civil turbulence. Such regimes habitually subordinate long-range prosperity to the consolidation of their own dominion, routinely sacrificing the economic diversification and human-capital investments that safeguard resilience. Wealth concentration among the governing class compounds inequity, alienating vast segments and entrenching social fractures. This inequitable substratum thwarts systemic regeneration, as economically and politically dislocated groups gravitate toward radical narratives that promise restitution. Simultaneously, authoritarian rule subverts the forging of a cohesive, inclusive national narrative, entrenching fissures that run along ethnic, sectarian, and ideological fault lines.

The systematic denial of minority rights, coupled with the monopolisation of political power, generates profound societal rifts that can swiftly escalate into violence and protracted instability. In the end, the orientation toward repression and domination—hallmarks of authoritarian governance—preempts the emergence of stability, economic development, and lasting peace in the region.

Institutional Weaknesses: From Corruption to Collapse

No analysis of the region's fragility can ignore the all-pervasive corrosion of governance that feeds instability and dissipates collective trust. Corruption has become endemic, permeating every stratum of the state and hollowing out its legitimacy. Cronyism, bribery, and embezzlement have not merely distorted procurement and personnel decisions; they have siphoned scarce resources from health, education, and critical infrastructure. The systematic evasion of scrutiny and the absence of redress have institutionalised the immunity of the political class, cultivating the conviction that wrongdoing will, at worst, be rewarded. Against this backdrop, the prospect of institutional collapse shifts from a remote possibility to an impending certainty. Apparatuses already frayed by intra-elite conflicts and foreign intervention lack the reserves—moral, fiscal, and technical—to respond to cumulative shocks. The result is a sclerosis of

governance where the policy cycle stalls, and even the rudi-
ments of statecraft break down, leaving administrative voids
that non-state actors and violence readily exploit.

As state structures deteriorate beneath the cumulative
pressures of sustained Corruption and administrative dysfunction, the implicit compact linking governments and
citizens collapses, and confidence in public institutions
plummets to unprecedented levels. This failure of governance, however, extends well beyond fiscal misconduct. Legal systems that lack both coherence and independence,
and whose personnel are drawn into party rivalries, further
weaken the institutional fabric. When the judiciary becomes
a partisan tool, the rule of law erodes, and powerful groups
are able to script legal outcomes that protect their interests.
Such manipulation extends the dominance of impunity and
poisons the public's belief in the fairness and neutrality of
adjudication.

The economic consequences of these cumulative institutional failures are equally pronounced. Corruption on a
systemic scale, combined with fractured regulatory regimes,
deters entrepreneurship and causes foreign capital to
flee, thus perpetuating stagnation. The shrinking economy, in turn, generates a steady contraction of employment
prospects, while widening socio-economic divisions magnify resentment and amplify the risk of instability. Remedial action, therefore, requires far-reaching reform agendas
that place transparency, accountability, and the rebuilding
of citizen confidence at the forefront. Only by uprooting
deep-seated Corruption and repairing the decay of public
structures can a foundation be built for governance that is

both enduring and capable of fostering equitable socio-economic progress.

Yet, the long march toward sustainable change depends not only on consistent political resolve but also on coordinated international cooperation. This global solidarity, coupled with mobilised community outreach, can erode the structural constraints that have lingered in the region for generations.

Political Elitism: Entrenched Interests and Exclusion

Political elitism erects a governance framework that privileges the consolidated interests of a narrow aristocracy and systematically excludes the wider citizenry from substantive influence. Emerging from long-standing configurations of power, the phenomenon materialises when dynasties, clans, or oligarchs monopolise statecraft and economic levers, thereby embedding cycles of exclusion for all who reside outside the concentric zones of privilege. This deficiency of openness transcends the absence of delegates in formal chambers; it infects the distribution of regulatory permits, the allocation of public contracts, and the upward mobility of social capital. Members of the consolidated elite exercise decisive control over security forces, bureaucracies, and courts, thereby fortifying the walls of privilege and circumscribing arenas in which accountability and innovation can flourish. Resilient networks of patronage, clientelist exchanges, and inherited offices reinforce loyalty while subduing dissent, and thus the original appearance of political competition becomes a facade accommodating the reproduction of oligarchic rule. The resulting concentration not only stifles effective policy experimentation but also institutionalises the inequities and injustices that reformers claim to oppose.

Political elitism heightens socioeconomic inequality by sustaining policies that favour a narrow elite group while neglecting the wider populace. This intensification of disparity sharpens social rifts and fuels anger among marginalised communities, thereby undermining societal cohesion and jeopardising stability. Simultaneously, the systematic exclusion of varied viewpoints and capabilities impoverishes the policy-making arena, denying societies the creativity and inclusivity essential for enduring progress. The recurring nurture of elite dominance cultivates a milieu of impunity, wherein the powerful evade legal scrutiny and retain immunity from the repercussions of their deeds. Such a climate of non-responsiveness weakens public faith in state institutions and spreads widespread disenchantment, posing a formidable obstacle to genuine reform and advancement. Additionally, elite persistence frequently aligns with sectarian or ethnic fissures, solidifying identity-driven politics and deepening societal polarisations. Redressing political elitism demands holistic reforms designed to uproot embedded hierarchies, promote participatory governance, and uplift marginalised constituencies. Through the active pursuit of transparency, shared responsibility, and merit-based advancement, societies can gradually erode elite hegemony and cultivate governance structures that are more just and accurately reflective of the populace.

Fostering diverse perspectives within open, inclusive conversations is essential for dismantling entrenched political elitism and for activating the creative potential inherent in the entire populace.

Economic Mismanagement: The Financial Dependencies

The region's economic trajectory has been shaped by repeated misjudgments and structural weaknesses, all of which reinforce financial dependency and obstruct the trajectory toward self-sustaining growth. At the core of this mismanagement lies a systemic culture of cronyism and Corruption, which has corroded trust in public institutions and distorted the distribution of resources. Powerful groups routinely craft policies that favour their narrow interests, magnifying social and economic disparities whilst stalling authentic advancement. Concurrently, the habitual recourse to external aid and loans has entrenched a cycle of indebtedness; the attendant conditionalities circumscribe policy latitude, infringe upon economic sovereignty, and prolong dependence on foreign transfers. This vulnerability to external dictates weakens the capacity for coherent domestic policy and exposes the region to the volatility of the global economic arena. Compounding these difficulties is the insufficient diversification of revenue bases and the patently low investment in human capital and infrastructure, which together render the economy fragile in the face of external shocks and circumscribe its capacity for adaptive resilience.

Syria and Lebanon's economies are so closely linked that downturns in one country quickly translate into heightened problems for the other. Agriculture, tourism, and manufacturing—industries essential for balanced development—have all contracted as wars and political crises have stifled investment and disrupted trade. Economic misgovernance has thus reinforced cycles of debt and instability, eroding the very foundations of future prosperity. Redressing these problems demands sweeping reforms anchored in transparency, accountability, and environmental sustainability. Curbing Corruption, designing inclusive fiscal frameworks, and nurturing domestic entrepreneurship and investment are immediate priorities. Simultaneously, enhanced regional cooperation and strategic cross-border partnerships could cushion the impact of shocks and shore up joint resilience against global volatilities. By confronting the structural drivers of mismanagement, both countries can gradually pivot toward diversified, self-sustaining economies, thereby enlarging their policy space and lessening dependence on precarious foreign credit.

Lack of Judicial Independence: Law as a Tool for Control

The lack of judicial independence in Syria and Lebanon decisively reinforces the ruling elites' capacity to exercise control and sensitive power consolidation. In both polities, the judiciary has fallen into politicised capture, disabling its function as an impartial mediator of legal disputes. The consequent weakness of judicial autonomy diffuses throughout the social order, corroding individual rights and undermining the legal order. In Syria, the judiciary has long functioned under the regime's shadow, with verdicts so correlated to power priorities that legal norms appear subordinate to political expedience. Encroachment by the executive, together with opaque procedures, has fostered an atmosphere of dread, mistrust, and anticipatory obedience. Litigants, however warranted, confront procedural saturation with procedural hurdles that favour political fidelity over equity. As a result, the foundation of public belief in judicial legitimacy and capacity withers under a regime that rewards loyalty and institutionalised discretion.

Compounding the crisis is the declaration of temporary emergency legislation, cited as necessary for national security, which permits the regime to circumvent normal judicial safeguards and thus tighten its control over both state power and judicial independence. Concurrently, Lebanon continues to confront persistent obstacles to judicial autonomy, whose viability is repeatedly compromised by the intertwining of sectarian loyalties and established political constellations. Lebanon's court system is routinely subjected to pressures from diverse sectarian blocs, which compromise its capacity to deliver decisions that are free from prejudice or partial advantage. Recruitment and promotion of magistrates routinely emphasise party or sectarian affiliation, rather than competence or seniority, thus corroding the meritocratic foundation that is vital to judicial credibility. As a result, public confidence in the Lebanese judiciary has diminished, with citizens increasingly regarding verdicts and rulings as extensions of particular sectarian or party imperatives rather than as vindications of universal legal principles. This compromised autonomy thus becomes a fundamental mechanism for sustaining the prevailing political order, permitting legislative and judicial instruments to be reconfigured into instruments of control rather than as effective safeguards for the rights and entitlements of the population at large.

Re-establishing public confidence in legal institutions, fostering openness, and reinforcing the underpinnings of democratic governance in Syria and Lebanon hinge decisively on safeguarding judicial independence.

Public Disillusionment: Erosion of Government Accountability

The widening rift between the governed and the governors has crystallised public disillusionment, exposing the fragility of state accountability in the region. Across the Levant, the latest cycles of violence and political stagnation have amplified long-simmering grievances, channelling popular anger into street protests, electoral boycotts, and everyday apathy. Citizens, fatigued by unmet promises, identify the crisis as systemic rather than accidental; they isolate three interrelated phenomena—systemic corruption, opaque decision-making, and the ham-fisted refusal of rulers to translate popular aspirations into policy.

Within this context, institutions once entrusted to audit public conduct and to prosecute malfeasance have either been co-opted or paralysed. Judges, prosecutors, and advocacy groups brought to the fore seemingly technocratic remedies, yet they soon revealed the vulnerabilities of their own hierarchies. Courts are perceived less as neutral ad-judicators than as arenas where political capital is offered and judicial sentences are bought. The result is a culture of impunity that has migrated from politics to everyday life, confirming for ordinary citizens the enduring separation be-tween law as aspirational text and law as instrument of elite preservation.

Additionally, limited access to information and exclusion from decision-making processes have further estranged the populace from state institutions. Secrecy and non-transpar-ent mechanisms have communicated to citizens that their voices and choices count for little, leaving many to feel that the democratic compact has been hollowed out. When the public is stripped of the tools to question, to assist, and to right its leadership, the entire edifice of accountability weakens and distrust seeps into the very core of society. Compounding this civic erosion is the continual failure to deliver the basic goods and services upon which democratic legitimacy rests. Crumbling infrastructure, unreliable public goods, and skeletal welfare nets demonstrate to the popu-lace that the state is either unwilling or incapable of sus-taining everyday life. Such failure magnifies the impression of governmental negligence, hardening the conviction that state institutions have passed beyond the point of practical credibility. Together, these failures have crashed public trust into the basement of public life, bespeaking a culture of exhausted scepticism and warded-away participation. The implications are wallpapered across the social canvas—dis-jointed social solidarity and, in fateful instances, the lur-ing of the disaffected into extremist currents. Re-establishing transparent, accountable governance thus becomes the non-negotiable preliminary for reviving both trust and civic vitality, paving the road to a resilient, genuinely responsive polity.

Governance vs. Sectarian Allegiances: A Symbiotic Relationship?

In Syria and Lebanon, the consolidation of state authority with sectarian loyalties has generated a pervasive and mutually reinforcing network of power relations. Each polity has, over time, institutionalised governance arrangements that privilege particular religious communities, endowing their elites with a concentration of authority that exceeds numerical representation. The result is a durable coupling of state mechanisms with sectarian identities, which has become the overriding logic of both political systems. Political coalitions, power-sharing pacts, and the distribution of state assets are anchored in communal membership, while the legitimacy of public authority is likewise measured against confessional representativity. The manifestation of this entangled order is evident in cabinet formations, electoral district boundaries, and the staffing of administrative and security institutions, whose structures are meticulously calibrated according to sectarian quotas. Legislative initiatives and executive decisions are, in turn, calibrated to reflect the variables of communal interest, ensuring that the imperatives of governance and the imperatives of sectarian loyalty remain reciprocally corroborative. As such, the state apparatus becomes not only a mediator of communal interests but the arena in which their reproduction is programmatically secured.

This ongoing entanglement has fortified profound fissures within society, as citizens frequently equate their sectarian affiliation with entitlements to political voice and resource distribution. The result is a persistent sectarian cycle that reaffirms its mutually beneficial links to governance, thereby obscuring the separation of allegiance from the larger contours of power. Foreign actors have further instrumentalised these realities, manipulating sectarian vectors to serve a wider geopolitical calculus, which in turn deepens the interdependence of statecraft and sectarian loyalty. The durability of this entanglement obstructs even the most committed endeavours to construct inclusive and responsive governance, since it solidifies fragmentation and diminishes the capacity for accountable, transparent institutions. Remediation of this interlace demands a layered strategy that recognises the entanglement of past grievances, social stratifications, and political imperatives, while nurturing governance frameworks that rise above sectarian boundaries and guarantee fair representation and opportunity for the entire polity.

External Interventions: Distorting Sovereign Governance

Outside interventions have decisively warped the perimeter of sovereign rule and governance across the contemporary, fractious Middle East.

Foreign powers have, motivated by strategic interests and geopolitical ambitions, consistently sought to penetrate and reshape the political landscapes of Syria and Lebanon, exacerbating pre-existing crises and accelerating the decay of sovereign governance. Central to this phenomenon is the concert of regional and global actors that the 2011 Syrian uprising and the subsequent Lebanese crises invited, each actor channelling resources to rival factions and armed militias, with the predictable effect of perpetuating pugilistic momentum and reordering power asymmetrically. The flow of arms, financial streams, and training from overseas sponsors has, therefore, dragged these societies into prolonged violence and delegitimised the centralised state, birthing de facto authorities that outmanoeuvre recognised institutions and further fission political cohesion.

The impact of third-party involvement, however, is not limited to kinetics. External actors have mastered the art of economic and diplomatic interference, eroding the latitude necessary for autonomous policymaking. Coercive measures—sanctions regimes, calibrated trade choke-holds, and conditional macro-financial packages—have been calibrated to yield compliance with foreign agendas, while simultaneously undercutting the fiscal and administrative bases of domestic governance and minimising the welfare of affected populations. Diplomatic levers are then manipulated, with foreign powers recalibrating recognitions and alliances according to shifting expediencies, thereby inducing a politics of transient loyalties that further muddies the calculus of local actors. Consequently, the internal governance architecture is rendered even more brittle, and the possibility of durable regional stabilisation recedes with each recalibration of external involvement.

Failures in Reform: Attempts at Change and Resistance

External interventions have profoundly shaped the governance landscape in the region, eroding the underpinning of sovereignty and self-determination while embedding a durable instability that thwarts the emergence of genuine reform. Acknowledging the weight of these interventions proves essential for decoding the multifaceted patterns of governance failure, and advocates the adoption of refined strategies that restore national autonomy and strengthen domestically grounded authority.

The trajectory of reform, marked by ambitious design yet constrained in effectiveness, epitomises the persistent friction of the regional context. Repeatedly, efforts to induce substantive change have collided with resilient structures of power that reconstitute themselves following each initiative, leaving a residue of stagnation and widespread disaffection. The difficulty of dislodging deeply seated institutions and of confronting consolidated interests generates a durable impasse. When external actors exert leverage in pursuit of reform, they intensify the clash between the wish for transformation and the principle of non-interference. Compounding the challenge, efforts to introduce new policies have routinely provoked mobilised resistance from elites who perceive reform as a menace to their monopolised privileges.

Those dominant actors—political, economic, or sectarian—press doggedly against genuine change, guarding their authority and material interests with equal resolve. Their unwillingness to forfeit control and privilege keeps governance stagnant, blocking the rise of systems that are genuinely accountable and inclusive. If well-designed, even good-faith reforms can, with a cruel irony, harden opposition: the threatened elite, fearing loss, rapidly consolidate to insulate their privilege. Public scepticism, however, compounds the dilemma. Citizens, conditioned by a history of broken pledges and dashed hopes, scrutinise fresh proposals with a jaded eye, breeding a climate of mistrust that openly resists even the mildest adjustments. This widespread disillusionment not only stymies reform tactics but also obstructs the critical consensus that sustainable change demands. At the institutional level, deep-rooted structural frailties further impede progress. Institutional inertia, regulatory capture, and administrative slowness conspire to render reform measures ineffectual. Scarce resources, a dearth of specialised knowledge, and the weight of bureaucratic habit together sap the energy of reform programmes, entrenching the status quo and prolonging governance deficiency. The convergence of these interwoven obstacles emphasises the complexity of the reform project and highlights the urgent necessity for strategies that are both comprehensive and integrative.

Addressing resistance entails tactfully negotiating entrenched interests, actively consulting disillusioned constituencies, and fostering governance frameworks marked by transparency and accountability, which in turn reinforce public trust and legitimacy. Furthermore, awareness of the interplay among political, economic, and social spheres is critical when crafting reform strategies that are both sensitive to local realities and aligned with overarching strategic objectives.

13
Diplomatic Efforts
Paths Towards Resolution

Diplomatic Channels: Historical Context and Present Dynamics

The diplomatic landscape between principal actors in the peace process is profoundly informed by a history of negotiations, accords, and hostilities that have crystallised the region's geopolitics over successive decades. From the inception of the United Nations to the eruption of the Arab-Israeli conflict and the later consolidation of peace treaties, diplomatic activities have advanced by way of decisive turning points that reveal recurring patterns of alliance formation, rivalry, and the pursuit of national interests. The 1947 partition of Palestine and the 1948 declaration of the Israeli state produced an immediate, durable state of friction and elicited multilayered diplomatic intervention. The Arab states' repudiation of the UN proposal precipitated the 1948 Arab-Israeli War, which institutionalised the expectation that diplomacy would intervene in militarised outcome cycles. The Cold War exacerbated the landscape, as superpowers inserted themselves into regional disputes, reshaping alignments in a manner that rendered diplomatic efforts increasingly contingent upon the larger global rivalry. The Suez Crisis of 1956 and the series of confrontations that followed demonstrated the difficulty of sustaining effective diplomatic pathways when rival global interests simultaneously pursued strategic objectives in the same theatre.

Yet, amid decades of upheaval, moments of diplomatic courage, such as the Camp David Accords of 1978, proved that even deep-seated animosities could yield to negotiated compromise, creating the possibility for enduring coexistence. The 1993 Oslo Accords further advanced this trajectory, as the Palestine Liberation Organisation and Israel publicly acknowledged each other's legitimacy, kindling hopes for a permanent settlement. Although the Camp David Summit of 2000 and the Annapolis Conference of 2007 did not produce the envisioned final status, they affirmed that sustained diplomatic engagement remained central to the Israeli-Palestinian conflict. Regional forums have equally addressed interstate rivalries; the Madrid Conference of 1991 and the 2002 Arab Peace Initiative exemplify efforts to construct a wider framework for peace. Today, the trajectory of diplomatic endeavours continues to be shaped by these earlier milestones. The unresolved legacies they left remind us that dialogue—properly sustained and politically supported—remains the primary mechanism for pursuing stability and reconciliatory progress across the Levant.

Against the changing landscape of multipolar competition and reconfigured alliances, grasping the formative history of diplomatic conduits is essential for, and not merely informative to, the contemporary regional peacemaking landscape.

Key Stakeholders in the Peace Process: Regional and Global Influences

Achievement of durable peace within the intertwined Syrian and Lebanese geopolitical space mandates meticulous mapping of principal stakeholders, both regional and extra-regional. The sheer complexity of the situation obliges scrutiny of actors who exert decisive leverage over negotiation trajectories. This section delineates the layered architecture of stakeholders, appraising their interests, resources, and functions in the constellations of mediation. Regional players remain irreplaceable in the construction of peace, as proximate states—including Turkey, Jordan, and Iraq—experience direct and indirect spillover from the Syrian conflict. Each country possesses distinct strategic imperatives, and the interplay of these imperatives constrains and channels diplomatic behaviour. Turkish emphasis on preventing Kurdish autonomy and the protection of borders, interlaced with the logistics of refugee management, has framed Ankara's calibrations. Jordan, motivated more by the imperative of regime survival and border security than by ideological alignment, prioritises an outcome that preserves internal cohesion. Iraq's stakes, compounded by sectarian and identity politics, further complicate the negotiation environment. The confluence of these regional imperatives thus intersects with external paradigms, compelling any viable peace architecture to account for the full spectrum of actors and motives.

At the same time, Iraq continues to confront domestic difficulties that shape Baghdad's response to the shifting regional balance. Beyond Iraq's borders, Riyadh and Tehran emerge as principal architects of the overarching security landscape, each leveraging pervasive political and economic networks throughout the Levant and the Gulf. Their persistent antagonism and divergent ideological visions further complicate any stabilising arrangement, as proxy support and funding consistently re-energise localised militias and political factions. In the extra-regional dimension, decisive engagement from Washington, Moscow, and the European Union remains essential for any prospect of lasting accord. A nuanced appraisal of their historic interventions, especially with respect to Syria and Lebanon, is required to formulate credible diplomatic plans. Parallel to these calculations, the United Nations and its auxiliary bodies occupy a central position, furnishing arenas for negotiation and institutional mechanisms for de-escalation. Equally, the influence of non-state networks—ranging from intergovernmental organisations to grassroots civil-society coalitions—deserves rigorous analysis. These actors can circumscribe the agenda of state leaders and introduce humanitarian-centred tracks that may, in the long run, reinforce the legitimacy of formal reconciliation efforts.

A thorough grasp of the varied stakeholders—their motives, capacities, and limits—is indispensable for navigating the intricate realm of diplomatic talks and for constructing enduring paths to peace.

Negotiation Frameworks: Understanding Existing Protocols and Agreements

Amid the diplomatic efforts to resolve the conflicts in Syria and Lebanon, a close familiarity with the prevailing protocols and treaties is essential. Examining these negotiation frameworks exposes the layered legal, political, and historical strata upon which the peace process is erected. The multi-dimensional character of these instruments mandates a systematic study to illuminate how the different players chart their course toward settlement. Foremost, the United Nations assumes a central role in supervising and facilitating the diplomatic architecture. Security Council Resolution 2254, adopted in 2015, delineates a political roadmap for Syria, insisting on a nationwide ceasefire, constitutional revision, and the holding of free and fair elections. Concurrently, the Arab League has contributed regionally by endorsing the 2012 Geneva Communique, which articulates the contours of a peaceful transfer of authority in Syria.

The structure inaugurated by the International Syria Support Group continues to offer a multilateral space within which principal states may deliberate and harmonise their contributions toward a durable peace. In parallel, the Astana and Sochi tracks have formed, orchestrated principally by Russia, Turkey, and Iran, which—though they may overlap—add layers of complexity and diverging terms to the overarching process. A review of comparable diplomatic precedents illuminates conceivable routes for contemporary negotiators. The Taif Agreement of 1989 constitutes a striking reference point: it concluded the Lebanese Civil War by recalibrating power-sharing among sectarian groups and embedding provisions for reconciliation into the constitutional order. The Camp David Accords of 1978, which settled differences between Israel and Egypt, further illustrate how judiciously framed engagements may yield durable accords. Yet, the execution of such pacts frequently faltered because of entrenched distrust, colliding national objectives, and the influence of third parties. The fragile equilibrium between respect for national sovereignty and the necessity of external support thus demands constant, informed calibration to sustain the integrity of negotiation structures. As novel instruments are crafted and extant road maps are revised, a granular comprehension of the tactical architecture of diplomacy remains essential for shaping the arc toward lasting peace and stability in Syria and in Lebanon.

Successful Initiatives: Analysing Past Diplomatic Triumphs

The historical record offers several cases in which concert-

ed diplomatic effort decisively altered the course of seemingly intractable regional disputes, underlining the effectiveness of sustained multilateral
engagement.

These earlier breakthroughs continue to inform and energise contemporary diplomacy within the Syria-Lebanon geopolitical arena. The Camp David Accords of 1978, which mediated the Israel-Egypt peace settlement with American facilitation, illustrated how focused, enduring negotiation can convert entrenched adversarial relationships into functional partnership, thereby offering a replicable framework for transforming animus into coexistence. The 1993 Oslo Accords, which secured mutual recognition between Israel and the Palestine Liberation Organisation, underscored how structured dialogue can articulate a pathway for addressing enduring, intricate disputes. The 1995 Dayton Accords, negotiated within a multilateral diplomacy that included the United States and European powers, arrested the Bosnian conflict and crystallised rules for power sharing and reconciliation, thereby validating the capacity of concerted multilateral pressure and persuasion to produce durable settlements. Parallel to these cases, the 2002 Arab Peace Initiative constituted a collective Arab overture that framed a two-state solution to the Israeli-Palestinian conflict, reiterating the principle that sustained regional collaboration is indispensable for stability and for the gradual normalisation of relations across the Levant.

The study of historic diplomatic breakthroughs yields valuable lessons about the strategic repertoires, negotiation architectures, and enduring dedication required to settle long-standing geopolitical conflicts. Each case illuminates how creative problem-solving, trust-building between erstwhile foes, and the cultivation of a consistent and credible diplomatic process can pave the way to lasting settlements. Critical to these successes have been transformative political leaders, expert mediators who anticipate and alleviate misperceptions, and combatants who forgo maximum expectations to achieve a more enduring peace. Such case studies encourage contemporaneous actors to persist amid fatigue, illustrating the capacity of diplomacy to overcome inherited animosities. They particularly illuminate the interaction between Syria and Lebanon, inspiring diplomatic action which, by embracing these lessons, can reconcile the present divergence and construct an interdependent future of bilateral stability.

Ongoing Dialogues: Current Efforts and Their Progress

In the present moment, a dense network of diplomatic conversations continues to navigate the region's inherited fractures. Formal and informal channels remain active, threading together bilateral, trilateral, and multilateral elements into a single, cumulative peace architecture.

The current round of peace dialogues involves a broad constellation of stakeholders: state officials, humanitarian and advocacy NGOs, neutral mediators from regional and multilateral bodies, and trusted leaders from conflict-affected constituencies. Each actor introduces a distinct blend of strategic objectives, normative values, and on-the-ground exigencies, thereby enriching the debate while simultaneously raising the level of difficulty inherent in any consensus-building endeavour. Principal agenda items under consideration include agreed timetables for ceasefire consolidation, unhindered humanitarian passage, the design of inclusive and representative post-conflict governance arrangements, and modalities for the dignified return and reintegration of refugees and internally displaced persons. Variation in the intensity and durability of each party's engagement confounds the viability of any single analytic or procedural frame. The interactive effects of shifting regional allegiances, the asymmetric influence of third-state sponsors, and occasionally contradictory economic incentives for local actors further obfuscate the trajectory toward a durable and just peace. An encouraging development within the dialogues is the deliberate embedding of grassroots constituencies and civil society coalitions, whose testimonies, data, and practical recommendations illuminate the risks and opportunities confronting the everyday security and livelihoods of affected populations. Concurrently, a growing network of track two initiatives—characterised by unofficial, closed seminars and collaborative research among former officials, academics, and influential civic leaders—continues to identify common ground that formal delegates sometimes underexplore, thereby widening the negotiators' shared understanding of feasible compromises.

Current dialogues continue to unfold, underscoring the necessity of trust, transparency, and attention to long-standing grievances in achieving lasting progress. Confidence-building measures, coupled with effective monitoring and enforcement mechanisms, remain indispensable for the durability of any agreements brokered. The involvement of international stakeholders—among them the United Nations, the European Union, and regional neighbours—provides legitimacy and technical expertise, thereby reinforcing the credibility of the overall diplomatic enterprise. An accurate assessment of developments in these dialogues requires a balanced appraisal of both concrete successes and enduring impediments. While select elements of the peace framework may appear encouraging, significant obstacles and recurrent setbacks thwart full reconciliation and long-term stability. Remaining alert to stalling strategies, peace spoilers, and unresolved grievances is therefore essential. The negotiations now shaping the futures of Syria and Lebanon require an unrelenting dedication, inventive diplomatic strategies, and a collective commitment to the sustainable peace both societies so urgently seek.

Challenges to Diplomacy: Obstacles in Reaching Consensus

Diplomatic initiatives directed at resolving intractable regional conflicts inevitably confront numerous hurdles that obstruct the attainment of a shared accord. A primary impediment is the persistence of historical grievances and collective memory, which solidify mutual distrust and obstruct cooperative engagement. Compounding this, geopolitical rivalries among influential external powers introduce competing agendas that fragment the quest for a unified compromise. Ideological and religious divergences further exacerbate the fracture, as fundamentally disparate world-views render the articulation of acceptable concessions exceedingly difficult. The presence of non-state actors—paramilitary organisations, insurgent movements, and surrogate forces—injects a variable unpredictability, frequently destabilising carefully calibrated negotiating tracks. Economic inequities and competition for vital resources exacerbate the situation; control over lucrative commodities is seldom a separate concern but rather becomes fused with political bargaining, hardening oppositional stances. Lastly, questions of sovereignty and territorial integrity frequently crystallise as decisive obstacles, particularly when rival, mutually exclusive claims over specific regions or border demarcations animate the conflict.

The involvement of global powers in fragile conflicts frequently complicates diplomatic efforts, as divergent external agendas can intensify pre-existing animosities or weaken sincere steps toward reconciliation. In addition, the absence of a cohesive, shared strategy among state, regional, and multilateral actors creates uncertainty and inconsistency in diplomatic signals, impeding the attainment of significant milestones in negotiations. A further critical obstacle is the exercise of sustained political will and leadership; shifting domestic priorities, along with competing partisan agendas, can dissipate the focus and resources necessary for a durable peace process. In such contexts, a lack of effective, ongoing communication channels permits gaps between intent and action, leading to damaging misinterpretations that undermine the fragile construction of reciprocity and trust.

Equally disruptive is the failure to safeguard continuity in dialogue: leadership changes, electoral volatility, or abrupt domestic crises can sever previously established conversational pathways and require the costly and time-consuming task of reconstructing the necessary domestic and interpersonal trust. To navigate this complex landscape, a comprehensive approach is required—one that identifies the multilayered nature of the obstacles and simultaneously forges incremental avenues of dialogue and cooperation. Success in this endeavour will depend on the cultivation of patient persistence, innovative problem-solving, and an unshakeable dedication to the long-term aspiration of sustained peace and regional stability.

Role of Multilateral Organisations: Facilitators of Regional Peace

Multilateral organisations are instrumental in promoting regional peace in multifaceted geopolitical contexts such as Syria and Lebanon. These institutions provide structured venues for dialogue, negotiation, and conflict resolution, thereby enabling multiple stakeholders to engage in a coordinated manner. Their external neutrality helps to distance the peace process from partisan influence, thereby cultivating the trust necessary for durable cooperation among conflicting parties. Moreover, these organisations are typically endowed with the expertise and material resources required to execute long-term peace initiatives effectively. In the specific contexts of Syria and Lebanon, several multilateral entities have been decisive in advancing peace-building endeavours. The United Nations has consistently facilitated diplomatic dialogue while coordinating humanitarian assistance in both countries, deploying its specialised agencies to tackle critical priorities such as refugee protection, post-conflict reconstruction, and security sector reform. The Arab League has complemented these efforts by functioning as a regional diplomatic forum, fostering dialogue and consensus among its members, while its mediation missions have aimed to mitigate tensions and encourage cooperative security arrangements throughout the Arab world. Concurrently, the European Union has sustained its engagement, providing technical assistance, monitoring, and financial support to strengthen peace and stability across the Eastern Mediterranean basin.

Through diplomatic outreach and targeted development assistance, the EU has fostered economic stabilisation, promoted governance reforms, and encouraged cross-border collaboration. These multilateral instruments complement national and bilateral strategies, collectively mitigating the drivers of conflict and fostering an environment where durable peace can take root. By providing an enduring forum for dialogue and negotiation, they create neutral territory where disputed parties can pursue constructive discourse. The participation of multilateral entities also confers legitimacy on peace processes, for their global mandates and heterogeneous memberships reflect an international consensus on the imperative of regional stability. Yet, realising the full capacity of such organisations in peace facilitation remains a work in progress. Difficulties persist in harmonising the disparate organs, in securing adequate financial support, and in institutionalising broad-based decision-making. Furthermore, external geopolitical rivalries and divergent national priorities can complicate the efficacy of multilateral interventions. Notwithstanding these hurdles, the foundational contribution of multilateral organisations to durable peace endures. Ongoing engagement and reinforcing support from these entities are indispensable for decoding the intricate politics of conflict resolution and for nurturing constructive relations in the Eastern Mediterranean.

Track Two Diplomacy: The Significance of Non-Governmental Actors

Non-governmental actors occupy a decisive space within the diplomatic arena, serving as essential brokers in both conflict resolution and the wider architecture of peace-building. Their actions, often shielded from the political pressures that constrain state diplomats, allow for more candid exchanges and the gradual erosion of mistrust.

Often designated as "Track Two diplomacy," this diplomatic practice supplements official intergovernmental talks by convening actors outside the state: civil society groups, academic institutions, interfaith leaders, and private-sector stakeholders. While Track One diplomacy consists of formal negotiations conducted by accredited state officials, Track Two creates a more fluid and informal space for conversation, thereby permitting the exploration of creative options and direct people-to-people engagement. Its principal contribution is the reinforcement of trust-building measures and the articulation of solutions that engage the root drivers of conflict. Such initiatives assume particular significance in lengthy and multifaceted disputes in which conventional state-centred efforts confront systemic impediments. Through their varied participation, Track Two processes illuminate a spectrum of viewpoints, elevate the concerns of marginalised constituencies, and cultivate comprehensive peace-building strategies. Non-state actors possess the flexibility and inventiveness often constrained within formal diplomatic frameworks, enabling the trial of innovative concepts and non-traditional remedies. Moreover, Track Two diplomacy plays a critical role in preserving diplomatic momentum during periods when official talks stagnate or remain fragile, thereby sustaining conversation and nurturing pathways for prospective political breakthroughs.

The participation of non-governmental actors bolsters the legitimacy of peace efforts at the community level, since these entities integrate local narratives and galvanise constituencies around initiatives for lasting peace. Nevertheless, Track Two diplomacy must also face specific constraints. Lacking state authority, non-governmental participants often struggle to impose resolutions and to monitor compliance. Furthermore, the array of viewpoints that characterises Track Two roundtables can introduce negotiation complexity and internal dissent, thereby requiring skilled facilitation and mediation. Yet, these very diversities also enrich the deliberative process. Thus, while Track Two diplomacy confronts difficulties, its contribution remains indispensable. Non-governmental actors go beyond supplementary involvement; they ignite broader societal transformation and exemplify people-centred diplomacy that is critical for embedding lasting peace within societies emerging from conflict.

Roadmaps for Long-Term Stability: Designing Sustainable Peace Strategies

Attaining long-term stability against the current geopolitical backdrop of Syria and Lebanon demands peace strategies that are comprehensive and layered. The deep-seated historical, political, and socio-economic interdependencies behind the region's recurrent crises call for a finely calibrated roadmap that confronts conflict drivers head-on while simultaneously nurturing reconciliation and sustainable coexistence.

A foundational principle of sustainable peace strategies is the comprehensive engagement of all relevant actors. This engagement must encompass not only formal state agencies and governmental entities but also marginalised populations, civil society organisations, women's collectives, youth representatives, and other non-traditional voices that are indispensable to the social fabric. By integrating these varied viewpoints and emphasising inclusivity, peace processes foster a sense of ownership and accountability among those directly confronted by conflict, thereby establishing a peace infrastructure that is both durable and resilient. Concurrently, any credible long-term stability strategy must focus on crafting governance systems that are effective, uphold the rule of law, safeguard human rights, and afford equitable access to resources and opportunities for every individual in the region. By bolstering the capacities of local institutions and by advancing transparent, accountable governance, the strategy effectively diminishes the likelihood that resumed conflict will arise from grievances of political exclusion, economic inequity, or social injustice. Holistic peace policies must also tackle the interrelated dimensions of security sector reform and transitional justice. Cultivating trust between communities and state security forces, demilitarising conflict-prone areas, disarming non-state actors, and instituting truth-telling and reconciliation processes are not merely complementary actions; they are indispensable for the attainment of sustained stability.

An effective environment in which communities feel secure from violence and intimidation is critical for the establishment of long-lasting peace. Likewise, any strategy intended for durable peace must deliberately nurture regional cooperation and solidarity. The Syrian-Lebanese context demonstrates the necessity of cross-border remedies: the ongoing refugee crises, escalating environmental decline, and deepening economic entwining all transcend frontiers. Therefore, concerted action that spans national boundaries is non-negotiable. Collaborative economic zones, coordinated stewardship of shared natural resources, and reciprocal trade accords can cultivate collective identity and mutual reliance, progressively entrenching the peace achieved. The conception of durable peace in Syria and Lebanon must therefore embody a comprehensive, inclusive, and integrative logic, interfacing governance, protection, accountability, and regional partnership. By confronting root conflict drivers and harnessing the shared insights of heterogeneous actors, such blueprints can offer a firm foundation for a future characterised by lasting stability and prosperity.

Conclusion: Evaluating Diplomatic Efforts and Learning from Historical Missteps

The appraisal of diplomatic interventions in the shifting geopolitical terrain of Syria and Lebanon discloses a layered challenge and a spectrum of promising trajectories toward resolution.

A review of past diplomatic efforts reveals that any durable peace strategy for the Middle East must be attuned to the region's evolving socio-political realities and must weave together engagement from both near and distant powers. Roadmaps for enduring stability can be credible only if they emerge from disciplined inquiry into previous initiatives and if they confront the conflict's layered and interactive dimensions. Current diplomatic endeavours must therefore be centre-stage in the analysis so that they can benefit from the insight that uninterrupted dialogue and multilateral engagement are the lifeblood of enduring settlements. Participation must extend to sovereign states, international agencies, civil-society organisations, and the dependent or displaced communities for whom peace is both an aspiration and a necessity. Historical failures teach that any viable diplomatic architecture must calibrate itself to the lived needs and future ambitions of all groups affected, mandating the design of inclusive spaces where sceptics can be heard and where negotiation can be elevated from coercive linkage to shared ownership. Such a method not only lays the groundwork for peace but also institutionalises early-warning and conflict-resolution capacities. Diversified results from earlier interventions across the Syria-Lebanon theatres contain the corrective knowledge indispensable for refining future mediation in the dual, yet interwoven, contexts.

Successful peace initiatives highlight several key diplomatic tenets: first, confirming the legitimacy of underlying grievances; second, instituting confidence-building measures; and, finally, crafting credible incentives for collaborative behaviour. Continual negotiation forums, in turn, offer a crucible for both periodic evaluation and recalibration of conflict-resolution tactics, fostering a flexibility that is essential for lasting peace. Nevertheless, the obstacles confronting diplomacy must also be candidly acknowledged; they include divergent objectives, entrenched historical enmities, and the shifting interests of external powers. Addressing these impediments requires a decisive and coordinated involvement of regional and international actors. Multilateral frameworks—ranging from the United Nations to sub-regional entities—demonstrate that peace-building is most effective when collective leverage is exercised. Additionally, track-two initiatives that engage non-state actors and grassroots movements create supplementary corridors for dialogue and healing, thus sidestepping the limitations of sovereign negotiations. Realising the full promise of these approaches demands that the capacities and voices of all relevant stakeholders be treated as integral to the peacemaking enterprise.

A systematic appraisal of past diplomatic efforts, coupled with a candid recognition of earlier failures, reveals that any credible route to stability within the Syrian-Lebanese theatre must be integrative and reflective of the full spectrum of societal actors. Such a route requires a decisive shift away from traditional, interest-driven models of diplomacy and a renewed emphasis on human security, the principles of transitional justice, and the cultivation of social cohesion. Engagement must reach beyond ceasefire delineations to confront the multilayered dimensions of the conflict and to centre on the structural roots of instability. Only then can peace strategies be calibrated to the lived realities of the people inhabiting the region. The ultimate aspiration, therefore, is to reconfigure the dynamics of conflict so that the shared resilience and coexistence of Syrians and Lebanese citizens outlast and ultimately disrupt the incentives for fracture and violence.

14

Reconstruction Programs
Building Stability from Chaos

The Foundation of Reconstruction Initiatives

The durability of post-conflict recovery hinges on reconstruction programmes that are thoughtfully designed from their inception. The foundation of such programmes is laid through a disciplined assessment of guiding principles and through deliberate early planning that anticipates future challenges. Essential principles include an unwavering focus on the priorities articulated by the communities themselves; the cultivation of local ownership, ensuring citizens are not merely recipients but active architects of the recovery; a commitment to transparency and accountability in the management of public resources; and a deliberate long-term vision that integrates immediate rehabilitation with the aspirations of sustainable development. When these principles are woven into every stage of the initiative, they provide the structural integrity needed for recovery efforts to evolve into lasting improvement.

International Aid and Investment Strategies

The successful navigation of post-conflict recovery demands a multidimensional framework in which international aid and investment are essential, synergistic components. Once the immediate violence subsides, the United Nations, the World Bank, and a consortium of donor nations deploy financial and technical resources that are calibrated to kick-start the rebuilding process. Their assistance is not unilateral but is harmonised with local governments and civil society organisations to guarantee that funds and investments are directed to the areas of greatest need. This partnership is underpinned by donor governments coordinating their contributions through transparent mechanisms, thereby enabling a predictable flow of resources that reinforces local capacities rather than dilutes them.

International aid offers critical early support to regions affected by conflict, delivering food, temporary shelter, and urgent medical supplies that alleviate immediate suffering. Once the immediate humanitarian crisis subsides, the conversation must evolve to sustainable, long-term reconstruction. Investments in infrastructure, education, healthcare, and economic revitalisation take centre stage, transforming temporary relief into durable progress. Such a deliberate pivot to sustainable development cultivates local self-reliance and institutional resilience, turning assistance into a platform for stability and future prosperity. Financial transfers are vital, but the contribution of international experts—through training, data sharing, and institutional development—is equally crucial. Partnerships formed between international agencies, local governments, and civil society create a shared framework for strategic planning, resource allocation, and skill development. This inclusive process grants local actors a central role, enhancing ownership and accountability, and ensuring that reconstruction aligns with the nuanced realities and aspirations of affected communities. Alongside aid and expertise, foreign direct investment (FDI) injects capital that is essential for reigniting shattered economies. By safeguarding investor confidence and facilitating market entry, post-conflict countries can modernise industrial bases, adopt better technologies, and better integrate into regional and global supply chains. Such capital inflows are not only engines of immediate job creation, but also create a virtuous cycle of sustainable development, allowing local enterprises to re-establish themselves and nurturing a new generation of private-sector innovation.

This infusion of capital bolsters economic underpinnings and simultaneously nurtures public optimism and confidence, thereby indicating a promising course toward stability. Yet, vigilance is required to prevent aid dependency and to ensure that investment strategies are commensurate with local development priorities. A judicious equilibrium must be struck between external support and reverence for indigenous knowledge and customs, for this equilibrium cultivates a reconstruction process that is both inclusive and culturally attuned. Furthermore, transparent governance and robust oversight are critical to averting misappropriation or diversion of funds. When international aid and investment frameworks are intricately aligned with the authentic aspirations of impacted communities, post-conflict societies are poised to initiate a transformative process that leads, ultimately, to sustainable development and lasting stability.

Local Governing Bodies and Community Engagement

Local governing bodies and community engagement remain central to the efficacy of reconstruction efforts in post-conflict settings, occupying the critical space between national authorities and the constituencies they serve. In the Syrian and Lebanese contexts, these local institutions contend with issues of legitimacy, limited administrative capacity, and resource constraints. Nonetheless, their effectiveness can be markedly enhanced through the deliberate encouragement of community participation and inter-institutional collaboration, thereby embedding development objectives within local ownership and advancing both reconciliation and long-term sustainability.

A pivotal strategy for strengthening local governance lies in instituting transparent and participatory decision-making procedures. Such procedures must create genuine channels for diverse voices while guaranteeing that decisions rest upon the informed consent of the communities affected. Through these mechanisms, authorities cultivate trust, thereby conferring legitimacy and accountability—cornerstones of a durable political order. Concurrently, fostering grassroots initiatives and community-led enterprises allows local actors to assume primary responsibility for the reconstruction agenda. By engaging residents in the assessment of needs, the design of interventions, and the execution of measures, authorities can tap the resident population's latent capacities and local expertise. This inclusive practice not only cultivates an abiding sense of ownership and civic identity; it also yields solutions that are culturally grounded and therefore more sustainable. Beyond community-driven empowerment, local administrations must cultivate synergistic relationships with humanitarian agencies, civil society organisations, and international partners. Such collaboration enables the effective alignment of technical know-how, financial resources, and operational capacities. When coordination is rigorous, resources are pooled, successful practices are disseminated, and reconstruction initiatives are harmonised with overarching development objectives, thereby enhancing both effectiveness and efficiency.

In post-conflict contexts, tending explicitly to the unique vulnerabilities of refugees, internally displaced persons, and historically marginalised groups remains a core responsibility of local governance. Targeted programmes in livelihood generation, educational access, and social integration are vital to fostering a sense of belonging and preventing the exclusion of any subgroup from the broader recovery effort. Concurrently, community engagement must include the revitalisation of public spaces and social infrastructure, which are critical for reconstructing social cohesion and providing environments conducive to collective healing. Local governments are well-placed to oversee the rehabilitation of cultural centres, community halls, and recreational facilities, thereby creating venues for dialogue, cultural exchange, and civic participation. Such investments in space must be matched by governance structures that are reflexive and responsive to the changing contours of community needs. Mechanisms for dynamic feedback, periodic consultations, and rigorous monitoring must be embedded to continually evaluate the efficacy of reconstruction initiatives and to recalibrate approaches in light of newly surfacing challenges and opportunities. When local authorities keep a responsive ear to the community's evolving pulse, they amplify their own relevance and the overall efficacy of the recovery enterprise.

Infrastructure Rebuilding: Roads, Schools, and Hospitals

As conflict-affected areas begin to recover from extensive destruction, the re-establishment of critical infrastructure ranks first among the measures required to restore normal daily life and to put sustainable development on a viable trajectory.

Reconstruction initiatives must first focus on the renewal and strengthening of key infrastructures—roads, schools, and hospitals—that undergird the re-establishment of any functioning society. Restoring the road network is indispensable, as it enables the fluid exchange of goods, services, and people, thereby jump-starting commerce and reconnecting dispersed communities. Strategic public and international investment in upgraded, resilient transport systems guarantees the swift movement of resources and fortifies the region's long-term sustainability. Equally critical is the re-creation of the school system, which provides the scaffolding for intellectual and civic development. Rebuilt classrooms restore access to formal instruction and embody a collective aspiration for brighter tomorrows; they impart the routines and frameworks that confer a sense of normalcy and security in the wake of upheaval. Alongside these, the re-establishment of hospitals and clinics must be viewed as an imperative—not a luxury—for protecting public health and treating both conflict-related injuries and chronic conditions that may otherwise fester in the absence of care. Quality health infrastructure is essential not only for immediate survival but for the gradual accumulation of human capital. Collectively, these undertakings reinforce the social compact; by restoring access to indispensable services, they rebuild local trust, encourage individuals to come back, and signal to potential investors that the region is on a progressive recovery path.

Reconstructing infrastructure following conflict presents a complex set of interdependencies and requires rigorous attention to logistics, funding, and multilevel collaboration. The seamless interaction of government agencies, humanitarian actors, and private investors is a prerequisite for the effective design and long-term viability of infrastructure projects. Transparent procurement practices, strict adherence to ethical guidelines, and robust oversight are indispensable for guarding against corruption and misappropriation of funds. When investments are persistently and judiciously directed towards roads, schools, and healthcare facilities, communities emerging from conflict can establish the initial pillars of durable stability, equitable growth, and adaptive capacity, thereby creating a climate that is amenable to comprehensive social advancement and long-term, sustainable development.

Economic Revitalisation: Boosting the Local Economy

The recovery of economies in post-conflict regions represents an ambitious yet non-negotiable step toward viable and durable peace. Economic recovery, in this context, is understood as a multidimensional undertaking that aims to reactivate local production, stimulate job creation, and cultivate a culture of entrepreneurship. A particularly effective strategy for invigorating the regional economy is the expansion of microcredit schemes and small loan programmes that target both nascent and established enterprises. By coupling financial resources with training and mentorship, such schemes equip individuals with the means and the skills to reconstruct their enterprises, thereby driving the wider process of communal economic revitalisation.

Nurturing a supportive environment for foreign direct investment (FDI) can channel essential capital into the region, energising the establishment of new sectors and the creation of sustainable employment. Formulating strategic alliances with international institutions, neighbouring nations, and multinational corporations can amplify this momentum by harnessing shared expertise, financial resources, and advanced technologies. In parallel, the introduction of vocational training initiatives tailored to the region's evolving industrial landscape can furnish the labour pool with the precise competencies demanded by emerging markets. Seamless trade promotion and enhanced market connectivity are equally crucial, weaving local enterprises into broader regional and global supply chains, expanding export avenues, and encouraging diversification of the economy. By fortifying market linkages and dismantling trade impediments, these endeavours can elevate the robustness and competitive edge of domestic markets. Nonetheless, overcoming economic constraints requires a concurrent focus on foundational obstacles, including the complexities of land tenure, insecure property rights, and outdated regulatory environments. Rationalising administrative processes, guaranteeing secure property ownership, and embedding transparent governance are indispensable for cultivating a climate that invites investment and for constructing the bedrock of durable economic prosperity. In the final analysis, effective economic revitalisation embodies the accomplishment of a broader humanitarian mission—reviving optimism, empowering local communities, and securing the sustained stability essential to post-conflict reconstruction.

Security Measures: Establishing Safe Zones

In the wake of conflict and widespread destruction, the creation of safe zones is crucial for both the recovery process and the restoration of public confidence. These zones become focal points for rehabilitation, laying the groundwork needed for enduring order. The security measures governing safe zones must be multilayered, protecting both bodily safety and mental reassurance. The participation of local authorities and international partners is vital in designing and executing comprehensive security plans. Core elements of these measures include stationing trained law enforcement units to sustain public order and the rule of law. This process necessitates the recruitment and ongoing education of indigenous police, in concert with international peacekeepers, to mount a joint and proportional counter to any signs of insecurity. The creation of checkpoints and managed entry and exit points further restricts unauthorised ingress, deterring any threatening groups from penetrating the zones' confines. Yet physical containment is only half the task; equally crucial is the rehabilitation of ordinary routines and the reconstruction of interpersonal trust throughout the community.

To achieve a lasting and sustainable foundation for safe zones, it is essential that programmes designed to strengthen social cohesion and build trust across diverse ethnic and religious communities are pursued with equal determination to security measures. Initiatives such as neighbourhood-level policing, impartial mediatory structures, and persistent advocacy for human rights create an environment that is both physically secure and socially welcoming. Complementing these efforts, the systematic provision of health clinics, schools, and basic infrastructure within the safe zones addresses both humanitarian imperatives and the developmental conditions necessary for recovery. Access to such crucial services alleviates immediate suffering and simultaneously fosters the conditions that reinvigorate local economies and facilitate the safe return and reintegration of displaced persons. Equally important are vocational training programmes and job creation schemes, which offer displaced and host community members a renewed sense of agency, thereby countering susceptibility to extremist, nihilistic influences. Moreover, the protection and maintenance of historical and cultural landmarks serve both to safeguard the tangible heritage that anchors collective identity and to foster psychological healing and communal pride. These landmarks are, for the residents, irreplaceable touchstones of memory and belonging. Ultimately, the effective deployment and longevity of safe zones rest upon the coordinated, persistent engagement of diverse actors, seamlessly weaving together security guarantees, social healing, and economic revitalisation.

This integrated strategy fosters resilience and hope within impacted communities, forging a solid foundation for enduring reconstruction and peacebuilding in the face of continuing adversity.

Cultural Heritage Preservation: Protecting Historical Assets

Protecting cultural heritage in periods of conflict is essential for maintaining a nation's collective memory and identity. Following periods of violence, historical sites and collections face heightened threats from destruction, looting, and the illicit antiquities market. Nevertheless, decisive and well-coordinated actions can limit these dangers and ensure that a society's heritage survives. Preservation in post-conflict settings requires a holistic agenda that unites local populations, government authorities, international agencies, and specialised practitioners. Initial steps include systematic documentation and evaluation of sites, objects, and living traditions in order to ascertain damage and devise precise recovery interventions. This phase depends on the mobilisation of archaeologists, conservators, and cultural heritage experts who carefully record and assess vulnerable resources. Complementing this, the creation of protective frameworks—ranging from designated buffer zones and routine security patrolling to contemporary surveillance technologies—reduces the likelihood of vandalism and illicit excavation at critical heritage locations.

Raising awareness and promoting education on the significance of cultural heritage cultivates a collective sense of ownership that actively deters theft and destruction. Collaborative initiatives among neighbouring states and international organisations create vital channels for cross-border coordination and information exchange, weakening the networks that facilitate the smuggling of antiquities. Embedding cultural heritage preservation within larger reconstruction programmes highlights its inseparable relationship to social and economic revitalisation. The careful restoration of historic sites and the active promotion of heritage tourism generate jobs, energise local markets, and knit a sense of pride and social cohesion among residents. Yet, numerous obstacles remain: limited financial resources, a shortage of specialised skills, and political volatility threaten the continuity of these efforts. Meeting these challenges requires unwavering commitment from state actors, philanthropic foundations, and international donor agencies to ensure that financial and technical resources are sustained over the long term. Further, governance must be characterised by transparency and probity to guard against corruption and the diversion of funds intended for heritage initiatives. Documented case studies of successful preservation efforts provide critical lessons and adaptable strategies that can be modified to suit a multitude of cultural contexts.

Ultimately, safeguarding historical assets serves as a powerful affirmation of a nation's resilience, identity, and collective memory in the midst of conflict and upheaval.

Challenges in Implementation: Transparency and Corruption

Transparency and accountability rank among the most vital prerequisites for the effective execution of reconstruction programmes. Yet corruption can disrupt these prerequisites, generating inefficiencies and misappropriation of resources. In post-conflict environments, notably Syria and Lebanon, the urgency for rapid reconstruction frequently collides with long-standing systemic weaknesses, magnifying the corruption challenge. A central obstacle is the absence of transparent procurement procedures. In the absence of effective oversight, contracts for reconstruction may be granted on the basis of personal connections or bribery, inflating costs and compromising workmanship. Furthermore, the lack of coherent regulations and enforcement mechanisms fosters atmospheres ripe for embezzlement and kickbacks, siphoning essential funds from their designated purposes. The tangled nexus of political and business interests in the region compounds these transparency deficits. The entrenchment of powerful stakeholders can throttle fair competition, inviting monopolistic conduct that inhibits both innovation and sustainable economic growth.

When the interests of elite actors coalesce around reconstruction assistance, reconstruction gains tend to be unevenly allocated, further entrenching existing social divisions and rendering entire neighbourhoods and social groups peripheral to the recovery process. The corrosive effects of corruption are felt not only in the waste and diversion of scarce resources but in the cumulative erosion of state legitimacy; once citizens perceive that officials are siphoning reconstruction funds, the social contract frays, and public trust in the institutions charged with recovery collapses. The resultant distrust is exacerbated by opaque bidding processes, missing audit trails, and the absence of responsive legal frameworks, spurring resentment, protests, and sometimes violent sabotage of the very infrastructures meant to restore livelihoods. The deterrent effect stretches beyond citizens, extending to the international community—donors and foreign investors recoil from environments where project viability is compromised by graft, diverting capital to lower-risk jurisdictions. A durable response to these interconnected hazards demands, first, the design and implementation of layered preventive infrastructures: legal statutes that criminalise procurement fraud, independent commissions endowed with prosecutorial autonomy, and public registries that permit civil society to track every Euro and dollar in reconstruction financing. Complementary to legal architectures is a normative shift: accountability must migrate from theory into practice, constraining politicians, procurement officers, construction firms, and international contractors alike. Finally, systemic corruption can only be dismantled in cooperative frameworks; donor countries and multilateral institutions must synchronise their due diligence with host governments, sharing investigative resources, forensic auditing teams, and anonymised corruption-risk indices, thereby extending best practices refined in earlier emergencies and embedding a culture of probity that can outlast the immediate donor cycle.

Further engagement with local civil society networks and the empowerment of citizen monitoring coalitions strengthen transparency by enabling persistent collective oversight and the timely reporting of irregularities. Addressing the interlinked challenges of transparency and corruption in post-conflict reconstruction demands resolute commitment from national authorities and the broader international community. By emphasising principled governance, strict observance of the rule of law, and the meaningful inclusion of affected populations, the transition from disorder to sustainable stability can decisively transcend the obstacles posed by corruption and opacity.

Empirical Illustrations: Successful Reconstruction Efforts

After violence and ruin, the task of reconstruction is staggeringly complicated, but several documented initiatives reveal how, through strategic choice and coordinated purpose, affected societies have turned crises into opportunities. Critical inside these narratives are the experiences of Syria and Lebanon, each presenting constants of hardship yet yielding lessons of resilience. In Syria, the post-Aleppo landscape illustrates how empowered local councils, international humanitarian partnerships, and organised neighbourhood collectives galvanised recovery. Their synchronous efforts focused on the systematic restoration of public utilities, educational centres, and health facilities, collectively re-establishing the institutional and social pillars needed to persuade displaced families to return and to signal that normal life might, at last, re-establish itself.

The execution of tailored economic revitalisation initiatives designed to rejuvenate local enterprises and sectors has been pivotal in advancing enduring development and in generating viable livelihoods for local populations. A compelling example of this principle in practice is the rehabilitation of Beirut, Lebanon, in the wake of political fragmentation and severe economic dislocation. By orchestrating coordinated action among state agencies, civil society organisations, and private sector partners, the city has experienced an impressive renewal, one that deliberately protects its cultural patrimony while upgrading essential civic infrastructure. Simultaneously, the meticulous restoration of the city's historic landmarks and architectural icons has enhanced both its visual character and its capacity to attract cultural tourism, thereby furthering civic renewal. These narratives highlight the necessity of involving local constituencies and of positioning them as primary agents in the rebuilding process. Genuine community participation has been decisive in aligning the renovated settings with the lived realities and long-term aspirations of those who endure the immediate consequences of conflict. Furthermore, the sustained security arrangements that protect these vulnerable environments from renewed threats are equally critical to the enduring safety and welfare of the inhabitants.

Through the study of these illustrative cases, policymakers, humanitarian agencies, and all those engaged in the long-term rebuilding of post-conflict societies can distil critical insights and foundational practices that will shape forthcoming recovery initiatives. The featured recoveries illuminate the measurable achievements possible when resilience, collective commitment, and strategic collaboration converge in the aftermath of violence. They affirm that the ruins of war can, with deliberate effort, become the substratum for reconstruction that is not only visible but is also enduring.

Future Outlook: Sustaining Reconstructed Stability

The enduring viability of any reconstruction programme hangs on its capacity to safeguard the stability it creates. When communities begin to repair structures and restore livelihoods, attention must immediately turn to a coordinated framework that consolidates achievements and obviates a relapse into violence. Sustaining the stability generated by successful recovery operations will therefore require integrated interventions that simultaneously address governance, economic development, security, and the strengthening of social cohesion. Institutions are the fulcrum of this effort; establishing governmental frameworks that are both functional and representative is vital to the long-term maintenance of peace. Transparency, legal accountability, and the empowerment of sub-national authorities are not merely recommended practices; they are the procedural backbone without which the temporary truce of reconstruction is unlikely to crystallise into a permanent peace.

In addition, collaboration with a wide range of stakeholders to craft and enact policies that tackle root grievances while advancing social justice will be essential for establishing an atmosphere conducive to enduring peace. On the economic front, durable stability hinges on revitalising the local economy and generating viable employment and growth opportunities. This may require the prudent channelling of international assistance and investment into priority sectors, the encouragement of entrepreneurial ventures, and the cultivation of regional trade networks. Complementary efforts to fortify financial architectures, widen access to credit, and deliver vocational education will help rejuvenate the economy, anchoring the achievements of reconstruction. Security, too, plays a decisive role in shielding recovered stability. Designing comprehensive security structures, disarming former combatants, and ensuring the dignified and secure repatriation of displaced communities must remain priority objectives in the post-conflict period. Ongoing partnership with international bodies and neighbouring states to monitor prospective threats and enforce deterrence will be indispensable to thwarting the relapse into violence. Finally, social cohesion and reconciliation must be regarded as the bedrock of sustainable stability in post-war landscapes. Valuing diversity, nurturing cross-community dialogue, and addressing the lingering psychological and emotional fallout of violence remain indispensable to reknitting the social fabric.

Educational initiatives centred on promoting tolerance, alongside community-driven truth and reconciliation programmes, are integral to forging trust and reducing the likelihood of renewed violence. Ensuring that the newly established stability endures requires strategies that exceed short-term recovery and embrace a sustained, long-range perspective. Such strategies must be underpinned by unwavering dedication, inclusive engagement of all relevant actors, and flexible approaches capable of adjusting to the multifaceted obstacles and unpredictable dynamics that define post-conflict periods. By prioritising the construction of resilient institutions, stimulating economic recovery, guaranteeing public safety, and nurturing social integration, societies leaving armed conflict can construct a credible vision of a future marked by lasting peace and progressive development.

15
Barriers to Progress
The Constraints of Change

Political Fragmentation and Factionalism

Political fragmentation and factionalism obstruct coherent governance across both Syria and Lebanon. In each case, multilayered political allegiances and rivalries prevent the adoption and execution of systemically sound policies. Syria's prolonged experience of autocratic rule under the Assad dynasty has hardened political divides. The Ba'ath Party preserves formal monopolisation of power, yet a spectrum of opposition forces—ranging across secular, leftist, and Islamist orientations—confront the regime with divergent visions. The resulting fragmentation has prolonged the civil war, confounding initiatives that seek a durable political settlement and orderly reconstruction. In Lebanon, the consociational model, ostensibly designed to balance sectarian communities, has solidified factional dominance. The distribution of state offices along sectarian lines nurtures a system of political patronage, institutionalising clientelism and barricading the rise of cohesive national referenda. Competing priorities among factional leaders, therefore, regularly overwhelm the procedural instruments of decision-making, fostering both policy paralysis and recurrent cycles of unrest. Foreign engagement compounds these internal fractures; external actors—motivated by geostrategic calculations—manipulate local divisions, thereby attenuating the possibility of externally mediated consensus. The cumulative effect of these embedded fractures is a political milieu in which the attainment of collective governance remains remote.

A prioritisation of sectarian or partisan ambitions over the common good erodes the foundations for durable reform. Overcoming these obstacles requires a multidimensional strategy that dismantles entrenched polarities and nurtures broadly representative political frameworks. Reducing sectarian factionalism and achieving greater political solidarity will depend on sustained diplomatic initiatives, open and accountable discourse, and a steadfast dedication to a unified and stable nation. Without deliberately redirecting energy away from factional rivalry, the chances that either Syria or Lebanon can attain enduring governance and measurable progress will remain severely limited.

Economic Weaknesses and Foreign Debt

The region's economic architecture is burdened by fragilities that obstruct sustained advancement. Prolonged deficiencies in fiscal discipline, budgetary oversight, and balance-of-payments equilibrium have generated a landscape of acute vulnerability. In Lebanon, the persistent elevation of foreign liabilities has produced a debt-to-GDP ratio that ranks among the most critical internationally. This escalating encumbrance has circumscribed the state's latitude to finance vital public goods and upgrade dilapidated infrastructure, thereby widening social inequities and reinforcing a recurring pattern of financial instability.

Above all, the dependence on outside financing has tethered the country to the ebb and flow of the global capital markets, exposing it to sudden changes in investor sentiment and deepening its vulnerability to global shocks and recessions. Syria, in yet another layer of economic distress, is grappling with the heavy legacy of chronic conflict and the persistent weight of international sanctions. The costs of reconstruction stretch far beyond fiscal budgets, encountering dire shortages of capital and severe damage to essential infrastructure, not to mention the irrevocable depletion of skilled and educated personnel. The conflict has thus compressed the nation's productive potential and amplified treasury volatility, obstructing the path to any sustained economic revival. Political volatility, entrenched corruption, and weak transparency have compounded the challenges in both countries, retarding confidence and new capital inflows. Whenever reform agendas have been drafted, they have invariably collided with entrenched interests, spawning yet another layer of obstruction. Unmonitored capital inflows, the proliferation of money-laundering schemes, and persistent illicit financial corridors further erode the stability of the economic landscape. To reverse this legacy of fragility, remedial action must be both deep and coherent, mandating fiscal discipline, structural position shifts, and the establishment of governance frameworks that enhance accountability and predictability.

Policies focused on bolstering domestic revenue generation, refining public financial governance, and instituting resilient and sustainable fiscal frameworks are critical for offsetting the deleterious effects of external debt and for fortifying the overall economic fabric. Equally, cultivating a private-sector-friendly climate, advancing economic diversification, and emphasising job generation rank among the non-negotiable pillars of a credible and sustainable recovery strategy. The active partnership of international financial institutions and donor nations remains instrumental in delivering the technical and financial resources necessary for macroeconomic stabilisation and the phased reconstruction of the region.

Security Concerns and Persistent Conflict

The futures of Syria and Lebanon remain inextricably linked, yet they continue to be beset by enduring security challenges and active conflict, which systematically compromise both stability and developmental prospects. The civil war in Syria has diffused instability beyond its borders, exacerbating pre-existing tensions in Lebanon and generating a new constellation of vulnerabilities. The large-scale arrival of Syrian refugees has strained public services and infrastructure, amplifying security risks and social polarisation. Concurrently, the enduring presence of rival armed formations and the unchecked circulation of illicit weaponry have convoluted the security environment, threatening civilian safety and eroding the institutional capacity of the Lebanese state.

The fragile sectarian equilibrium within Lebanon persists under strain as historical resentments and sharp political divides merge with pervasive security vulnerabilities. The risk to public order extends beyond domestic actors; external geopolitical dynamics have decisively shaped the region's security fabric. The entanglement of state and non-state sponsors has recurrently revitalised confrontations and obstructed the slow, uneven path to durable peace. The prevalence of proxy intervention and geopolitical manoeuvring has solidified sectarian rifts and stymied the resolution of key disputes, overshadowing any immediate prospects for a coherent, collective security architecture. These layered insecurities have radiated outward, disrupting social cohesion and stalling sustained developmental and reconciliatory efforts. Humanitarian actors report soaring demands for assistance, while public agencies, strained and under scrutiny, struggle to deliver basic services in a patchwork of shifting, militarised zones. Laying durable, peace-oriented foundations will therefore require strategies that engage political, social, and economic undercurrents in a coordinated, persistent manner. Systematic disarmament of non-state militias, advancement of accountable, inclusive governance, and the cultivation of interstate, region-wide collaboration must converge. Additionally, the cultivation of sustained, multifaceted international backing for peace building programmes will remain crucial to lessening the security interdependencies binding Syria and Lebanon.

Institutional Corruption and Governance Issues

No less critical is the pervasive affliction of institutional corruption and governance deficit, which alike encroach upon the political economies of both Syria and Lebanon.

The widespread corruption embedded within these state institutions has decisively eroded public confidence, magnifying structural inefficiencies that obstruct the delivery of essential services and entrench social and economic inequities. The Corruption Perceptions Index, published by Transparency International, has repeatedly classified Syria and Lebanon among the nations most afflicted by corruption, thus intensifying the already acute challenges of governance. Malfeasance has infiltrated every tier of administration, manifesting in bureaucratic obstruction, nepotistic hiring, opaque procurement, and the misappropriation of public resources. The virtual absence of oversight mechanisms has permitted these practices to proliferate, diminishing the perceived legitimacy of state institutions and stoking popular grievances. Simultaneously, the politicisation of strategic appointments and the abandonment of meritocratic hiring criteria have eroded the professionalism and integrity of public offices, further entrenching institutional corruption. Compounding these deficiencies, both countries have witnessed policy-making processes that lack transparency and efficacy, frequently dominated by a centralised decision-making elite that excludes diverse constituencies and reinforces authoritative governance. Such concentration of authority has stifled meaningful civic engagement and consolidated elite monopolies, thereby obstructing the emergence of inclusive and equitable governance structures.

The fragility of the rule of law and the compromised independence of the judiciary have deepened the difficulties facing these states in confronting pervasive corruption and in championing democratic values, thereby creating a persistent climate in which the powerful and well-connected can act without fear of sanction. The continuing shadow of past authoritarian rule, coupled with the entrenched presence of security forces in political life, has inhibited the development of administrations that are both accountable and capable of responding to citizens, perpetuating a pervasive atmosphere of intimidation that suppresses dissent and limits civil society mobilisation. Such systemic failures have corroded public trust in governmental institutions, widening social rifts and undermining the conditions necessary for long-term security and sustainable development. Effective countering of institutional corruption and governance deficits requires a coordinated strategy that deepens transparency, fortifies mechanisms of accountability, and restores the integrity of the rule of law. Priority reforms must include the depoliticisation of the civil service, the adoption of meritocratic hiring standards, and the creation of autonomous anti-corruption agencies endowed with broad investigative authority. Simultaneously, the promotion of civic participation, the safeguarding of free expression, and the reinforcement of judicial independence are indispensable for embedding a durable culture of accountability and for nurturing governance that is genuinely participatory.

Understanding how institutional corruption, governance failures, and citizens' well-being reinforce each other compels us to pursue integrated reforms that foster institutions capable of being both resilient and accountable, serving the interests of the entire population.

External Influences and Geopolitical Pressures

External actors and geopolitical calculations are decisive in the Syrian-Lebanese sub-system. The competition among global and regional powers has generated an intricately connected environment that renders both stability and development contingent upon multiple transnational vectors. Iran remains a principal external actor; it has deepened military and political integration with Hezbollah while providing a lifeline to the Assad state, a policy that intensifies sectarian polarisation and deepens Iran's confrontation with Israel and Saudi Arabia. Russia's military engagement has recalibrated the internal balance, empowering the Assad military, yet it has also complicated the search for political compromise. U.S. interests have further complicated the calculus, where support for Syrian Kurdish forces and the enduring alliance with Israel are conceived as measures to constrain Iran, yet risk entrenching divisions and permitting the persistence of non-state actors. Each actor's calculations are therefore interlaced, limiting the prospects for a cohesive trajectory toward stability in both Syria and Lebanon.

The continued engagement of these powerful external actors has entrenched cycles of proxy conflict and military escalation, obstructing any movement toward enduring, comprehensive solutions. The overlapping strategic competitions among them affect every facet of domestic governance and conflict settlement, inhibiting local actors' autonomy and postponing any prospect of durable peace. Within this environment, the escalating rivalry between Saudi Arabia and Iran—projected through their respective proxies in Lebanon and Syria—has deepened sectarian polarisation, fortified political fragmentation, and scarred the political economy of the Levant. Their divergent and mutually exclusive regional imperatives, aggravated by aspirations for hegemonic dominance, have further taxed an already unstable strategic context. The repercussions of external intervention and geopolitical contestation are not confined to military escalation; they radiate into economic and social spheres. Competing efforts to secure strategic energy reservoirs—with both states seeking enduring control of oil and gas deposits—have aggravated economic fragility and widened the spatial and sectoral holes in regional sub-systems, inhibiting coherent pathways for sustainable development. Simultaneously, the flow of global humanitarian and financial assistance—often conditioned by the competing interests of donor states—has generated disjointed and uneven impacts on civil institutions and local governance, the results of which complicate longer-term prospects for social cohesion and resilience. The analytical challenge, therefore, lies in disentangling these overlapping layers of external engagement to identify leverage points for policies that could align diverse global interests with the local imperatives of peace and development.

Social Divisions and Sectarian Tensions

Social divisions and sectarian tensions continue to underpin the fraught situation and demand urgent attention. These issues between Syria and Lebanon, concealed under the surface of their relations, are what both countries confront: their intertwined histories, cultural traditions, surface, and chronic internal divides that consistently amplify regional volatility. Lebanon's precarious sectarian political architecture, accommodating Maronite, Sunni, Shia, and Druze constituencies, frequently collapses into deadlock, breeding both overt confrontation and latent animosities. Across the border, the Assad regime's systematic repression and its calculated patronage of the Alawite minority have alienated the Sunni majority and other excluded groups, entrenching similarly harmful antagonisms. These social divisions, once confined to domestic arenas, have, over the decades, exported instability, prompting cross-border conflicts and massive population movements. The older Sunni–Shia confrontation, now reinforced by the ambitions of Tehran and Riyadh, has transformed sectarian identity into a calculative instrument of regional rivalry, prolonging cycles of violence and mistrust. Compounding this is a matrix of economic marginalisation and uneven development, wherein disparities in wealth and public goods are mapped onto sectarian or ethnic identity. As constituent groups compete for scarce resources and equitable political voice, accusations of systematic injustice burgeon, inhibiting any shared, forward-looking national project.

Efforts to close these divides and soothe sectarian discord confront powerful obstacles, since entrenched elites and foreign meddling frequently deepen, rather than lessen, the cracks along communal fault lines. Yet, for Syria and Lebanon, the recognition of shared futures and mutual vulnerability offers a hopeful path to partitioned partitions remaining a prerequisite for meaningful inclusion and enduring stability.

Infrastructural Challenges and Development Gaps

Infrastructure undergirds national life, enabling economic flourishing, social integration, and cumulative development. In Syria and Lebanon, dilapidated networks present enduring impediments to durable order and prosperity. Years of conflict have laid waste to main arteries, vital bridges, power stations, and telecommunication grids, necessitating the extent of the devastation that forestalls coordinated reconstruction, compounding already uneven paths of advance. In parallel, haphazard urban development and a shortage of affordable housing burden cities and towns, curtailing sustainable expansion and quality of life. Continuing dilapidation of schools, clinics, and public services prolongs institutional fragmentation, limiting the prospects for recovery. Citizens, therefore, endure daily friction, from sporadic electricity to congested travel and inadequate services, deepening popular frustration and eroding future trust.

Disparities in access to essential services continuously reinforce inequalities among regions and demographic groups, solidifying socio-economic divides across both Syria and Lebanon. Coupled with clear developmental rifts between urban centres and rural hinterlands, this reality highlights the urgent requirement for broad and deep infrastructural renewal. Bridging these divides will depend on significant and sustained capital investment, demanding disciplined resource distribution, forward-looking planning, and coordinated strategic partnerships. Effective narrowing of the development chasm requires layered, overlapping interventions that unite transport corridors, energy grids, digital communications, and public utilities into a coherent framework. The resilience of this framework rests on integrating sustainable design, leveraging emergent technologies, and embedding systematic maintenance into project design. In parallel, public-private partnerships, bolstered by international advisory and financial support, represent critical avenues for overcoming persistent structural barriers. Together, these efforts can progressively transform infrastructural capacity and interconnectivity, triggering broad, positive reverberations across local economies, societies, and political institutions. The systematic resolution of these infrastructural challenges thus remains a precondition for advancing sustainable development, reinforcing societal resilience, ensuring inclusivity, and cultivating a shared and prosperous future for both states.

Humanitarian Needs and International Dependence

The humanitarian situation in Syria and Lebanon has evolved into a multi-layered crisis whose drivers and impacts routinely transcend national borders, raising considerable concerns for regional stability and international humanitarian architecture.

Both states have been severely impacted by the enduring conflict in Syria, resulting in a dramatic rise in refugee and internally displaced populations that now number in the millions. The sudden demographic shift has overwhelmed transport networks, housing, and public health systems, generating a humanitarian situation that, by its very breadth and depth, now threatens stability across the Levant. The dimensions now surpass what any single government can absorb, and therefore, the afflicted societies find themselves increasingly dependent on multilateral assistance and humanitarian corridors. The spectrum of exigencies is expansive, encompassing the immediate need for safe shelter, food supplies, psychiatric and medical care, educational continuity, and protective safeguards for women, elderly persons, and unaccompanied minors. In light of the scale, UN agencies, international NGOs, and a coalition of donor capitals have mobilised simultaneously to deliver lifesaving aid and to conceive resilience-based programming. Still, the reliance on external financing raises pressing questions about durability: recurrent financing shortfalls trigger operational pauses that jeopardise the gradual shift to community-driven recovery. It is crucial to balance emergency relief with incremental, transparent efforts to restore governance and livelihood systems, ensuring the sustainability of aid and preserving the continuity of care and preventing the gradual shift to community-driven recovery. Compounding this, aid has occasionally been harnessed as a diplomatic leverage point, and the fragmentation of security governance on the ground has rendered needs assessments and logistical movements liable to sudden obstruction. These layered concerns insist on a refined approach that balances emergency relief with incremental, transparent efforts to restore governance and livelihood systems.

The protracted nature of the crisis has steadily eroded local capacities and deepened the vulnerability of host communities, thereby intensifying competition for already scarce resources. In this setting, fostering self-reliance and enabling affected populations to engage meaningfully in their recovery becomes non-negotiable. It is crucial to empower affected populations and reduce chronic dependence on outside aid. Aspects of every humanitarian strategy. Additionally, the interdependence of humanitarian needs with economic, social, and security dimensions necessitates a comprehensive and integrated response. Although international assistance remains vital for immediate lifesaving interventions, a parallel and sustained investment in local capacity, infrastructure, and livelihood opportunities is essential for fostering resilience and reducing chronic dependence on outside aid. Placing the dignity and agency of affected communities at the centre of the response is critical to offsetting the adverse effects of prolonged humanitarian assistance and to forging durable pathways toward recovery and reconstruction. Ultimately, the challenge of managing humanitarian needs and international dependency requires a sophisticated recognition of interlocking challenges and a persistent commitment to collaborative, rights-based, and people-centred interventions.

Legal and Constitutional Hurdles

The legal and constitutional context in Syria and Lebanon imposes critical barriers to reform and sustainable progress in both countries.

In each country, prevailing statutes and constitutional frameworks have repeatedly been wielded by ruling elites to solidify their dominance and muzzle opposition. The absence of an independent and effective judiciary has intensified a climate of impunity surrounding individuals in high political and security offices, stalling any prospects for sincere legal and constitutional advancement. In Lebanon, divergences among sectarian-based legal systems further hinder the pursuit of an integrated legal order that acknowledges the rights of all citizens. The resultant tangle of legal variables constitutes a significant obstacle to the adoption of substantive reform. In tandem, constitutional clauses in both states have, over time, reinforced the concentration of authority within designated political or sectarian blocs, precluding genuinely inclusive governance and equitable representation. The difficulty of reforming these foundational statutes is compounded by an unresolved debate over the character of the state and the corresponding rights and obligations of its populace. Additionally, the persistent shadow of authoritarian governance in Syria, coupled with the fragile sectarian equilibrium in Lebanon, has fortified the legal and constitutional hurdles that stand in the way of reform.

The continuing imposition of emergency laws in Syria alongside the unfinished legacy of the Taif Agreement in Lebanon exemplifies the enduring character of these impediments; both phenomena continue to sculpt the political terrain while preventing the advent of genuine transformation. Compounding these legacies, the interplay of foreign actors and the volatility of regional politics imposes additional complications on the legal and constitutional domains. Interventions by external powers have, on occasion, exacerbated pre-existing fissures, producing cycles of institutional stagnation and fortifying the very barriers reform efforts seek to dismantle. Any viable roadmap to progressive change, therefore, must confront these legal and constitutional impediments in their totality—engaging, in parallel, the reform of specific laws and constitutional clauses, the fortification of judicial independence, the establishment of transitional justice frameworks, and the creation of inclusive, deliberative constitutional dialogue. Surmounting these challenges requires strategies that faithfully account for local particularities while striving to cultivate a legal environment capable of sustaining equality, justice, and the fulfilment of the most fundamental human rights for every citizen.

Cultural Reticence and Resistance to Reform

Cultural reticence and resistance to reform pose formidable barriers to achieving enduring change across the region.

The social fabric of Syria and Lebanon is so thickly woven with inherited values and practices that reform proposals frequently meet with muted rejection. Many citizens interpret attempts to alter business regulation, constituency boundaries, or personal-status law as efforts to dilute the inherited systems of communal identity and patronage that confer certainty and order. Chief among these inherited values is the allegiance to hierarchy, be it familial, sectarian, or tribal, which is ritually reinforced within parochial schools, unofficial courts, and publicly sanctioned commemorations. Any ambitious programme that seeks to redress sectarian inequality is thus experienced as a potential fracturing of the loyalties that grant both status and protection to the incumbents of these customary tiers. Parallel to this hierarchy is the insistence that respectable women remain within circumscribed public spaces, a principle so deeply embedded that its subversion is frequently interpreted as a repudiation of local dignity. Consequently, proposals for quota-based parliamentary inclusion, for example, are frequently dismissed as externally funded provocations instead of constitutionally sanctioned abstentions from masculine monopoly. Furthermore, the reflexive protection of boundaries extends to territorial claims and dispute resolution, where communal memory and customary law are summoned to negate the legitimacy of unfamiliar negotiation techniques—even, or especially, when those techniques are prescribed by international law. This blend of autobiography and inter-generational obligation reinforces a communal threshold of tolerable reform, beyond which innovations are classified as alien intrusions and hence repudiated.

Proposed reforms frequently face scepticism and opposition from groups that regard them as threats to long-held customs and identity. To counter this cultural hesitation, the strategy must prioritise engagement with local leaders, faith authorities, and cultural figures who can promote dialogue, neutralise misunderstandings, and embed reform in indigenous narratives and ethical frameworks. Such efforts are complicated, however, by the residue of external meddling, geopolitical rivalries, and historical resentments that continue to shape the regional sociopolitical environment. Proxy contests and foreign meddling have fostered antagonistic frames of reference that deepen cultural reluctance, entrenching divisions and obstructing meaningful advancement. The overlapping legacies of history, geopolitics, and identity formation magnify the difficulty of dissolving cultural resistance as a structural hindrance to progress. Confronting these layered obstacles demands a finely calibrated grasp of local realities, uninterrupted dialogue, and cooperative initiatives that will rebalance power structures and prevailing social norms in a manner congruent with the shared ambition for inclusive, just, and future-oriented societies.

16

Three Scenarios for the Future

Predicting Regional Outcomes

Future Scenarios

We reach a decisive moment in the inquiry, confronting the intricate contingencies marking the prospective evolution of the region. By systematically interrogating the prevailing sociopolitical arrangements, the intricate webs of the economy, and the sedimented legacies of the past, we construct a referential frame for projecting future trajectories. A layered assessment of current political currents and shifting geopolitical alignments allows us to delineate selections of plausible pathways. Essential to this inquiry is the recognition of the mutual entanglement of local and external agents, each wielding varying degrees of leverage. Interdisciplinary lenses, inclusive of technological studies and environmental sociology, will be brought to bear, permitting us to gauge the transformative pressures exerted by innovation and climate oscillations upon the regional order. Our purpose here is to foster a granular grasp of the region's multilayered fabric, thereby permitting a circumspect valuation of emergent courses. By clarifying the syntactic and diachronic interdependencies of earlier formations and present predicaments, we intend to furnish a coherence that accommodates conceivable optimistic, stasis, and adverse outcomes. In this manner, we secure the analytical ground for a rigorous and layered elucidation, ensuring that the reader possesses the requisite intellectual instruments to interpret the complex territories of forthcoming regional constellations.

Optimistic Scenario: Pathway to Stability and Reconciliation

The optimistic scenario envisages a convergence of deliberate choices that together cultivate regional stability and reconciliation, a vision that, while ambitious, is animated by the cumulative power of constructive agency. Constructing this future requires simultaneous innovation across the socio-political, economic, and diplomatic spheres, sustained by a commitment to collaboration and enlightened leadership that deliberately redirects the momentum of rivalry and disintegration. Inclusive governance is the cornerstone of this prospective order; political frameworks that deliberately discount sectarian affiliation and instead foreground the common good begin to alter the foundational social contract. Complementing this governmental reorientation, a suite of multidimensional policies is deployed to promote national unity and recognise cultural pluralism, embedding the rule of law and equal citizenship as normative templates for everyday life. Economically, the same spirit of collective endeavour galvanises coordinated revitalisation initiatives that mobilise latent regional assets and distribute gains equitably among all constituencies. Through deliberate, recurring investments in human capital, resilient infrastructure, and sustainable job creation, this scenario anticipates the gradual dissolving of structural inequities, tending instead to a shared landscape of opportunity in which the dividends of stability are both visible and widely accessible.

Similarly, the diplomatic stage may evolve into a platform for meaningful dialogue and consensus cultivation, so long as regional actors remain dedicated to addressing long-standing grievances through principled engagement and conflict-resolution instruments. Peace building architectures and intercommunal dialogue initiatives, when reinforced, become essential for closing divides and nurturing enduring trust among disparate groups. The encouraging scenario further embeds strategic partnerships with international players committed to non-interference and meaningful engagement, thereby heightening the likelihood of durable peace and security. The vision also acknowledges the transformative potential of technological innovation, particularly digital interconnectivity and renewable energy, both of which may drive inclusive development and ecological stewardship. Amid this generative context, the foundational conditions for lasting harmony and advancement are nurtured, presenting a compelling model of a future in which shared purpose overcomes division and resilience outmatches hardship.

Stagnant Scenario: The Status Quo Persistence

In the stagnation scenario, the future of the Syrian-Lebanese region is projected to replicate the present configuration, with political, societal, and economic arrangements reproducing themselves without meaningful alteration or advancement.

The situation illustrates an absence of decisive progress in confronting entrenched conflicts, sectarian divides, or the pursuit of genuine reconciliation. In this context of inertia, the overlapping layers of regional rivalries, proxy networks, and legacies of past grievances remain essentially unchanged. The consolidation of present arrangements threatens to prolong the suffering of forcibly displaced populations, obstruct meaningful development, and keep sectarian factions firmly entrenched within state structures. In Lebanon, the brittle confessional framework shows signs of entrenchment, resisting pressure for meaningful reform and contributing to re-energised sectarian rivalries and weakened state capacity. In Syria, the unresolved competition among domestic factions and rival outside powers risks reproducing cycles of violence and vengeance that deepen societal fractures. From an economic perspective, the current trajectory signals persistent vulnerability, limiting the space for coordinated recovery initiatives. Core sectors such as tourism, trade, and agriculture are unlikely to regain solid ground, impeded by persistent geopolitical volatility and domestic disruptions. Absent durable institutions and transparent governance, prospects for investor engagement dim, further complicating the formulation of credible and long-term economic policies.

Internationally, the continuation of prevailing patterns is likely to perpetuate chronic regional volatility, encumbering external actors as they confront the layered repercussions of the Syrian crisis and its spillover into Lebanon. Diplomatic impasses and ongoing geopolitical discord may frustrate the orchestration of united responses designed to restore stability and security across the theatres of conflict. In this fraught environment, civil society collectives, humanitarian agencies, and locally driven movements may yet preserve limited spaces of agency, alleviating humanitarian distress and nurturing resilience within besieged populations. Despite these marginal gains, the inertia of the present order confronts exertions for systemic change with substantial barriers, amplifying the need for rigorously critical analysis, anticipatory planning, and coordinated strategic engagement as stakeholders contend with the shifting realities of the Syrian-Lebanese theatre.

Pessimistic Scenario: Escalation of Conflict and Division

Within the intricate geopolitical architecture of the Eastern Mediterranean, a pessimistic trajectory reveals an unfolding of intensified hostilities and deepening fractures. This projection posits a further sharpening of sectarian allegiances and elite-driven power contests, amplifying the existing volatility in both Syria and Lebanon.

Deep-seated grievances rooted in history, when combined with ongoing violence, now sustain a grinding situation that darkens any realistic hope for regional order. A faltering economy, worn thin by conflict, creates a spiral of poverty, population displacement, and civilian unrest. Key goods and services, already scarce, become prizes that communities violently contest, sharpening divisions and deepening dangerous rivalries. Public infrastructure, already damaged, collapses further, while clinics and schools, barely functional, become sites of desperation that humanitarian agencies cannot adequately relieve. Surrounded by despair, extremist recruiters find eager ears among those who feel abandoned by the state and the world, spreading a radicalism that matures into terrorism that endangers the region and the far-off capitals that ignore the early warnings. External efforts, instead of unifying support, fracture into rival agendas, multiplying factions and delaying any negotiated end. As fighting expands, the number of refugees surges far beyond forecasting, placing impossible burdens on transit nations whose banks, services, and societies fracture faster than governments can adapt. The resulting backlash against newcomers, combined with eroding public order, threatens to turn a humanitarian displacement into a geopolitical disaster that destabilises entire continents.

Rising tensions between host communities and refugee

populations are widening already deep political and social rifts, complicating efforts at cohesive coexistence and undermining hopes for durable reconciliation and peace. Although humanitarian imperatives and moral arguments continue to urge open accommodation, such goodwill cannot mask the unravelling of local social contracts and the widening of grievance registers. Multilateral diplomatic mechanisms, already strained, are losing the consensus necessary for even minimal protective frameworks. If the current trajectory is not decisively reversed, the region faces a self-reinforcing cycle of insecurity, deepening humanitarian crises, and external militarised responses, each exacerbating the others and locking the populations into a chronically explosive dynamic.

Socioeconomic Indicators Influencing Future Outcomes

Socioeconomic variables constitute a decisive framework for forecasting the trajectories of both Syria and Lebanon. A systematic analysis of these variables is not merely academic; it informs the design of policies capable of steering the countries, and by extension the region, away from crisis and toward sustainable development. The critical domains of inquiry encompass real GDP per capita, labour-market participation, multidimensional poverty, the concentration of wealth, the accessibility of essential public goods, and the integrity of transport and utility networks. Each of these measures is now historically low in both states, and the cross-border effects of Syria's extended conflict—including capital flight, inflation-induced erosion of real wages, and the fragmentation of supply chains—have intensified the deterioration in Lebanon and weakened the resilience of communities hosting refugees.

Persistent displacement, shattered livelihoods, and widespread infrastructural damage have combined to generate profound economic contractions, deepening pre-existing vulnerabilities and inequalities. The demographic pressures arising from the influx of refugees have stretched public and private resources, weakening the capacity of affected communities to absorb additional economic shocks. Concurrently, the loss of skilled labour and eroded organisational knowledge has diminished productive potential, entrenching the long-term scars on recovery trajectories. Countering these interrelated obstacles demands a comprehensive strategy that prioritises deliberate investment in vocational training and education, the revival of productive sectors, and policies that ensure growth remains inclusive. Equally critical is the deliberate reconstruction of social trust and cohesion; without these, fragmented communities will undermine any recovery effort. The deliberate adoption of digital and clean technologies offers additional leverage for economic diversification and vulnerability reduction. The successful reintegration of displaced individuals into formal labour markets, coupled with the expedient restoration of transport, energy, and social infrastructure, will provide the bedrock for durable recovery. Finally, guaranteeing universal access to healthcare, education, and essential public services will address inequities at their roots and foster a more cohesive and equitable society. Viewed through a constructive lens, these demands are not intractable barriers, but rather actionable, interrelated corridors toward genuine renewal and social reconstruction.

By engaging every sector of the population and drawing upon the distinctive advantages embedded within our varied communities, the region is uniquely positioned to move beyond present difficulties and to outline a trajectory leading to lasting stability, broad-based prosperity, and equitable advancement for all.

Political Developments and Their Potential Trajectories

An examination of recent political developments in Syria and Lebanon reveals that the future of both states will remain closely linked to the trajectories now being charted by their political elites. In the aftermath of violent conflict, the durability of any trajectory toward peace will hinge on the quality of governance, the interplay of leadership blocs, and the depth of institutional renewal. Lebanon's enduring sectarian power-sharing system complicates this calculus, rendering every policy debate a negotiation over the fragile balance of communal representation. This equilibrium, though ostensibly stabilising, may impair Lebanon's capacity to absorb the tremors of a volatile region, for external powers, each pursuing rival interests, frequently intervene to tilt the balance and deepen domestic rivalries. Syria, by contrast, bears the cumulative scars of a prolonged civil war that shattered state and society alike. The ongoing fragmentation of authority—exemplified by the consolidation of the Assad regime, the survival of rival military and political oppositions, and the emerging autonomy of Kurdish-led governance—compels the pursuit of genuinely inclusive political forums. Only such forums can negotiate a common future that reconciles these opposing, and often mutually exclusive, visions.

Moreover, external interventions and competing geopolitical calculations have transformed Syria's political recovery into a high-stakes contest, with outcomes that affect both national and regional stability. Syrian and Lebanese political arcs cannot be disentangled from the broader regional power chessboard, where Iran, Saudi Arabia, and Turkey treat both states as arenas for pursuing complementary and conflicting objectives, exponentially complicated by the legacies of the Syrian war. The overlapping of grand strategies with clandestine proxy operations constrains national sovereignty and reframes any political reform as a negotiated settlement among external sponsors as much as between local actors. A thorough projection of political futures in Syria and Lebanon, therefore, must foreground governance modalities, the evolution of state-society contracts, and the architecture of transitional justice. Only by charting pathways for genuinely inclusive dialogue, patient consensus-building, and serious institutional overhaul can regional actors cultivate a semblance of sustainable peace. The analytical task requires a layered reading of historical cleavages, shifting power constellations, and the dense braid of domestic and transnational determinants that guide political choices, illuminating the differing roads still available.

Geopolitical Shifts and International Involvement

The current and future architecture of the region is being quietly but decisively remade by international actors whose commitments, both visible and covert, will determine whether Syria and Lebanon emerge as cohesive states or as fragmented arenas of perpetual contest.

The overlapping alliances, rivalries, and military interventions by world powers create ripple effects that endanger the stability and security of Syria and Lebanon alike. At the heart of the shifting geopolitics lie the strategic calculations of the United States, Russia, and China, each of which has moved to expand its influence over the Eastern Mediterranean. Each power regards the region as a vital arena for both geopolitical competition and operational reach. Their involvement has not merely intensified pre-existing disputes; it has also layered fresh variables onto the landscape, determining the longer-term contours of both states. Regional players—Turkey, Saudi Arabia, and Iran—further entangle the situation by advancing contradictory priorities that sustain proxy confrontations and heighten the risk of broader destabilisation. Meanwhile, the European Union, preoccupied with the humanitarian fallout of the refugee crisis and limited attempts at diplomatic mediation, introduces yet another dimension of external engagement. Collectively, the contest for pivotal geopolitical assets—strategic maritime routes, hydrocarbon reserves, and the siting of military facilities—attests to the substantial stakes that compel both local and global contenders to intensify their presence.

The escalating race for influence in the Eastern Mediterranean has increased fears of unintentional escalation and miscalculation, suggesting that a wider conflict with far-reaching international consequences could emerge. For that reason, a close examination of the interwoven geopolitical changes and external involvement becomes essential for any credible anticipation of the paths that Syria and Lebanon are likely to follow in the coming years.

Role of Regional Actors in Shaping the Future

Regional actors remain central to the fate of the Eastern Mediterranean, and their influence continues to dictate the region's political, military, and economic intricacies. This section evaluates their varying capacities to foster either stability or renewed instability. Lebanon and Syria, caught in the crossfire of competing interests, reveal how external powers now help to choreograph their converging futures. The first focus is Turkey, whose historical linkages and ongoing interventions confer upon it a decisive role. Ankara's military operations across northern Syria and its alliances with select Lebanese factions recalibrate the regional equilibrium and compel neighbouring stakeholders to recalibrate their own strategies in response.

The complex dynamics among Turkey, Iran, and Saudi Arabia weave a narrative whose outcome remains in flux. In parallel, Israel's geopolitical calculations and military readiness continue to inform anticipated trends. Enduring hostilities with Lebanon and Syria feed broader volatility, exacerbated by the tentative Israel-Turkey relationship, which shifts alignments and tilts the regional equilibrium. Iran's sustained leverage, notably via Hezbollah, remains pivotal; its objectives, the hostility toward Israel, and competition with Saudi Arabia amplify Tehran's capacity to mould future events. Gulf States, led by Saudi Arabia and Qatar, exert substantial financial and diplomatic leverage. Their backing of diverse Lebanese factions, alongside involvement in Syria's proxy battleground, reinforces their stature as architects of the unfolding narrative. The United Arab Emirates, through assertive actions across Syria and Lebanon, further reconfigures the environment. Collectively, these regional players inhabit an intricate lattice of partnerships, enmities, and calibrated moves, each one marking the trajectory toward an uncertain horizon.

The interplay among these actors shapes political alignments, exacerbates existing fault lines, and influences the prospects for peace and stability.

Impact of Emerging Technologies on Regional Dynamics

Emerging technologies are now central variables in the geopolitical evolution of the Middle East, exerting simultaneous pressure and opportunity across critical domains. Artificial intelligence, cybersecurity frameworks, and blockchain architecture are proving instrumental in reconfiguring the architecture of power, governance, and everyday life. In cybersecurity, the maturation of advanced intrusion techniques has redefined the perimeter of vulnerability, confronting both state and irregular formations with asymmetric exposure. Governments, militias, and transnational networks employ advanced persistent threats not only for intelligence gathering but also for kinetic-like disruption of critical utilities, thereby transgressing the boundaries of traditional warfare. Consequently, the escalation of cyber hostilities, alongside the viral spread of state-sponsored disinformation, erodes the basis of trust among rival actors and amplifies the velocity of pre-existing sectarian and ideological rivalries. Artificial intelligence, for its part, is serving as a multiplier of military efficiency and political control. Algorithms governing predictive maintenance, facial recognition, and autonomous decision-making are steadily recalibrating the calculus of deterrence, while simultaneously embedding heightened surveillance in the civilian sphere. Through these mechanisms, the region is witnessing a re-resolution of power in which technical capability translates directly into political leverage, reinforcing both strategic advantage and societal fragmentation.

The rapid deployment of AI-driven autonomous weapon systems and surveillance technologies raises urgent ethical and existential questions, exacerbating fears of unbridled arms competition, unintended escalation of hostilities, and the diminishing role of human decision-making on the battlefield. At the same time, the region's embrace of blockchain innovations has generated promising responses to entrenched governance deficits and economic fragility. When embedded in public administration, distributed ledger technologies can simplify regulatory workflows, bolster accountability, and inhibit corrupt practices. Layered upon those gains, blockchain-oriented payment networks enhance financial inclusion and provide buffers against external shocks, potentially softening the destabilising effects of regional economic turbulence. Alongside these advances, the proliferation of social media and digital communication technologies has altered public debate, mobilisation, and civic agency across Syria, Lebanon, and the broader Levant. Digital ecosystems facilitate rapid information circulation, grassroots movements, and transnational solidarity while also linking diasporas and local communities. Yet, the same channels afford extremist currents, misinformation, and sectarian rhetoric fertile ground to expand, exacerbating polarisation and undermining social cohesion.

The rapid integration of emerging technologies across the Middle East is no longer an incremental change; it is a systematic reordering that will decisively alter state behaviour, security architectures, and the foundations of governance. As these technologies mature, responding to their cross-cutting effects will not only determine the trajectory of state and non-state actors but will also compel policymakers to construct anticipatory governance that is reflexive and resilient to technological disruption. The imperative is to frame policy that calibrates military, economic, and social instruments in a manner that mitigates risk while still harnessing the developmental potential these technologies offer.

Comparison and Analysis of Forecasted Scenarios

A systematic comparison of Syria and Lebanon's prospective futures mandates a triadic evaluation of optimistic, stagnant, and pessimistic trajectories. Each trajectory must be interrogated not merely as a probabilistic horizon, but as a lens through which the agency of both internal and external actors can be discerned. The optimistic pathway is predicated upon decisive and coordinated diplomatic engagement that is complemented by transparent economic reform and inclusive national dialogue; in this frame, a gradual reconstitution of governance is accompanied by visible socio-economic dividends. The stagnant trajectory, by contrast, acknowledges the operational persistence of entrenched elites whose rivalries and clientelistic networks continue to impede meaningful reform; in this state of play, the absence of decisive external pressure or reformist agency preserves, but does not reinforce, socio-economic decay and security lapses. The pessimistic trajectory foresees the fractionation of state authority, the erosion of boundary lines between security, economic, and militant networks, and an incremental yet compounding spiral of violence. Analysing these folded futures clarifies the stakes and underscores the limits of deterministic forecasting in an environment where the interaction of agency, technology, and geopolitics generates non-linear outcomes.

A more pessimistic scenario anticipates the intensification of conflict and fracture, marked by deepened sectarian antagonisms, intensified external intervention, and the entrenchment of lasting humanitarian catastrophes. Such a path risks disintegration into smaller, heavily militarised zones of power, geopolitical ossification, and widespread, enduring civilian destitution. A thorough understanding of these courses requires meticulous evaluation of the dynamics shaping the region's trajectory.

First, socioeconomic metrics remain fundamental, including demographic growth rates, the balance of productive employment, widening income inequalities, and the availability of health and educational services. Second, political trajectories—including leadership changes, the durability of governing institutions, and the responsiveness of civil sentiment—demand vigilant and granular observation.

Third, the regional geopolitical environment and international commitment are decisive, for global and proximate state actors can recalibrate alliances, orchestrate intervention, and redefine strategic calculations with surprising velocity. Fourth, the diffusion of technologies—especially in communication, information warfare, autonomous systems, and cybersecurity—introduces variables that must be systematically incorporated into risk assessment.

A concurrent evaluation of divergent futures—rooted in these interdependent variables—permits a probabilistic mapping of contingencies that will determine the political and human future of Syria and Lebanon.

This integrative perspective facilitates a detailed appreciation of the intricate interconnections involved, equipping policymakers, analysts, and engaged members of the public with the informed viewpoints necessary to steer through the unpredictable challenges that lie ahead.

17
Conclusion
Lessons from Fragile Geopolitics

Revisiting Historical Patterns: Insights from the Past

Revisiting the interwoven histories of Syria and Lebanon reveals the temporal substratum from which today's geopolitical tensions emerge. A comprehensive analysis of the two polities compels recognition of persistent feedback loops among strategic alignments, mobilised grievances, and contested sovereignty. Under the French Mandate and into subsequent moments of contested independence, decision-makers and social movements in both territories reciprocally recalibrated their boundaries—physical and discursive—while the legacies of political patronage, sectarian demography, and economic interdependence crystallised into persistent determinants of legitimacy. An inquiry into the transactional dimensions of border policing, territorial arbitration, and the circulation of political elites highlights the longer arc conditioning contemporary security discourses. Colonial cartography, interwar administrative practices, and the post-1950s reification of sectarian quotas cannot be disentangled from the genealogy of current insurgent, militia, and state discourses. Revisiting the Lebanese Civil War and the subsequent Syrian military presence further elucidates how commemorative politics and security retrofits perpetuate fault lines across the bifurcated sectarian and nationalist registers. These historical flashpoints do not reside in the past as discrete moments, but rather as internally embedded narratives that sediment within transnational identities and influence current diplomatic calculus. Attentiveness to these recursive temporalities offers the essential matrix for interpreting the concurrency of fractured sovereignty, enduring grievance, and the generative politics of exclusion that characterise the Levant today.

Understanding the historical engagements between Syria and Lebanon is crucial in identifying the forces that contribute to both fragility and resilience in the region. This historical perspective provides a robust foundation for crafting policy interventions that are sensitive to the complex dynamics of the region's past and present.

Understanding Geopolitical Precariousness: A Critical Analysis

Geopolitical vulnerability embodies the uneven interplay

of power, contested borders, and the actions of both sovereign and non-sovereign agents in a confined spatial frame. Its analysis requires unpacking the sedimented legacies, layered identities, and mutual economic dependencies that inform present-state conduct. A methodical inquiry of geopolitical vulnerability reveals a dense tapestry of alliances, antagonisms, and fluid hierarchies that now structure the Levant, and particularly the Syrian-Lebanese theatre. Such an inquiry compels us to identify the exposed seams where divergent ambitions converge, often precipitating disorder. It further obliges us to discern the motives and strategic calculations that animate the full roster of actors: official governments, transnational movements, and incumbents of regional hegemony.

This critical engagement traces the historical currents that flow into the present moment of geopolitical instability, illuminating the differential yet convergent trajectories of power, ideology, and strategy. It then interrogates the consequences of asymmetrical power distributions, competition for scarce resources, and tensions mobilised around identity, seeking to chart their cumulative effect on regional equilibrium. Through a granular analysis of these intersecting dynamics, it aspires to identify the latent motors of conflict and to clarify the shifting alignments that constitute a precarious balance of forces. Moreover, the study maps the circuits of influence, intimidation, and reluctant collaboration that inhabit the geopolitical space, demonstrating that statecraft, diplomacy, and the calculus of military readiness must all adapt to a moving target. By doing so, it aspires to furnish a conceptual instrument for parsing the diverse strands that constitute geopolitical precariousness, revealing the layered and often contradictory relationships that resonate beyond the regional theatre into the larger architecture of international security.

Regional Interconnectivity and Its Complexities

Syria and Lebanon persist as coeval laboratories of geopolitical interdependence, their fates intricately intertwined by history, demographics, and competing national narratives. Understanding this interconnectedness is not just important, but urgent for any comprehensive analysis of the region's geopolitical landscape.

These two states are linked not only by their borders but by a dense weave of history, culture, trade, and demography. Grasping this web is crucial for any analysis of regional power constellations and for forecasting the spillover of domestic upheavals. Central to the regional weave is a set of ties that defy the boundaries of the modern state. Common historical experiences, shared religious and ethnic groups, and permeable economic sectors reveal the resilience of this interconnection. The Syrian civil war demonstrated how the fracture of one polity can generate a chain reaction across the perimeter, amplifying rifts and burdening Lebanon. The flow of armed groups, refugees, and humanitarian exigencies from Syrian territory into Lebanese space illuminates the regional circuitry. The picture is further complicated by a mosaic of external sponsors and operators. Global and regional capitals, drawn to both capitals by different calculations, have etched overlapping layers of leverage that erode the viability of non-intervention. The heterogeneity of their objectives and the rivalries they entail now enter into the local calculus, transforming familiar dynamics into a terrain of unpredictable congestion. Economic ties, which encompass cross-border trade, remittance channels, and the so-called informal markets, add yet another stratum of volatility to the regional circuitry.

Trade routes, seasonal labour migration, and joint arrangements for water and energy have for decades linked Syria and Lebanon in a fragile, mutually dependent network. This interdependence, however, exposes both states to cascading shocks when conflict erupts. The recent surge of Syrian refugees into Lebanon highlights the strain on Lebanon's public services and labour markets, while simultaneously revealing the limits of national policy in a region where economies and social orders are permanently intertwined. A thorough study of such entanglements is therefore necessary to craft conflict-resolution strategies that go beyond temporary ceasefires and address the structural factors perpetuating instability. Understanding the layered connections that foster both vulnerability and adaptive capacity is not just important, but a significant part of shaping effective policy strategies.

Lessons from External Interventions: Strategies and Consequences

External military assistance, diplomatic mediation, and economic sanctions directed at both Syria and Lebanon have reverberated across the region, often with unintended and asymmetric effects.

From the initial phase of the Syrian civil war through the intricate and fragmented politics of contemporary Lebanon, the influence of external powers has remained both pronounced and multifaceted, frequently yielding outcomes that exceed the planners' original intentions. A principal insight emerging from successive interventions is the layered character of strategic positioning by both global and regional states intent on embedding their interests within the Syrian theatre. Russia, Iran, the United States, Turkey, and an array of Gulf monarchies have each intensified the geopolitical density of the Levante, demonstrating how layered and often contradictory agendas coexist. External policies have encompassed military assistance, the cultivation of proxy forces, diplomatic overtures, and conditional economic measures, with each modality embedding new fault lines within the war-torn polity. The dual temporal dimension of these interventions—distinguishing transient tactical successes from durable political logistics—has amplified analytical caution. Immediate alterations in frontline dispositions or diplomatic countenance have invariably refracted through the prisms of regional security, sociopolitical fragmentation, and the erosion or mutation of state sovereignty, raising pointed questions about the sustainability of the resultant order and the resilience of civil society under externally mediated equilibria.

The steady flow of arms and fighters into Syria, propelled

by clashing foreign patrons, has done more than lengthen the war; it has aggravated sectarian fractures and spun a tangle of shifting alliances and rivalries. Crucially, the strategic takeaways from these interventions demonstrate the necessity of grasping the multi-layered nature of influence, particularly when rival and overlapping interests collide. Geopolitical rivalries now intertwine with ideological contests, complicating any effort to obtain a durable settlement, as the goals of foreign states fuse with those of domestic factions and communities. This dense crossover of interests has fortified opposing camps and stalled the emergence of coherent governance and lasting coexistence. Moreover, the record of foreign involvement reveals how intervention practices are adapting in the face of hybrid warfare and information warfare. Military deployments alone are giving way to a multiplex toolbox in which proxy forces, economic pressure, and cyber tools are orchestrated to mould perceptions and exert control, thereby thickening the web in which interventions unfold. To assess the wider effects of outside involvement, analysts must therefore map the entwined currents of coercive and persuasive power.

In sum, distilling lessons from the regrets and recalibrations made by external actors in the unsettled geopolitics of Syria and Lebanon requires, above all, an appreciation of the layered, long-lived strategies employed and the records they now leave. As the region bears the continuing weight of those interventions, embedding these lessons in tomorrow's policy design and in negotiations at all tiers of governance will be critical for constructing a trajectory that is, at once, more durable and more peaceable.

Domestic Political Dynamics: Stability Through Inclusivity

Seated firmly within the emergent geopolitical edifice, domestic political dynamics remain the decisive engine of a nation's propensity for stability or for renewed fragility. In Syria and Lebanon, the fraught interaction of communities organised by sect, ethnicity, and party has circumscribed the region's past and shapes its unsettled present. To move from chronic turbulence to predictable stability, the principle of inclusivity must stand at the forefront of political design. When state and society are arranged such that every major segment can be heard and has fair representation, the thresholds that normally invite external meddling or internecine violence are raised; the polity is, in effect, tamed from within. Historical experience in both countries substantiates this proposition. Decades that have approached stability have tended to be coextensive with governing arrangements that deliberately acknowledge and normalise the region's heterogeneity. In contrast, the eruption of violence has reliably followed policies that marginalise or deliberately disadvantage entire communities.

An inquiry into the centrality of inclusivity must begin with an analysis of institutional mechanisms that allow political systems to absorb a spectrum of diverse voices. Such absorption cannot be limited to the presence of formal political representation; it must extend to empowering marginalised communities, institutionalising ongoing and meaningful dialogue, and rigorously protecting minority rights. Stability secured through inclusivity requires, in addition, a candid reckoning with historical grievances and the cultivation of a societal ethos that prizes pluralism and coexistence. Systematic examination of comparative case studies and recognised best practices across different contexts yields pragmatic lessons on how states can negotiate the complexities of governance in heterogeneous societies. Complementing this, a rigorous inventory of challenges and structural barriers to inclusivity offers a fuller comprehension of the systemic intricacies that decision-makers must confront. As communities embark on the deliberate reconfiguration of political dynamics, it is imperative to scrutinise the conditioning role played by leadership, formal institutions, and civil society in sustaining the absent fractures. Investigating, in parallel, the synergies that emerge between governance reforms and sustainable socio-economic progress reveals the interdependence of governance, social equity, and economic viability. The overarching imperative is a coordinated, multipronged strategy that integrates political, social, and economic domains, proceeding from the conviction that long-term stability can be attained only through a sustained commitment to inclusivity.

Although the journey toward governance that inclusively represents all segments of the polity encounters persistent barriers and pushback, historical evidence corroborates its critical importance in cultivating societies that are both resilient and cohesive against the backdrop of geopolitical instability.

Socio-Economic Dimensions: Building Resilience in Fragility

As we analyse the multidimensional socio-economic factors embedded in fragile geopolitical contexts, it becomes clear that they are decisive in the creation and re-creation of regional stability. Syria and Lebanon, whose fortunes have for decades been mutually dependent, illustrate how socio-economic variables can present simultaneous pressures and openings for resilience. Central to the argument is the study of their economic interdependence: historic flows of trade, migration, and investment have, until recently, constituted vital lifelines across the international frontier. The onset of civil war in Syria, however, severed many of these links, causing mutually reinforcing contractions in production and employment. Disentangling the fragile equilibrium between integrative advantage and systemic vulnerability thus emerges as a pedagogic prerequisite for policy-makers intent on cultivating robust, place-sensitive resilience. The intimate relationship is further complicated when we turn to the socio-economic effects of the Syrian refugee influx into Lebanon. The dramatic demographic and fiscal shocks to Lebanon invite a granular examination of how overstretched public utilities, housing markets, and social protection systems can become both a catalyst for policy innovation and a harbinger of conflict if mismanaged.

Simultaneously, this arrival has also catalysed entrepreneurial ventures, deepened cultural exchange, and underscored the vital role of international assistance and collective action in surmounting the socio-economic aftermath of forced displacement. Advanced investigation of energy and water regimes further reveals decisive socio-economic facets. Competition for water and energy has profoundly shaped the region's geopolitical order, shifting power hierarchies and diplomatic ties. Confronting water scarcity and establishing sustainable resource governance, therefore, constitute non-negotiable building blocks for socio-economic resilience in contexts where fragility is entrenched. Concurrently, both vertical and horizontal inequalities within Lebanese and Syrian communities have crystallised into fault lines that intensify overall instability. In response, fostering inclusive economic expansion, empowering historically marginalised groups, and nurturing socio-economic solidarity emerge as strategic imperatives. This chapter dissects the complex socio-economic interdependencies and argues for integrated policy frameworks that simultaneously cultivate resilience, social cohesion, and pro-poor growth. Strategic investment in inclusive entrepreneurship, applied innovation, and cross-border economic integration is therefore essential for navigating the socio-economic intricacies characterising fragile geopolitical environments.

Role of International Collaboration: Pathways to Sustainable Peace

Continued international solidarity functions as the bedrock for advancing sustainable peace in environments where geopolitics remain volatile and interdependencies are acute, providing a sense of security and hope.

The deep interdependence among states and the way local turmoil reverberates worldwide highlight the pressing need for concerted action and collective stewardship in confronting complex crises. This portion of the analysis examines how a multilayered international partnership serves as a route to durable peace in Syria and Lebanon, and it sketches strategic architectures and diplomatic ventures capable of fostering an enduring order. At its foundation, international partnership articulates the principles of cooperation, dialogue, and reciprocal comprehension among a broad array of actors. It embraces an array of instruments, including multilateral diplomatic assemblies, peacekeeping deployments, economic cooperation, and humanitarian operations. Concerning Syria and Lebanon, the aligned engagement of great powers, regional states, and intergovernmental organisations is indispensable for untangling the compounded political, security, and socio-economic constellations. Effective international action, however, must extend to local communities, civic groups, and grassroots movements, honouring the agency and adaptability of individuals even in strained settings. This engagement also requires the harmonisation of policy aims and the integration of initiatives targeting conflict settlement, the rebuilding phase, and sustainable development.

Diplomatic dialogue, structured mediation, and integrated peace-building programmes—when advanced through cooperative international networks—can cultivate reciprocal trust, reduce friction, and establish the foundations for participatory governance. Bilateral and multilateral economic pacts, paired with investment pledges, can drive growth, broaden employment capacity, and narrow economic inequalities, thereby reinforcing the framework of durability. Further, combined efforts in education, healthcare, and social welfare can strengthen societal resilience and human security, creating a fertile ground for peace to evolve. The international dimension of peace-building encompasses more than crisis intervention and humanitarian responsiveness; it represents a persistent pledge to reconciliation, empowerment, and coexistence. By consistently fostering dialogue and intercultural understanding, multilateral bodies and diplomatic missions can lower hostilities and reveal intersecting interests. Through continuous diplomatic presence and pooled financial and technical support, the international community can help reactivate governing institutions, restore infrastructure, and ensure the availability of vital public services, thus creating a sustaining peace architecture. Achieving this vision demands that the international ecosystem remain resolutely committed, genuinely inclusive, and capable of adjustment, always aware of the shifting geopolitical landscape and the changing realities of the communities it strives to serve.

By drawing on the deep resources of global solidarity and coordinated action, we can translate the hope for enduring peace in conflict-affected regions into a purposeful reality, paving the way for stability, prosperity, and a reconciled future, instilling a sense of optimism in the audience.

The Human Element: Agency, Movement, and Adaptation

Agency, movement, and adaptive capacity are the decisive forces that, interwoven, chart the volatile geopolitical landscape of Syria and Lebanon. Populations and neighbourhoods refuse to be mere bystanders before the pressure of nations and armies; they enter the fray, modifying and being modified by the unfolding catastrophe. Agency, in this context, signifies the power of individuals and collectives to deliberate and to choose, however constrained the socio-political frame. Within the Syrian war and its Lebanon-based shocks, a spectrum of responses emerges, each marking the shifting edges of resilience, defiance, and adjustment. A rigorous examination of these responses is necessary to register the totality of lived experience in a shattered environment. Movement, here, is more than migration. It is the recurrent act of crossing not only borders and checkpoints but also the hidden topographies of identity, obligation, and belonging, each crossing rewriting the narrative of the self and of the community.

Displacement wrought by armed conflict, economic precarity, and environmental exigencies has generated far-reaching population movements, giving rise to expansive refugee settlements and intricate demographic reconfigurations. The consequences of such migration exceed the bodily act of leaving, infiltrating the psychosocial fabric and altering identities, kin networks, and communal bonds. Adaptation, in these circumstances, surfaces simultaneously as a survival strategy and as a negotiated response to enduring uncertainty. Individuals and collectives traverse a landscape marked by discontinuity by reengineering livelihoods and reframing future aspirations. This process of adjustment is inherently multi-dimensional, traversing economic, social, and cultural registers. It demands a fragile equilibrium between the retention of inherited practices and the acceptance of new modalities, frequently animated by a twin consciousness of mourning and resolute endurance. The human phenomenon, therefore, constitutes the indispensable vantage point for interpreting the intricate convergences of agency, mobility, and accommodation within the wider geopolitical parameters of the Levant. Grasping these subtleties enables the formulation of more integrative strategies that confront the region's exigencies, surpassing reductive analytical and policy paradigms that neglect the primacy of lived experience and autonomous human agency.

Strategic Frameworks for Conflict Resolution

Facing the intertwined and layered geopolitical crises of Syria and Lebanon, the articulation of coherent strategic frameworks for conflict resolution is critical. Such frameworks should illuminate pathways to a durable peace and enduring stability throughout the Levant.

An effective resolution demands a comprehensive strategy that integrates diplomatic, economic, and security dimensions. On the diplomatic front, the immediate priority must be to convene an inclusive dialogue that engages all relevant regional and global stakeholders. Negotiations should be structured around genuine reciprocity and the acknowledgement of each party's legitimate grievances, thus enabling the identification of durable, principled compromises. Existing instruments—such as the UN-led modalities and regional mediation bodies—should be harmonised to ensure continuity and coherence in facilitating dialogue.

Concurrently, economic dimensions cannot be ancillary to the political and military tracks, but must be treated as fundamental enablers of sustained peace. Well-sequenced development and reconstruction initiatives—targeted at shared infrastructure, cross-border economic corridors, and inclusive community livelihoods—can translate immediate grievances into collective stakes in stability. Greater trade linkages between Syria, Lebanon, and the surrounding economies would institutionalise interdependence, rendering the costs of renewed hostilities prohibitively high for all parties.

Security considerations must undergird and reinforce the political and economic pillars. Comprehensive disarmament, demobilisation, and reintegration (DDR) programmes, tailored to the local context and supported by international expertise, are necessary to translate ceasefires into permanent cessation of violence. Such programmes must be bolstered by transparent, independent verification mechanisms that monitor arms holdings, troop redeployments, and local security governance, thereby cultivating the trust that underpins any viable settlement.

Additionally, strengthening cooperative mechanisms in counterterrorism and border management can diminish the likelihood of cross-border threats originating from the region. Yet, an effective response must also confront the underlying drivers of discontent, with the goal of fostering societal healing and reconciliation. Reckoning with historical disparities, advancing mechanisms for justice and accountability, and establishing truth and reconciliation processes are all vital to restoring trust and social cohesion. Moreover, the participation of local communities, civil society, and grassroots networks in conflict management is not merely advantageous; it is obligatory. Their involvement ensures that conflict-resolution efforts are grounded in the lived realities and aspirations of the populace, enabling the peace-building architecture to reflect the most pressing local priorities. When diplomacy, economic incentives, security guarantees, restorative justice, and broad-based participation are interwoven, the outcome is a coherent strategic framework capable of producing the transformative and sustainable peace that the volatile geopolitical environment of Syria and Lebanon so desperately requires.

Future Perspectives: Towards a New Paradigm in Regional Stability

Achieving lasting stability in the Middle East requires the adoption of innovative paradigms and forward-thinking policy orientations. As we look ahead, it is critical to devise an integrative strategy that surpasses conventional geopolitical configurations.

Advancing a new paradigm for regional stability now demands a comprehensive reassessment of current frameworks combined with an openness to unconventional trajectories. The essential insight guiding this evolution is that durability cannot stem from isolation or unilateralism. Rather, it proceeds through a collaborative, inclusive strategy that confronts the layered causes of conflict and disruption. Consequently, any forward-looking strategy must elevate domestic actors as primary architects of change, affirming their capacity to steer regional dynamics. This shift effectively moves the locus of agency from external imposition to locally anchored resilience initiatives that promote self-determined, sustainable trajectories. The new stability paradigm must also anticipate and collaboratively address common, transboundary challenges, from widening socioeconomic inequalities to environmental pressures and rapid technological shifts. Creating enduring multilateral forums for cross-border cooperation enables states to pool expertise and resources, thereby neutralising shared threats while converting them into avenues for joint prosperity. Equally vital is the deliberate cultivation of plural narratives and intercultural dialogue, forming a solid bedrock for lasting peace and coexistence. Realising this vision further necessitates a deliberate unravelling of inherited power hierarchies and the productive re-examination of past grievances, thereby nurturing a reconciliatory ethos that prioritises both transitional justice and progressive, forward-looking governance.

Facilitating the inclusion of varied perspectives demands

that we rethink institutional arrangements so that decision-making structures provide fair representation for all stakeholders. Such efforts thrive on international cooperation nourished by principled diplomacy and reciprocal respect, which together chart a course for a regional order anchored in common values and a united commitment to peace and shared prosperity. Moving forward, we must weave lessons from earlier attempts into the very sinews of the emerging paradigm. This entails a candid appraisal of both achievements and failures, distilling wisdom from past experiences to shape flexible, forward-looking policies, and then progressing with resolute determination paired with reflective humility. By committing to a future oriented around regional stability, empathy, and cooperative, anticipatory approaches, we can nurture a constructive inheritance that benefits the generations yet to come.

Bibliography For Further Reading

Chapter 1: Introduction – Intertwined Destinies

English Sources:

Hourani, Albert. (2013). A *History of the Arab Peoples*. London: Faber & Faber.

- Traboulsi, Fawwaz. (2012). A *History of Modern Lebanon*. London: Pluto Press.

- Harris, William. (2012). *Lebanon: A History, 600-2011*. Oxford: Oxford University Press.

- Salibi, Kamal. (1988). A *House of Many Mansions: The History of Lebanon Reconsidered*. Berkeley: University of California Press.

French Sources:
- Corm, Georges. (2012). *Le Liban contemporain: Histoire et société*. Paris: La Découverte.

- Picard, Elizabeth. (2016). *Liban-Syrie, intimes étrangers: Un siècle d'interactions sociopolitiques.* Paris: Sindbad-Actes Sud.

Chapter 2: Historical Context

English Sources:

- Khoury, Philip S. (1987). *Syria and the French Mandate: The Politics of Arab Nationalism, 1920-1945.* Princeton: Princeton University Press.

- Zamir, Meir. (2014). *The Secret Anglo-French War in the Middle East: Intelligence and Decolonization, 1940-1948.* London: Routledge.

- Thompson, Elizabeth. (2000). *Colonial Citizens: Republican Rights, Paternal Privilege, and Gender in French Syria and Lebanon.* New York: Columbia University Press.

Arabic Sources:

- Al-Hakim, Yusuf. (1991). *Suriyya wa al-intidab al-faransi.* Bayrut: Dar al-Nahar.

- Zeine, Zeine Noureddine. (1973). *Nushu' Lubnan.* Bayrut: Dar al-Nahar.

Chapter 3: The Syrian Civil War

English Sources:

- Lesch, David W. (2019). *Syria: A Modern History*. Cambridge: Polity Press.

- Phillips, Christopher. (2016). *The Battle for Syria: International Rivalry in the New Middle East*. New Haven: Yale University Press.

- Heydemann, Steven & Leenders, Reinoud (Eds.). (2013). *Middle East Authoritarianisms: Governance, Contestation, and Regime Resilience in Syria and Iran*. Stanford: Stanford University Press.

- Lynch, Marc. (2016). *The New Arab Wars: Uprisings and Anarchy in the Middle East*. New York: PublicAffairs.

French Sources:

- Balanche, Fabrice. (2018). *Géopolitique du Moyen-Orient*. Paris: La Documentation française.

- Burgat, François & Paoli, Bruno (Eds.). (2013). *Pas de printemps pour la Syrie*. Paris: La Découverte.

Chapter 4: Lebanon's Sectarian Balance

English Sources:

- Makdisi, Ussama. (2000). *The Culture of Sectarianism:*

Community, History, and Violence in Nineteenth-Century Ottoman Lebanon. Berkeley: University of California Press.

- Hanf, Theodor. (2015). *Coexistence in Wartime Lebanon: Decline of a State and Rise of a Nation.* London: I.B. Tauris.

- El-Khazen, Farid. (2000). *The Breakdown of the State in Lebanon, 1967-1976.* Cambridge: Harvard University Press.

Arabic Sources:
- Baydoun, Ahmad. (2012). *Lubnan: al-islah al-mardud wa-l-kharab al-manshud.* Bayrut: Dar al-Saqi.

- Al-Sulh, Nasib. (1988). *Lubnan wa-l-uruba: al-huwiyya al-wataniyya wa-takwin al-dawla.* Bayrut: Dar al-Ilm lil-Malayin.

Chapter 5: External Powers and Proxies

English Sources:
- Hokayem, Emile. (2013). *Syria's Uprising and the Fracturing of the Levant.* London: IISS/Routledge.

- Hinnebusch, Raymond. (2015). *The International Politics of the Middle East.* Manchester: Manchester University Press.

- Pierret, Thomas. (2013). *Religion and State in Syria:*

The Sunni Ulama from Coup to Revolution. Cambridge: Cambridge University Press.

French Sources:
- Donati, Caroline. (2009). *L'exception syrienne: Entre modernisation et résistance.* Paris: La Découverte.

Chapter 6: Hezbollah and Iran

English Sources:
- Norton, Augustus Richard. (2014). *Hezbollah: A Short History.* Princeton: Princeton University Press.

- Blanford, Nicholas. (2011). *Warriors of God: Inside Hezbollah's Thirty-Year Struggle Against Israel.* New York: Random House.

- Azani, Eitan. (2011). *Hezbollah: The Story of the Party of God.* New York: Palgrave Macmillan.

- Alagha, Joseph. (2011). *Hizbullah's Identity Construction.* Amsterdam: Amsterdam University Press.

Arabic Sources:
- *Hizb Allah wa al-dawla fi Lubnan: al-ru'ya wa-l-masar.* Nasrallah, Fadl. (2018). Bayrut: Dar al-Farabi.

Chapter 7: The Israel-Hezbollah Dynamic

English Sources:
- Kober, Avi. (2008). *Israel's Wars of Attrition: A Historical Perspective*. London: Routledge.

- Achcar, Gilbert & Warschawski, Michel. (2007). *The 33-Day War: Israel's War on Hezbollah in Lebanon and Its Consequences*. London: Saqi Books.

- Harel, Amos & Issacharoff, Avi. (2008). *34 Days: Israel, Hezbollah, and the War in Lebanon*. New York: Palgrave Macmillan.

Chapter 8: Refugees as Catalysts

English Sources:
- Chatty, Dawn. (2018). *Syria: The Making and Unmaking of a Refuge State*. Oxford: Oxford University Press.

- Dionigi, Filippo. (2016). *The Syrian Refugee Crisis in Lebanon: State Fragility and Social Resilience*. LSE Middle East Centre Paper Series.

- Janmyr, Maja. (2017). *Protecting Civilians in Refugee Camps: Unable and Unwilling States, UNHCR and International Responsibility*. Leiden: Brill.

French Sources:
- Doraï, Kamel & Puig, Nicolas (Eds.). (2012). *L'urbanité des marges: Migrants et réfugiés dans les villes du*

Proche-Orient. Paris: Téraèdre.

Chapter 9: Water Security

English Sources:
- Allan, J.A. (2001). *The Middle East Water Question: Hydropolitics and the Global Economy*. London: I.B. Tauris.

- Amery, Hussein A. & Wolf, Aaron T. (Eds.). (2000). *Water in the Middle East: A Geography of Peace*. Austin: University of Texas Press.

- Wessels, Joshka. (2015). *Coping with Climate Change and Water Scarcity in the Euphrates-Tigris Basin*. London: Routledge.

Chapter 10: Economic Interdependencies

English Sources:
- Schiff, Maurice & Winters, L. Alan. (2003). *Regional Integration and Development*. Washington: World Bank.

- Owen, Roger. (2013). *State, Power and Politics in the Making of the Modern Middle East*. London: Routledge.

- Cammett, Melani et al. (2018). *A Political Economy of the Middle East*. Boulder: Westview Press.

Arabic Sources:

- Ghosn, Antoine. (2010). *Al-iqtisad al-lubnani: qira'a fi al-tahawwulat wa-l-afaq*. Bayrut: Dar al-Farabi.

Chapter 11: Sectarian Fault Lines

English Sources:

- Haddad, Fanar. (2020). *Understanding 'Sectarianism': Sunni-Shi'a Relations in the Modern Arab World*. Oxford: Oxford University Press.

- Makdisi, Ussama. (2017). *Age of Coexistence: The Ecumenical Frame and the Making of the Modern Arab World*. Berkeley: University of California Press.

- Weiss, Max. (2010). *In the Shadow of Sectarianism: Law, Shi'ism, and the Making of Modern Lebanon*. Cambridge: Harvard University Press.

Chapter 12: Governance Failures

English Sources:

- Heydemann, Steven. (2004). *Networks of Privilege in the Middle East: The Politics of Economic Reform Revisited*. New York: Palgrave Macmillan.

- Cammett, Melani. (2014). *Compassionate Communalism: Welfare and Sectarianism in Lebanon*. Ithaca: Cornell University Press.

- Leenders, Reinoud. (2012). *Spoils of Truce: Corruption and State-Building in Postwar Lebanon*. Ithaca: Cornell University Press.

Chapter 13: Diplomatic Efforts

English Sources:
- Hinnebusch, Raymond & Tür, Özlem (Eds.). (2013). *Turkey-Syria Relations: Between Enmity and Amity*. Farnham: Ashgate.

- Seale, Patrick. (1988). *The Struggle for Syria: A Study of Post-War Arab Politics, 1945-1958*. London: I.B. Tauris.

- Rabinovich, Itamar. (2008). *The View from Damascus: State, Political Community and Foreign Relations in Syria*. London: Vallentine Mitchell.

Chapter 14: Reconstruction Programs

English Sources:
- Salloukh, Bassel F. et al. (2015). *The Politics of Sectarianism in Postwar Lebanon*. London: Pluto Press.

- Dibeh, Ghassan (Ed.). (2007). *The Political Economy of Postwar Reconstruction in Lebanon*. UNU-WIDER Research Paper.

- Najem, Tom. (2012). *Lebanon: The Politics of a Penetrated Society*. London: Routledge.

Chapter 15: Barriers to Progress

English Sources:
- Dagher, Albert (Ed.). (2000). *L'avenir du Liban après les événements*. Paris: LGDJ.

- Young, Michael. (2010). *The Ghosts of Martyrs Square: An Eyewitness Account of Lebanon's Life Struggle*. New York: Simon & Schuster.

- Khalaf, Samir. (2012). *Lebanon Adrift: From Battleground to Playground*. London: Saqi Books.

Chapter 16-17: Future Scenarios and Conclusion

English Sources:
- Bahout, Joseph. (2016). *The Unraveling of Lebanon's Taif Agreement*. Carnegie Endowment for International Peace.

- Khashan, Hilal. (2020). *Lebanon's Political System: The Enduring Legacy of Sectarianism*. Middle East Quarterly.

- International Crisis Group. (2021). *Lebanon: Reform or Bankruptcy*. Middle East Report No. 223.

Policy Papers and Reports:
- ESCWA. (2020). *Syria at War: Eight Years On*. United

Nations.

- World Bank. (2021). *Lebanon Economic Monitor*. Washington: World Bank.

- UNDP. (2020). *Impact of the Syria Crisis on Lebanon*. United Nations Development Programme.

This bibliography provides a solid foundation for academic research on Syrian-Lebanese relations. Each source has been selected for its scholarly rigor and relevance to the chapter themes.